The Films of the Sixties

ALSO BY DOUGLAS BRODE
The Films of the Fifties

The Films of the Sixties

DOUGLAS BRODE

A CITADEL PRESS BOOK   Published by Carol Publishing Group

First Carol Publishing Group Edition 1990

Copyright © 1980 by Douglas Brode

A Citadel Press Book
Published by Carol Publishing Group

Editorial Offices
600 Madison Avenue
New York, NY 10022

Sales & Distribution Offices
120 Enterprise Avenue
Secaucus, NJ 07094

In Canada: Musson Book Company
A division of General Publishing Co. Limited
Don Mills, Ontario

Designed by A. Christopher Simon

Queries regarding rights and permissions
should be addressed to: Carol Publishing Group,
600 Madison Avenue, New York, NY 10022

Manufactured in the United States of America
10 9 8 7 6 5 4

Library of Congress Cataloging in Publication Data

Brode, Douglas, 1943–
    The films of the sixties.

    1. Moving-pictures—Plots, themes, etc. 2. Moving-
pictures—United States. I. Title.
PN1997.8.B7   791.43'75   80-12340
ISBN 0-8065-0798-5

FOR MY WIFE, SUE,

who shared with me
the films of the Sixties
and all the films since.

ACKNOWLEDGMENTS

With grateful thanks to those people who generously helped me on
this project in various ways, and especially to Nat Segaloff, Jack
Clark and Jack Jordan of *Cinemanational,* Dave Outjean and Claudia
Raddo of WTVH, John and Anna Astin; Sherry Larrison, Larry Edmond's
Bookstore; and all the people at Allied Artists, American-Inter-
national, Buena Vista, Columbia, Continental Films, Embassy Films,
Metro-Goldwyn-Mayer, Mirisch, Paramount, Seven Arts, 20th
Century-Fox, United Artists, Universal, and Warner Bros.

Contents

Introduction

More than any other decade in twentieth-century history, the sixties marked an era of transition. In every field from fashion to philosophy, from politics to lifestyle, from mass entertainment to personal outlook, our world changed so drastically—and, in many cases, irrevocably—in this ten-year period of time that some among us doubted we were even able to cope with the changes. In one of the decade's most widely-read books, author Alvin Toffler explained this modern syndrome by assigning it the label *Future Shock,* his concept being that change had become so constant, and so rapid, people were finding themselves numbed by their own unsuccessful attempts to keep up with the latest trends. In earlier, more relaxed times, a fellow might peruse the latest styles in men's fashions and then consider, at length, the possibility of purchasing one of the innovations in clothing with the assurance he would get several years' wear out of his investment. In the Sixties, we felt no such assurance. Whether it was the Madras look in 1962 or the Nehru jacket in 1967, one had to buy and enjoy the product at once, for fear that the style might go out as quickly as it came in. He who hesitates, an old axiom tells us, is lost. In the Sixties, that notion became the order of the day. And whether or not one had read or even heard of Toffler's treatise, we all suffered from the syndrome he described. Styles in popular music, books, and especially films changed with amazing rapidity: in 1965, Billy Wilder's relatively innocuous comedy *Kiss Me, Stupid* could not be released until the filmmaker reshot his ending and eliminated the implication that Dean Martin had slept with Ray Walston's wife; in 1967, mass orgies onscreen were the order of the day. Likewise, ideology ranged from Transcendental Meditation to the Jesus Movement; all such movements were absorbed, then abandoned, before most people had adjusted to their existence. The result of all this was the death of the notion of permanence in an era marked not so much by any one emerging lifestyle or set of values as by the constant state of flux from one to another.

The Sixties began with Richard Nixon stating, after his defeat first for President and then for Governor of California, that we would not have him to kick around anymore; the era ended with Richard Nixon sitting in the Oval Office. The decade began with young people extolling the new President John Fitzgerald Kennedy for returning a sense of class and style to the White House, and ended with the vast majority of young people turned off to the very notions of class and style. This was an era that be-

gan with the Peace Corps and ended with the Peace Movement, that began with the country's youth feeling, after Kennedy's inauguration, they would have a greater say in government than ever before, and ended with youth feeling politically disenfranchised. The Sixties began with the introduction of the space program, designed to conquer the last great frontier, and ended with the giant step forward for man, the moon landing; it began with teenagers twisting to the synthetic, simplistic sound of Joey Dee and The Starlighters in New York's small, dingy, but unaccountably popular Peppermint Lounge, and ended with teenagers dancing naked in the sun to the psychedelic sounds of Jimi Hendrix in the open-air fields of Woodstock. At the decade's opening, Jack Kennedy was the clean-cut hero of youth; at the close, he had been supplanted by Ché Guevara, and the only similarity between the two was that each had died under highly questionable circumstances. In 1960, everyone looked forward to conquering what Mr. Kennedy optimistically referred to as the New Frontier, while in 1969, we were preoccupied with entering what a popular song termed the Age of Aquarius; in 1960, the most popular play on Broadway was *Camelot* and, in 1969, that distinction went to *Hair.* Perhaps most tellingly of all, the Sixties began with a rejection of everything the Fifties—that period of apathy and quiet desperation—had stood for and ended, ironically enough, with a wave of nostalgia for that decade—or, for that matter, *any* period from the past that allowed us to temporarily forget the turbulence of our own times.

In retrospect, the Sixties might be diagrammed as a hollow tube extended between two funnels, one marked 1963, the other 1968. For these were clearly the two watershed years of the decade, the points in time when the social currents at work in society were at last redirected into the mainstream of American life. Both those years were marked, perhaps not coincidentally, by an assassination of a Kennedy. And if the assassiniation of young Robert Kennedy—civil rights and anti-war candidate for the presidency, and the man who appeared about to at last end the vacuum of emotion the country had suffered through since the death of his brother five years earlier—might be considered the final straw that led to the outburst of radicalization in America, then the assassination of his brother Jack—the man who had, during his thousand days in office, offered us a new sense of idealism, purpose, and commitment that was sharply silenced when gun blasts tore through Dallas—was the event which ended what the Sixties at first promised, simultaneously beginning what they were instead going to be.

They were, we soon learned, to be disquieting times of doubt and anxiety. Yet how ironic that they began as a shimmering renaissance of beauty and elegance. There were those who argued Jack Kennedy was the first truly "modern" president, if only because he was the first to be elected owing in part to the impact of television. In his famous debates with Nixon, Kennedy assured himself of the election not by anything he said but by the way he said it. In 1960 people were, for a variety of reasons, ripe for style, and Kennedy's sparkling, classy charisma appeared eminently preferable to Nixon's frumpy grayness, a holdover from the bygone days of the Fifties. No matter what the two actually said to one another during their historic broadcast, the viewing audience embraced what Kennedy clearly stood for: a fresh start. And just as people lined up, every evening, to see Richard Burton extoll the virtues of Camelot to his new queen Julie Andrews in Broadway's most popular show, so did we all enjoy knowing that Jack and Jackie were entertaining in the White House in a grand style that had, during the bland, apathetic years of the Eisenhower era, all but disappeared. Ike had enjoyed reading Zane Grey in privacy; Jack, we learned, liked listening to Robert Frost recite his own verse in the company of the country's best, brightest, and most beautiful people. What we chose to ignore, of course, was the unhappy ending of the President's favorite play, the lines in which Arthur speaks of the "one brief shining moment" of Camelot. Little did we suspect this lavish musical entertainment contained a prediction of the fate in store for our own modern Camelot.

And so, for a time, we felt secure in knowing the likes of cellist Pablo Cassals, poet André Malraux, and composer Leonard Bernstein were appearing before the President and his chic, sophisticated wife; that whenever they travelled to foreign lands, people swarmed through the streets in order to catch a glimpse of the young and beautiful figure-heads of freedom; that the President played football on the beach with his family and friends, and that in the Oval Office he surrounded himself with a group of intelligent Ivy League men who had been hand-picked to ensure the safest and most exciting future for us all. That the President was rumored to be involved in affairs with such glamorous movie stars as Marilyn Monroe and Jayne Mansfield only made him all the more attractive; though we may have been momentarily frightened by the Cuban Missile Crisis, we trusted that, like the good soldier he was,

WHY ARE WE IN VIET NAM?: Norman Mailer raised the question in his controversial novel, but moviemakers were slow to deal with the complex issue. Two films that did tackle the topic early were *Lost Command* with Anthony Quinn and *A Yank in Vietnam* with Marshall Thompson.

11

Jack would see us through. Khrushchev, all bloated and out of control, might shout and make loud threats, but our calm, self-assured leader could be counted on to deal with them effectively. Could there be anything to worry about with Jack Kennedy in the White House? We had listened closely and well to his Inaugural Address of January 20, 1961, and his promise that "the torch has been passed to a new generation of Americans." We trusted that the glow from that fire could truly "light the world."

And yet, for all the exuberance of the Peace Corps volunteers, who intensely set out to spread American ideals to backward parts of the globe, and their domestic counterparts who, with equal enthusiasm, worked to eliminate illiteracy and poverty here at home—all of them deriving their course of action from Kennedy's liberal vision of constant progress as a force that could lick the problems of the world—the seeds of unrest were already sprouting. What emerged as the first great cause in an era of causes was the civil rights movement. Though the controversy over segregation in education and public facilities in the deep South dated back to the mid-Fifties, it was in the Sixties that the movement reached the dimensions of a crusade—first non-violent and idealistic, matching the country's mood at the time and then, later, militant and terrifyingly bloody, once again paralleling the overall pattern at work in our corner of the world. Civil rights was a movement that would take Americans from Selma to Watts, and many places—Washington, D.C., included—in between. It began with the disclosure that, in numerous southern states, blacks were being consciously denied their constitutional voting rights by a vicious cycle that refused them the vote if they were illiterate, and kept them illiterate so they would not be able to vote. Thousands of clean-cut, Kennedy-inspired northern liberals and serious-minded white college students poured into the South in order to draw the media's—and thereby the nation's—attention to civil rights. During the summer of 1964, three young people—two whites and one black—disappeared during one such march, and an F.B.I. investigation disclosed they had been murdered by members of the Ku Klux Klan. "We shall overcome . . ." became the victory chant of the civil rights activists, and massive demonstrations in Washington brought the problem home to the capital itself. No man better represented the integration-oriented style of the movement than Dr. Martin Luther King, Jr., who stated, at one of the Washington rallies, "I have a dream!";

no man better symbolized the segregationist attitude of his opponents than Governor George Wallace of Alabama, who insisted, in his Inaugural Address, "I draw the line and toss the gauntlet!" Eventually, King had to make way for more militant Negro spokesmen, who took the old term "black" —once an insulting word when applied to Negro Americans—and turned it into a word representing pride. H. Rap Brown spoke of waging "guerrilla war" on the whites, forsaking King's plea for non-violence; Elijah Muhammad, founder of the Black Muslims, spoke out against King's dream of integration, calling for the black man to remove himself from white society; Malcolm X insisted that "the day of non-violent resistance is over," while Stokely Charmichael used a new pharse, "Black Power." Younger black leaders emerged: some, like Julian Bond, hoped to change the system from within as Martin Luther King had done, while others, such as Eldridge Cleaver or Huey Newton, took more radical stands. But even before the assassination of Dr. King, riots and burnings had devastated cities from Detroit, Michigan, to Newark, New Jersey. Northern cities were now under attack for being every bit as racist, though in more subtle ways, as their southern counterparts. Still, all the hostility and hysteria eventually led to a new identity for blacks. The phrase "Black Is Beautiful!" formed the basic philosophy for the emerging "Afro American" who no longer desired to be assimilated into white society but rather hoped to express a pride in his own particular heritage. The number of blacks who had their hair straightened dropped drastically, while the Afro haircut—along with styles of clothing to match—emerged as a hallmark of dignity in one's own culture. The desire to rediscover ties to the past eventually led one black author, Alex Hailey, to embark on a personal odyssey in search of his "roots."

Yet for all the impact the civil rights movement had on the Sixties—and for all the drastic changes it would cause—there was another great issue that eventually dwarfed the race problem and became forever identified as the most significant controversy of the decade. The escalation of a full-scale war in Vietnam took place only after years of gradually growing involvement. In the post World War II period, Truman had sent three dozen "military advisors" to the newly created country of South Vietnam in order to keep that vulnerable area from falling into Communist hands; Eisenhower had increased the force to close to a thousand; Kennedy upped the number of men to 20,000. The original concept had been for the American advisors to train the South Vietnamese to defend themselves, but when the Communist forces threatened to overthrow the area, Americans abruptly found themselves in active combat—and, before very long, doing the lion's share of the fighting. Kennedy had himself helped create the Green Berets, an elite corps of professional warriors; they formed the spearhead of the American involvement. For years, politicians had spoken knowingly of a "domino theory" in Southeast Asia, and the dangers of all those countries falling over to the Communists once the first was allowed to go. Few eyebrows were raised when, following the reported 1964 attack on U.S. destroyers by the North Vietnamese, then-President Johnson ordered the beginning of the bombing; quickly, American involvement in the war escalated. The Senate backed Johnson's action while the American public, thoroughly confused as to the realities of the situation, applauded the President's "get tough" attitude.

Gradually, though, an anti-war movement began to take form. Surely, some of the people involved were "professional pacifists" who would have opposed our involvement in *any* war. But others pointed out that the Vietnam War was *not* like any other war. They questioned whether the President had a right to involve us in a full-scale conflict without in fact openly declaring that we were indeed at war. They questioned whether our boys' lives were spent to defend a free state against Communist aggression or merely to prop up a corrupt puppet dictatorship while involving ourselves unfairly in another country's civil war. They wondered if what we were doing in Vietnam might in effect constitute genocide, since it necessitated our dictating the outcome of a dark people's problem with our own best interests in mind. "Dove" was the term used to describe such protesters and, though their number was at first small and they were written off as radicals by the vast majority of Americans, their influence grew steadily, especially when the Vietnam conflict took on a "quicksand" quality—the more men and money we poured in, the deeper we seemed to be mired in it. Vietnam became, in the words of one nightclub comic, the longest running show on TV, thanks to the evening newscasts which broadcast terrible—and often bizarre—images of battle each and every evening. Vietnam had somehow been reduced from a grand cause to a media circus, and Lyndon Johnson—who had introduced his term as President of "The Great Society" with bright hopes of making progress for civil rights,

found himself mired in this ugly, endless war to the exclusion of almost all other concerns.

He was not without his supporters. "Hawks," they called themselves proudly, and they were mostly conservative, mostly middle-class people. They were, ironically enough, the very people Johnson's extreme integrationist domestic policies tended to offend, but they rallied behind their President and their nation. "My country, right or wrong!" was one of their most popular button slogans, "Love It or Leave It!" another. In a gesture of fervent patriotism, they applied small American flag decals to the rear right windows of their cars. At any other time in our history, such a gesture would have seemed innocuous enough. But in the mid-Sixties, the sight of a flag decal caused the anti-war people to wince with anger, taken as a symbol of something more than just general love of one's country. The decals came to signify unquestioning loyalty to the war cause. The protesters, then, had to find some way to counter this jarring symbolism, and they did so by burning American flags or desecrating them by making flags a part of their clothing. Somehow, blind support of a questionable and possibly illegal war had become identified with patriotism, while opposition to it on moral grounds was transformed into an anti-patriotic action. There seemed no middle ground anymore, and Americans woke one morning to discover we had become, for the time being at least, two separate and antagonistic nations existing simultaneous with one another.

Though many of the protesters were well on in years (Dr. Benjamin Spock, the baby expert, was one of the first celebrities to voice opposition to the war), the movement nonetheless became associated with the nation's youth. Joan Baez, long established as an "ethnic" (as opposed to "commercial") folksinger, lent her music a strong anti-war edge; Arlo Guthrie, son of the great folksinger Woody Guthrie, recorded a long walking, talking blues ballad about his experiences as a draft dodger, calling it "Alice's Restaurant." For a while, the country's youth—college students included—were as confused and divided over the issue as the rest of the country and, as late as 1966, a calm debate on the war issue could be heard on almost any campus. Only two years later, the majority of the country's youth—and almost all of the educated youth—had mobilized against the war. The campus emerged as the center for their activity, especially after the draft calls jumped from several thousand a month to tens of thousands, and educational deferments were done away with. There was, evidently, no greater spur toward radicalization than immediate and personal threat.

During the five-year period between 1963 and 1968, the very concept of the college campus was redefined. The bright-eyed, Peace Corps mentality disappeared overnight; in its place was the Peace Movement. College radicalism had, in fact, begun in Berkeley over a question of students' rights and freedom of speech, when an outspoken young man named Mario Savvio was photographed being carted away by police; at that time, the image of radicalism had turned off the majority of America's college students. But by 1967, they were seizing control of their administration buildings, joining such groups as Students for a Democratic Society, and reading books with titles like *Revolution for the Hell of It* and *We Are the People Our Parents Warned Us Against*. Confrontation—at first peaceful, eventually violent—took place on once conservative campuses, as National Guardsmen and local police were called in by anguished administrators. Finally, the long respected Columbia University, once a bastion of traditionalist liberalism, was seized in a student takeover and actually closed down until helmeted police violently bore away the student demonstrators.

In the beginning, many of the anti-war activists believed that they could work for peace within the system, and fell in behind Eugene McCarthy, the Minnesota Democrat who challenged Johnson in the primaries. The kids decided to "look clean for Gene," and canvassed first New Hampshire, then other states in what came to be called "The Children's Crusade," proving in nominally conservative areas that the majority of middle-Americans were now sick of the war, too. But when, despite numerous primary victories and the embarrassed, begrudging withdrawal of Johnson from the presidential race, the Democratic party still ignored McCarthy and his followers, a great many of them decided to drop out of the system entirely. The Chicago Convention of 1968 was the turning point. When thousands of anti-war students wandered the streets, Mayor Richard Daly ordered police to protect the convention center from threats, real or imagined. The subsequent beatings of the students, and the accompanying chant of "The Whole World Is Watching!"—an acknowledgment of the presence of TV cameras broadcasting the melee live—proved to be the final straw for many young people who, up that time, had trusted in the old assurance that they did have a voice. The debacle in Chicago was interpreted as the ultimate proof that working

within the system—indeed, within the society—was, for a growing number of people, no longer an option.

Out of this grew the vast though strangely shortlived Youth Movement. Never in the history of American culture had so much emphasis been placed on the interests and the tastes of the nation's young. Records and movies were designed to please them, and fashions were modelled after their oftentimes fickle tastes. In the early Sixties, a hippie movement had emerged in New York's East Village and San Francisco's Haight-Ashbury district. At first, it appeared nothing more than an isolated phenomenon, as the Beat Generation had been ten years earlier, though instead of the drab, olive and black garb, downbeat attitudes, and intellectual mien of the beats, the hippies went for bright colors, a life-celebrating attitude, and a wide-eyed innocence. They sampled marijuana, decked themselves out in body paint and bizarre clothing that combined old-fashioned shirt-tops with the new bell-bottomed jeans, enjoyed free love and communal living. Likewise, they found a cultural form to reflect their attitudes. The New Rock began, for many, on February 9, 1964, the evening that the Beatles first appeared on *The Ed Sullivan Show* and immediately did away with the old notion that rock 'n' roll was a form of music fit only for morons. For others, it began shortly thereafter, when folksinger Bob Dylan traded in his acoustic guitar for an electric one. The lyrics were suddenly complex, sensitive and aesthetic, and rock music became socially acceptable overnight. With their dashingly outdated clothes, their long hair and sexually charged, sometimes drug-inspired lyrics, the Beatles exerted a cultural influence that has never been fully been measured. Rock lyrics were at once interpreted in college classrooms as serious poetry; rock performers could suddenly be treated as avant garde celebrities. The music grew louder as the lyrics became less simple, and all the while more and more youths slipped into the counterculture lifestyle, trying communal living, LSD trips, and psychedelic forms of art.

Quickly, though, there emerged a counter force. Nixon's vice-president, Spiro T. Agnew, became a hero to millions of middle-Americans by exploiting the anger, anxiety, and outright aggression of those working class citizens who could not comprehend what was happening to their country or bear to think of their way of life being threatened. "The Silent Majority" was the Administration's pet term for such people, and it gave them a sense of identity they cherished and clung to in the light of the catastrophic changes taking place around them. The music on the radio was suddenly louder than ever, the lyrics attacked everything they believed in; movies, once their favorite retreat, were now "X-rated" and contained scenes of nudity and lovemaking that once had been the sole domain of stag films. Much has been made of the Generation Gap of the Sixties, the escalation of a conflict between fathers and sons who could no longer communicate; the hippies helped foster that notion with their catchphrase, "Don't Trust Anybody Over 30!" In fact, though, many of their heroes—be it the LSD spokesman Timothy Leary or the anti-war spokesman George McGovern—were well over 30; meanwhile, many of those wearing "Love It or Leave It!" buttons were in their teens. A generation gap did exist, but far more notable was the conflict between two cultures living side by side, in a state of mutual antagonism. In small towns, farming communities and, for that matter, in large, provincial cities, the old values—Fourth of July parades, Sunday morning church sessions, family picnics and state fairs—were still enacted in the same old manner, even if there was now the fear that some "hippies" might show up to laugh at the "squares."

But for all that, too much had happened too fast for their world to ever again be the same. Popular culture underwent one extreme transition after another: in the early Sixties, the smart young modern woman wanted to look like Nancy Sinatra, with a micro-mini skirt and plastic knee boots; a few years later, she traded in her synthetic image for the more natural hippie fashions. Slender women have always been held at a premium, but in the Sixties, that syndrome was often taken (like everything else) to the point of absurdity: the high fashion model Twiggy and the popular actress Mia Farrow sported waif-like haircuts and figures that resembled bean sprouts. In the wake of the Beatles, the influence from England increased immeasurably, and Carnaby Street fashions were soon the in thing. "Do your *own* thing!" became the catchphrase for clothing, and every day was Halloween as the latest trends in fashions took on a science-fiction quality. A young writer named Susan Sontag coined the term "camp" to describe the values of popular, rather than traditional, culture, and her doctrine was spread by such social critics as Tom Wolfe. Before very long, freshman English courses at major universities were replacing Joseph Conrad's *Victory* with Ken Kesey's *One Flew Over the Cuckoo's Nest* as the novel for required reading, in

a desperate bid to be "relevant" to students' current anti-Establishment views. The go-go discos of the frenetic early Sixties were replaced by rock palaces where the new music was performed. Eventually, even television felt the influence, first as camp came to the tube in the form of comic strip shows like *Batman,* then in the presence of *Laugh-In,* which brought the fragmented quality and accelerated pace of life in the Sixties to a weekly television format, and quickly emerged as the most popular show on the air. Whether it was Tiny Tim warbling in falsetto imitation of great singers of the distant past, Gore Vidal's novel *Myra Breckinridge* with its sexually transformed hero/heroine, or Peter Max's psychedelic posters that earned him the reputation of being the Disney of the Sixties, this was an era marked by put-ons, pop art, and high camp.

And, as Marshall McLuhan had prophesied, an era that would witness the beginning of the end of literacy. *The Saturday Evening Post, Look* and, shortly thereafter, *Life* magazines all died. More and more people watched more and more television, that "mosaic mesh," as McLuhan called it. But TV proved to be a medium of style over substance, of form over content: *Laugh-In* demonstrated audiences would accept radical changes in format as long as the content was not upsetting; when *The Smothers Brother Show* offered Pete Seeger a forum for a softspoken anti-war number, the series was summarily cancelled. Still, there was no denying the importance of the television medium as it made us, again in McLuhan's words, a "global community"; whether it was sending us images of Lada Edmund, Jr., *Hullabaloo*'s disco-dancing "girl in the cage," television's watered down version of James Bond, *The Man from U.N.C.L.E.,* or live and instantaneous images of President Kennedy's funeral, the murder of Lee Harvey Oswald by Jack Ruby, or the first landing of men on the moon, it was clear that TV had long since passed its experimental stage and had emerged as the most significant, powerful, and omnipresent force in our society.

Thus, when the girls of *Laugh-In* danced in their bikinis with their bodies colorfully painted, TV loudly announced it had embraced the sexual revolution—a full five years after every other element of society had acknowledged this new force. In the early Sixties, people whispered about the results of the Kinsey Report, and its findings concerning the frustrations of the average American housewife. A few years later, the names Masters and Johnson were most closely associated with popular styles in

THE YOUTH MOVEMENT: At the decade's beginning, our image of teenagers came directly from Dick Clark's *American Bandstand,* but the war in Viet Nam and concurrent cultural changes would alter that vision drastically. Drop-outs congregate in *Riot on Sunset Strip* and join in an orgy in *The Magic Garden of Stanley Sweetheart.*

16

sexual expression. But other, less expert (at least in terms of educational qualifications) persons also made their influence felt. In her book *Sex and the Single Girl*, Helen Gurley Brown openly catalogued the ways in which a bright young woman could use sex to achieve success, and a few years later went on to turn the fading *Cosmopolitan* magazine into a monthly sex guide for swinging single women. Hugh Hefner, meanwhile, whose *Playboy* magazine had been established back in the Fifties, found the ambience of the Sixties particularly conducive to his publications, clubs, and other related enterprises. Before the decade was out, the pill was in, and so were such establishments as singles bars and singles only apartment houses, all catering to young, affluent professional people desiring to live out what Federico Fellini had called, in 1960, *La Dolce Vita*—"The Good Life."

The more traditional minded among us complained of widespread permissiveness and total breakdown of morality. But the changes were not going to go away. No longer was it considered "sinful" for a woman to live with a man without marrying him; more and more, women insisted on a liberation from the old double standard which approved such actions in men but frowned on them for females.

Simultaneously, though, another force was making itself felt, with far more frightening implications than the sexual revolution. From the beginning of the decade, the presence of violence in our lives—and, subsequently, in our popular entertainment—

17

THE FIRST BLACK SUPERSTAR: With the changing face of the civil rights movement in the early portion of the decade, Sidney Poitier was able to metamorphose from popular character actor to full-fledged superstar. Two of the films that helped him achieve that status were *Lilies of the Field* with Lilia Skala (for which he won an Academy Award) and *Guess Who's Coming to Dinner?* in which he joined the great team of Spencer Tracy and Katharine Hepburn.

A CHOICE OF HEROES: A good measure of how far we came during the decade was our shifting taste in heroes. In the early Sixties, President John Fitzgerald Kennedy was portrayed by Cliff Robertson in *P.T. 109*, but a scant five years later, people were more interested in seeing communist guerrilla leader Ché Guevara played by Omar Sharif in the film *Che!*

caused voices to be raised in controversial reaction. Two of the most noteworthy examples of "the new violence" occurred early in the decade. One involved a young woman who, while returning to her New York apartment building, was attacked by an assailant in clear view of the open windows of her neighbors. The attacker fled when the girl screamed for help but returned and killed the young woman after it became apparent that, despite the fact hundreds of people had obviously heard her shouts, no one was going to do anything about it. The people in the apartment house had, it turned out, merely turned up the volume on their TV sets in order to drown out the shrieks for help, and refused to call the police for fear of "getting involved." At about the same time, a man named Richard Speck captured the nation's headlines with one of the most grotesque sex crimes on record, imprisoning a group of attractive young student nurses and doing away with them, one by one. Was it any wonder that Ian Fleming's James Bond novels, which had been around for a number of years in hardcover, were suddenly best-sellers in their paperback printings? Bond—the cool, calculated, licensed-to-kill professional, who amorally seduces women in a relaxed manner, then swiftly does away with them like so many disposable objects after sexual involvement is over—emerged as the most significant pop-culture hero of the era. Meanwhile, the levels of violence escalated on all sides, from the Hell's Angels motorcyclists, who tore through towns with little opposition, to the political assassinations of Dr. King and the Kennedy brothers. The murder of Lee Harvey Oswald, broadcast live on TV from his Dallas prison, brought the immediacy of violence directly home and, before long, the reformers among us were lobbying for a clean-up of violence on television. In the movie houses, however, violence grew ever more extreme: this was the decade that began with *Psycho* and ended with *The Wild Bunch*.

It also ended with a great technological triumph: the landing of three astronauts on the moon. No wonder, then, that science fiction made an incredible comeback in popularity during the Sixties. Once written off as a junk-art form fit only for adolescents, sci-fi emerged as one of the most popular genres with adult readers and audiences. On TV there was *Star Trek;* in print, the novels of Kurt Vonnegut, Jr.; and on film, *2001: A Space Odyssey, Barbarella,* and *Planet of the Apes,* all major studio productions in sharp contrast to the grade B sci-fi films of the previous decade. When, early in his ad-

A CHOICE OF SYMBOLS: In the Sixties, our tastes in sex goddesses ran the gamut from Amazonian Raquel Welch, who outfought dinosaurs in *One Million Years B.C.,* to the passive Ewa Aulin, who was seduced by half the big-name stars in Hollywood in *Candy.*

PHALLIC SYMBOLS: In an era of new permissiveness, phallic symbols flourished onscreen. Faye Dunaway fingers Warren Beatty's gun in *Bonnie and Clyde*, and Jane Fonda bites down on Michael Caine's saxophone in *Hurry Sundown*.

HOLY HIGH CAMP! Following the publication of Susan Sontag's shattering essay, comic-book heroes were elevated to high art. Adam West and Burt Ward brought *Batman* to movie, as well as TV, screens as the perfect example of "low camp," and the sexier, more sophisticated capers of Monica Vitti and Terence Stamp gave *Modesty Blaise* a "high camp" appeal.

ministration, President Kennedy predicted we would reach the moon by decade's end, he created ripples of genuine excitement, for this seemed the ultimate test of American ingenuity, and a thoroughly engaging technological problem for us to solve during the upcoming, intellectually adventurous era; after the scathing experience of Vietnam and the race riots, as well as the radicalization of half a nation against their government, many people had nearly forgotten the space project. But even as various issues were tearing us apart, the scientists doggedly continued their quest. When, on July 20,

1969, Apollo 11 successfully landed on the moon, and astronauts Neil Armstrong, Michael Collins, and Edwin Aldrin actually walked on the surface of that heavenly body, an incredible cooling off took place in the nation's mood: at least some of the hostility which had divided Americans more completely than they had been since the Civil War some hundred years earlier evaporated. We were reminded of the ideals with which we had begun this decade and realized, with amazement, that all had perhaps not been lost. Our innocence was gone, surely, and much of our trust and optimism, too. But there were certain things that could still make almost all of us proud to be Americans, in spite of the unprecedented divisiveness we had experienced.

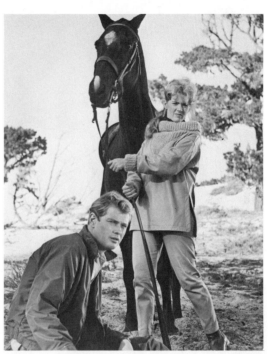

The Sixties were an era when our lifestyle was best symbolized by the computers which began to run our world, taking over everything from the control of our credit cards to the management of dating services. It was an era when the sophisticated new "jet set" lifestyle of the opening years was ultimately offset by a rejection of that very sophistication as being basic to the corruptness in which we had become mired, and was offset by a strong back-to-nature, ecologically minded approach to life. Finally, it was an era when the shock and despair of violence in our midst was replaced by a deep-rooted fear of conspiracy to do away with our great leaders. And, as with all eras in twentieth-century social history, the Sixties proved to be a period of time that was clearly reflected in its movies. Like our society, Hollywood began the era in the last bright light of its innocent years, and ended the period in a state of radicalism.

Few qualities of American movies are quite as fascinating as the ability of films, designed primarily as escapist entertainment, to reflect the moods, the emotions, the trains of thought at work in our world. Sometimes consciously but more often unconsciously, the individuals who collaborate in this art form offer us works that may say more about life in our time than any of those various artists and craftsmen involved in the act of creation intended. The films of the Sixties offer a social history of that age disguised as popular entertainment: the civil rights movement, the sexual revolution, the Vietnam conflict, the growth of a generation gap, the radicalization of the young, the challenge of conquering space, the formation of a vast counterculture—these, and all the other great themes that haunted us, somehow found their way into the most important pictures then being made. Here are one hundred of the most memorable of them.

PERFECT COUPLES: Every era produces its perfect couples, those boy-girl teams that create magical sparks onscreen. In the Sixties, three of the most popular were Jim Hutton and Paula Prentiss in *The Horizontal Lieutenant*, Troy Donahue and Connie Stevens in *Susan Slade*, and Elvis Presley and Ann-Margret in *Viva Las Vegas*.

THE SPY CYCLE: Following the success of the James Bond films, numerous spy heroes dominated the screen. Two of the most popular were James Coburn as *Our Man Flint* and Dean Martin as Matt Helm (seen here with Sharon Tate in *The Wrecking Crew*).

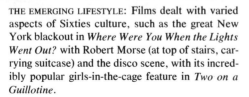

THE EMERGING LIFESTYLE: Films dealt with varied aspects of Sixties culture, such as the great New York blackout in *Where Were You When the Lights Went Out?* with Robert Morse (at top of stairs, carrying suitcase) and the disco scene, with its incredibly popular girls-in-the-cage feature in *Two on a Guillotine*.

THE SEXUAL REVOLUTION: Nowhere was the dramatic change in lifestyle more apparent than in the depiction of romance onscreen. In 1960, Doug McClure gave Roberta Shore a quiet kiss in the malt shop in *Because They're Young*, but at the decade's end, Don Johnson took a more direct approach with Victoria Racimo in *The Magic Garden of Stanley Sweetheart*.

DON'T RAIN ON MY PARADE: The Sixties witnessed the decline of the elaborate and expensive musical films. Two of the last were *The Music Man* with Robert Preston and *Hello, Dolly!* with Barbra Streisand

JAMES BOND'S WOMEN: The popularity of the 007 spy flicks catapulted not only series star Sean Connery, but also some of his voluptuous co-stars, to instant fame. As Honey Ryder, Ursula Andress created the prototype not only of the James Bond female, but also of the new era's idea of a sex symbol, when she emerged out of the sea, clad only in a brief white bikini, like some ancient Amazonian goddess in *Dr. No*. As Pussy Galore, Honor Blackman provided the ultimate Bond woman—ambiguously sexual, seductively sadistic, and delightfully deadly—in *Goldfinger*.

1960

The opening image of *La Dolce Vita:* Federico Fellini began the new decade with a highly symbolic shot of a helicopter lifting a statue of Christ out of Rome, representing the removal of God from the modern city.

LA DOLCE VITA

ASTOR PICTURES

Produced by Giuseppe Amato; screenplay by Federico Fellini, Tullio Pinelli, Ennio Flaiano, and Brunello Rondi; directed by Federico Fellini.

CAST

Marcello Rubini (Marcello Mastroianni); *Photographer* (Walter Santesso); *Maddalena* (Anouk Aimee); *The Prostitute* (Adriana Moneta); *Marcello's Mistress* (Yvonne Furneaux); *The Hollywood Star* (Anita Ekberg); *The Producer* (Carlo Di Maggio); *Robert* (Lex Barker); *Paola* (Valeria Ciangottini); *Marcello's Father* (Annibale Ninchi); *The Clown* (Polidor); *Nadia* (Nadia Gray); *The Matinee Idol* (Jacques Sernas)

In the years following World War II, Federico Fellini rose in 'the ranks of those Italian directors who composed the Neorealist School; but with each successive picture, he appeared more a singular artist with an important, universal theme that was even then being developed by other world artists, working independently of one another. It is hardly coincidental that in 1960—the first year of the new decade—Fellini offered one of the first examples of world cinema to capture the emerging lifestyle of the Sixties.

Fellini noticed an abrupt change in the quality of life, both in his own homeland and in the world at large. In Italy, young people were leaving the farms, the small towns, and the rural communities for the big cities—leaving their old values behind. They moved to Rome, where they collected and cohabited in hedonistic youth groups, dedicating themselves to living for the moment. Some social critics insisted such migrations were a direct result of the atomic bomb and ensuing Cold War; the fear of instantaneous oblivion caused people to embrace "the good life." Others suggested complex social forces were actually at the root of the problem. What was clear was that the texture of life was in transition. A new style of human interaction—more decadent even than that of the Lost Generation of the Twenties in their search for excitement and escape from the present predicament—had developed. In his three-hour epic study of modern life, Fellini analyzed what was happening to society.

The first image is of a helicopter carrying a piece of statuary up into the air and out of Rome.

The ultimate orgy: Marcello Mastroianni and friends enjoy "the good life." *(La Dolce Vita)*

Quickly, though, the viewer realizes it is a statue of Christ, and his presence is being removed from the city where bikini-clad girls are luxuriating in the sun. The shot at once established the moral framework for the entire film which follows and *La Dolce Vita* is, like all Fellini's films, a highly moral (but never simplistically moralistic) movie: here, he announces that his subject is a God-abandoned world; the machinery of modern living has removed religiosity, and the people now live for sensual pleasure. No one ever says this in words, of course: Fellini's language is the language of the cinema.

The deceptively rambling drama centers around Marcello (Marcello Mastroianni), a young newspaperman who stands for the superficiality of his world; instead of tracking down important stories of social or political significance, Marcello madly dashes from the glamorous to the grotesque, from interviews with a movie starlet (Anita Ekberg) to a pair of little children who believe they have witnessed a miracle. In each case, Marcello exploits the sensationalism of the incident at that moment;

A modern lifestyle: *paparazzi* snap pictures of Marcello Mastroianni and Anita Ekberg in *La Dolce Vita*.

there is nothing of lasting values in any of his stories. The contrast between his superficiality—and the sincerity of life as it was lived in the past—is made clear when Marcello is visited by his father (Annibale Ninchi), an elderly man who is shocked at the ease with which his son slips in and out of bed with various young women. Marcello boasts an elegant mistress (Yvonne Furneaux) and a fair amount of public notoriety; but he is, essentially, nothing more than a hanger-on with the fast living set of beautiful people, an emotionless member of the jet set who attends their endless orgies with ever increasing desperation.

This conflict between old and new values, as well as Fellini's own moral stance on the issue, is made clear in the final shot. Halfway through the film, Marcello briefly encounters a young peasant girl who has not changed with the changing times; she is simple, pure, honest. Much later, following the wildest of all-night orgies at their beach house, the revelers wander, in the light of dawn, down to the seashore where they discover the ultimate sensa-

Sex without commitment: Marcello Mastroianni and Anita Ekberg in *La Dolce Vita*.

Freedom or anarchy? Marcello (in the driver's seat) grows bored with the ever-more-bizarre antics of his friends. *(La Dolce Vita)*

29

tion: a kind of monster-fish that has washed up on the beach—a natural creature turned into a disgusting, freakish creation by radioactive fallout. Marcello, in the house, hears their voices, but as he walks across the beach, he vaguely hears another voice: adjacent to their house is the home of the peasant girl, who calls to Marcello to join her. In Fellini's conception of the incident, he is making his moral choice. As the voices of his companions drown out the peasant girl, he briefly waves to her, then turns and walks down the beach to gaze at the grotesque creature with his companions. He is, at last, lost—his one chance for possible redemption gone.

The glorification of superficiality: Newspapermen interview and snap pictures of a vapid movie star (Anita Ekberg) in *La Dolce Vita*.

THE APARTMENT

UNITED ARTISTS

Produced by Billy Wilder; screenplay by Billy Wilder and I. A. L. Diamond; directed by Billy Wilder.

CAST

C. C. "Bud" Baxter (Jack Lemmon); *Fran Kubelik* (Shirley MacLaine); *Jeff D. Sheldrake* (Fred Mac-Murray); *Joe Dobisch* (Ray Walston); *Al Kirkeby* (David Lewis); *Dr. Dreyfuss* (Jack Kruschen); *Sylvia* (Joan Shawlee); *Miss Olsen* (Edie Adams); *Margie MacDougall* (Hope Holiday); *Karl Matuschka* (Johnny Seven); *Mrs. Dreyfuss* (Naomi Stevens); *The Beautiful Blonde* (Joyce Jameson)

No filmmaker ever combined sentiment and cynicism in quite the same manner as Billy Wilder. In *Sunset Boulevard,* he lambasted the mythology of the Old Hollywood, kicking off the 1950s with the decades first great film. In *The Apartment,* he provided an equally strong starting point for a new era.

The story, concocted by Wilder and his constant collaborator, I. A. L. Diamond, offered the sort of ironic morality play which is typical of their best work. C. C. Baxter (Jack Lemmon) is the most popular young employee in a major New York city office building, simply because he is a bachelor who can loan out his apartment to the various middle-level executives he comes into contact with so they may enjoy their current mistresses without resorting to tacky hotel rooms. In return, they promise to put in a good word with the boss, the aloof Mr. J. D. Sheldrake (Fred MacMurray). But Baxter has begun to doubt he will ever enter the executive suite, and instead concentrates on trying to make a date with an attractive, elusive elevator operator named Fran Kubelik (Shirley MacLaine). Then, Baxter suddenly receives the promotion he's been waiting for: large office, bowler hat, personal secretary, the works—and is amazed his friends were actually able to exert such a strong influence on Sheldrake. In fact, Sheldrake has caught on to the little game, and wants Baxter to loan the fabled apartment only to him. Baxter's victory quickly proves a hollow one, for Mr. Sheldrake's mistress is none other than the lovely Fran Kubelik.

The resultant problems range from sophisticated situation comedy to strong social satire. As in all their films, the collaborators opted for a highly moralistic ending to their seemingly easygoing fable

Trapped by a lifestyle: Jack Lemmon and Shirley MacLaine in *The Apartment*.

Room at the top: Jack Lemmon, captured by the camera as he moves in a different direction from everyone else at the office party, turns his physical distinction into a moral uniqueness as well. *(The Apartment)*

31

A time for status: Jack Lemmon, Shirley MacLaine, and Fred MacMurray pose in derby hats, the symbol of "making it," in *The Apartment*.

The good life gone sour: Jack Lemmon and Jack Kruschen attend to Shirley MacLaine after she attempts suicide. (*The Apartment*)

about immoral characters. The old values are reaffirmed when Ms. Kubelik, after a near-tragic suicide attempt in the apartment, spends a bittersweet holiday season with Baxter, where Fran gradually gets over her feelings for her cool but contemptible boss, falling in love instead with the sycophant schlemiel who strains spaghetti through tennis rackets. Shirley MacLaine had already established her elfin character in several popular pictures, but the role of Fran particularly suited her peculiar talent; she was, of course, nominated for the Academy Award, but that year the Best Actress Oscar was handed to Elizabeth Taylor for *Butterfield 8,* one of that actress's lesser performances; it was clearly a case of sentiment, since Taylor had been

suffering from various illnesses all that year. Interestingly enough, though Taylor won for her portrayal of a prostitute, a clear sign that the industry was already able to accept—and respect—more mature screen roles. Lemmon was likewise passed over, despite the fact he delivered the most exquisite variation he would ever do of his own particular screen character: the button-down executive hero of the Sixties, trying desperately to get in on the good life and never realizing that it is his basic warmth as a human being that keeps him from ever succeeding. If the performers were slighted, the film and its director were not: both the Best Picture of the Year Award and the Best Director statuette went to *The Apartment* and Billy Wilder, respectively.

Wilder introduced the "new morality" of the Sixties to films by dealing with such matters as adultery in a light, rather than sombre, tone, and by suggesting such things were not so much tragic as comic, he poked fun at the absurdity of amoral behavior. Audiences of the early Sixties could cheer for a little-guy hero like Baxter in much the same manner that audiences of the thirties could cheer for Frank Capra's Mr. Deeds and Mr. Smith; instead of to town or Washington, the protagonist now went to New York to work in advertising and was not nearly so innocent as Gary Cooper or James Stewart. But he was still the little guy, the common man as we then still liked to believe in him.

ELMER GANTRY

UNITED ARTISTS

Produced by Bernard Smith; screenplay by Richard Brooks, based on the novel by Sinclair Lewis; directed by Richard Brooks.

CAST

Elmer Gantry (Burt Lancaster); *Sister Sharon Falconer* (Jean Simmons); *Jim Lefferts* (Arthur Kennedy); *Lulu Bains* (Shirley Jones); *William L. Morgan* (Dean Jagger); *Sister Rachel* (Patti Page); *George Babbitt* (Edward Andrews); *Rev. Pengilly* (John McIntire); *Preacher* (Rex Ingram); *Rev. Garrison* (Hugh Marlowe); *Prostitutes* (Jean Willes and Sally Fraser)

If Billy Wilder's *The Apartment* set the pace for the comic films of this new decade, then Richard

Burt Lancaster as Elmer Gantry, the role for which he won an Academy Award.

The con man meets the committed woman: Burt Lancaster and Jean Simmons in *Elmer Gantry*.

The moment of truth: Burt Lancaster wins a convert in *Elmer Gantry*.

Brooks' *Elmer Gantry* did the same for drama. But while Brooks' approach to a Hollywood dramatic film was indeed modern, his story was a period piece based on a novel by Sinclair Lewis. When that author created the character of Elmer Gantry in 1927, he gave us not a hero but a case study: an out-and-out opportunist who uses people's sincere religious convictions in order to achieve personal power and pleasure, a lustful charlatan the author constantly criticized in his prose. Over thirty years later, writer-director Brooks kept Gantry's essential characterization but noticeably changed the tone. In his version—and as played by the egregious and charming Burt Lancaster, in the role which won him an Academy Award—Gantry performs the same acts but receives little of the harsh condemnation. His con-man turns out to be as pleasant as the actor playing him, and audiences thus encountered the prototype of one popular character who would recur throughout the films of this era, as played by various actors from Paul

Jean Simmons as Sister Sharon Falconer in *Elmer Gantry*.

Newman in *The Hustler* to Robert Preston in *The Music Man:* the huckster as non-hero.

Brooks realized early in the process of revitalizing this American classic that a faithful adaptation of the book—which chronicled most of Gantry's life and contained numerous sermons, essays, and digressions in which the author expressed his point of view—would be irrelevant and uninvolving. Instead, he opted for a loose interpretation, in which certain key elements, ideas, and characters were retained but rearranged into a screenplay which would be more cinematically effective. Gantry was thus changed from an ordained preacher to a travelling salesman who shouts the name of "Jesus" as a sales pitch; his old seminary friend Jim Lefferts was transformed into an atheistic newspaperman of the H. L. Mencken variety; and Gantry's various adventures were whittled down to a particularly dramatic moment from the book: his infatuation with Sister Sharon Falconer (Jean Simmons), a tent show evangelist who falls in love with the smooth-talking stranger and is eventually destroyed by the effect of his wild ways.

Significantly, the first major drama of the new decade dealt with religious conviction and, while it never drew any conclusions for its audience, the three central characters were clearly symbolic of the philosophic poles which people would necessarily choose between. First, there is Gantry's hucksterish approach to religion, amorally using the simple faith of the common people to manipulate them to his purposes; then there is Sister Sharon's naive but admirable faith, which touches us as much as it does the people she speaks to; finally, there is Lefferts' (Arthur Kennedy) honest atheism, which he articulates with intellectual cynicism. Questions of faith were being raised in films as diverse as Stanley Kramer's *Inherit the Wind* and Federico Fellini's *La Dolce Vita.* Elmer Gantry brought this debate to the nation's screens by providing dramatic representations for three significant points of view.

Thus, *Elmer Gantry* replaced the message movies

In the fifties, prostitutes were disguised as bar girls in movies like *From Here to Eternity;* in the sixties, films like *Elmer Gantry* proved the new maturity of the screen by dealing directly with such topics.

of the Fifties with a more complex form of socially oriented drama. The complexity of the title character—his deceitfulness and, conversely, his engaging qualities—would show up with constant regularity in other screen protagonists; the courage to deal with controversial issues in a big budget, mass-market release would make for some interesting film properties instead of old-fashioned, conventional fare; such settings as brothels and speakeasies quickly ceased to shock audiences and were absorbed as an acceptable part of movies that took place in the real world instead of on a Hollywood set. One of Hollywood's favorite nice girls—Shirley Jones of *Oklahoma!* and *Carousel*—portrayed a prostitute and, instead of scorn, won a Best Supporting Actress Oscar for her efforts. It was no longer necessary to thinly disguise a prostitute as a "conversation companion," as had been the case with *From Here to Eternity* less than seven years earlier, when Donna Reed—another good girl gone "bad" in order to prove her acting ability—also won an Oscar for a similar role. *Elmer Gantry* proved that American films were at last willing to deal with reality in literal, rather than disguised, terms.

PSYCHO

PARAMOUNT

Produced by Alfred Hitchcock; screenplay by Joseph Stefano, from the novel by Robert Bloch; directed by Alfred Hitchcock.

CAST

Norman Bates (Anthony Perkins); *Marion Crane* (Janet Leigh); *Lila Crane* (Vera Miles); *Sam Loomis* (John Gavin); *Milton Arbogast* (Martin Balsam); *Sheriff Chambers* (John McIntire); *Dr. Richmond* (Simon Oakland); *Tom Cassidy* (Frank Albertson); *Caroline* (Pat Hitchcock); *Menacing Policeman* (Mort Mills); *Man Standing Outside Office in Cowboy Hat* (Alfred Hitchcock)

For three decades, Alfred Hitchcock reigned supreme as the master craftsman of suspense in the cinema. His English films in the Thirties explored the touchy international situation preceding World War II; his Hollywood epics for Selznick reflected the war and post-war mentality; his work at various studios in the Fifties perfectly captured the mass paranoia of America in the decade following the creation of a Cold War climate. Always, the basis of Hitchcock's appeal rested on his ability to adjust his own popular formula—terror, romance, and comedy carefully mixed in equal proportions—to the demands of the latest popular nightmare. Then, at the onset of the Sixties, Hitchcock's style changed drastically, as he dropped the guise of popular entertainer. With *Psycho,* Hitchcock ceased to be the beloved director who delighted audiences with frightening fun; all at once, he was at the forefront of a controversy which would rage, oftentimes out of control, throughout the upcoming decade: the question of explicit violence in films.

Psycho begins with one of Hitchcock's favorite devices for making the audience an accomplice in the action: the camera pans past the Phoenix, Arizona, skyline and seemingly randomly picks out a window of a hotel, then glides in to watch two people, Marion Crane (Janet Leigh) and Sam Loomis (John Gavin) involved in an adulterous affair. But if they are guilty of a sexual indiscretion, we are guilty of voyeurism. Their affair—sordid and sad, since the man cannot afford to divorce his wife and marry his lover—was in itself a mild shock, for it was still unconventional for movie stars to play such unglamorous roles. But Hollywood convention would be flouted even more strikingly in the next sequence: Marion compulsively steals a large sum of money from the safe at the real estate agency where she is employed as a secretary, hurriedly packs her belongings, and drives in the direction of San Francisco, where Sam lives. Still, adultery and larceny prove to be mild jolts from our "heroine," at least compared with what happens next: when Marion checks in at a roadside motel she is suddenly, shockingly murdered by a mysterious figure while showering in her room.

The killing itself breaks with one of the most basic conceptions of American movies—i.e., nothing can happen to the central character, at least until the end of the story. But the manner in which the killing was filmed provided a far greater furor than the shock of the incident itself. Marion is stabbed over a dozen times by what appears to be an old woman—the mother of the proprietor, Norman Bates (Anthony Perkins). We learn later, of course, that Norman—who has a second identity in which he masquerades as his long deceased mother—actually killed the woman. The shower sequence—long, terrifying, and bloody—set the pace for a decade of ever more graphic violence which was to blossom in *Bonnie and Clyde,* then come to a head

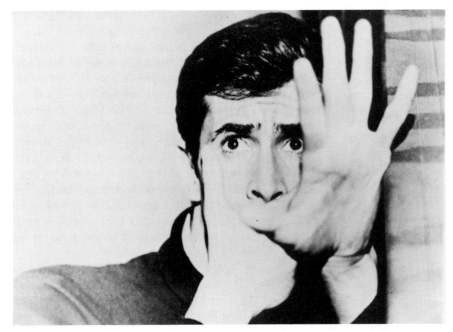

Anthony Perkins as Norman Bates in *Psycho*.

Even in an Alfred Hitchcock entertainment film like *Psycho*, illicit love was now treated in a more casual manner. Janet Leigh and John Gavin.

The classic Hitchcock shot: Despite the changes in film styles, the great director still clung to his most impressive techniques, including the use of the mirror to show a central character at a moment of conflict, in *Psycho*.

Sudden fear: Vera Miles recoils in terror. *(Psycho)*

in *The Wild Bunch*. In retrospect, though, the graphicness (if not the intensity) of the violence in Hitchcock's classic sequence has been overstated. We never actually see the knife make contact with the woman's body, though audiences *think* they see it; as a result of the brilliant editing—from the woman's screaming face, to the water streaming down, to the assailant wielding the knife, to the blood at the bottom of the tub—audiences believe they see the knife penetrating Marion Crane's body, though the penetration takes place in each viewer's mind. Future films would in fact actualize the violence that *Psycho* only suggested, but it was nonetheless this film—Hitchcock's first screen venture in the Sixties—that introduced the new style for the new decade.

In many respects, *Psycho* may be regarded as typical of Hitchcock in terms of his theme. First, there is the fact that Gavin and Perkins look alike, re-establishing Hitchcock's old theme of a hero and villain who are in fact the opposite sides of a single coin, with the implication being that the guilt for the crime is a morally complex issue, and no one character is finally responsible. Then there is "The MacGuffin," or final solution to the entire affair, which becomes clear when policemen restrain Mrs. Bates and discover it is, in fact, Norman in disguise. Finally, there is the sensation of an unexplainable—almost supernatural—situation that, in the end, is seen to be logically motivated. But despite these links to the great tradition of Hitchcock thrillers, *Psycho*'s impact derived from its demon-

The new violence: Suddenly, the normal boy down the street appeared as a dangerous force. Anthony Perkins and Janet Leigh in *Psycho*.

38

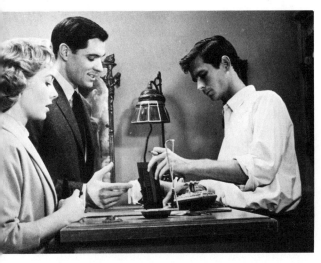

Vera Miles, John Gavin, and Anthony Perkins in *Psycho*. Note the mirror, which suggests an unknown side to "good guy" John Gavin's personality, as well as the striking physical similarity between hero (Gavin) and villain (Perkins), implying they are not as different as they might seem.

stration of Hitchcock's perceptive view of the upcoming decade. Our old enemies were gone: the fascists of the Forties had been replaced by the threat of the Communists in the Fifties, but even the Russians seemed somehow less dangerous in the Sixties than the forces of potential violence within our own society. In *Psycho,* the threat comes from that nice cleancut boy down the street. The theme would be re-echoed throughout the next ten years, not only in Hitchcock's films, but in those of other American filmmakers as well.

SPARTACUS

UNIVERSAL

Produced by Edward Lewis, in collaboration with executive producer Kirk Douglas; screenplay by Dalton Trumbo, from the novel by Howard Fast; directed by Stanley Kubrick.

CAST

Spartacus (Kirk Douglas); *Marcus Crassus* (Laurence Olivier); *Varinia* (Jean Simmons); *Gracchus* (Charles Laughton); *Antoninus* (Tony Curtis); *Batiatus* (Peter Ustinov); *Julius Caesar* (John Gavin); *Helena* (Nina Foch); *Tigranes* (Herbert Lom); *Crixus* (John Ireland); *Marcellus* (Charles McGraw); *Claudia* (Joanna Barnes); *Draba* (Woody Strode); *David* (Harold J. Stone); *Caius* (John Hoyt); *Julia* (Jill Jarmyn)

In the mid-Fifties, moviemakers had faced the ever greater threat posed by television; as an alternative, the superspectacular was born: widescreen, full color, stereophonic sound, all-star extravaganzas quite unlike the classic movies currently being rerun on TV. But as Hollywood filmmakers attempted to offer ever more elaborate pictures—each calculated to top the last in terms of "bigness"—their films grew repetitive and, by 1959, audiences were tiring of the super-spectaculars. In the first year of the new decade, executive-producer Kirk Douglas was responsible for a film which provided a fascinating transition between the type of movie that had reigned supreme in the late Fifties and the new themes that would dominate the upcoming decade.

The story follows a young slave who, at an early age, is enraged by the treatment he and his fellows receive in the salt mines where they labor. Through his training as a gladiator in the school of Batiatus (Peter Ustinov), a self-serving yet agreeable salesman of human flesh, Spartacus befriends a strong fellow slave, Crixus (John Ireland), who experiences doubts as to whether he could kill his friend for the pleasure of the decadent Romans. At first, Spartacus feels no such compunctions, but when he is matched against a strong black man, Draba (Woody Strode), in the ring, Spartacus is amazed that the man is unable to kill him, and instead sacrifices his own life by attempting to assassinate a cold-blooded Roman observer, Marcus Crassus (Laurence Olivier). When Spartacus is taunted over his love for a slave girl, Varinia (Jean Simmons) he suddenly rebels and kills one of the trainers; at once, the entire company of slaves rebels with him. They overthrow their masters and engage in a colossal slave rebellion against Rome itself, which greatly worries even the most humanitarian member of the senate, Gracchus (Charles Laughton), as well as his young manipulative cohort, Julius Caesar (John Gavin). But it is Crassus, desiring to rule Rome with a fascistic amount of power and wanting to possess Spartacus' woman, who dedicates himself to crushing the rebellion.

Years later, Kirk Douglas—reminiscing on his career in movies—would say: "I tended to be attracted to roles of people fighting society. The focus is on a man bucking the system and getting destroyed in the process." Such militant rebellion against "the system" would become the most significant popular movement of the late sixties, and it was Douglas who introduced it as a major movie theme.

Kirk Douglas as Spartacus.

Significantly, *Spartacus* marked the first time screenwriter Dalton Trumbo's name appeared on a movie screen since he was blacklisted during the heyday of McCarthy-era madness. Stanley Kubrick, who turned out interesting little B-movies until Douglas gave him his first big break with *Paths of Glory* in 1957, was chosen as the director, and used *Spartacus* as a vehicle for what would soon emerge as his dominant theme: the lack of relationship between "the humanities" and true human feelings. In *A Clockwork Orange,* Alec commits a murder while using a bust of Beethoven as his weapon; in *Barry Lyndon,* characters display inhuman traits while standing in the presence of great works of art from the past. *Spartacus* opens with an image of a bust of a Roman leader slowly crumbling, and deals throughout with the ironic contrast between the Ro-

Rebellion on foot: Kirk Douglas and John Ireland lead an attack on the Roman Establishment in *Spartacus.*

40

mans' appreciation of great art and the degree to which they have not been in any way humanized by their experience with "the humanities."

Spartacus also marked steps forward in other respects. Jean Simmons enjoyed a bathing scene which came very close to total nudity, paving the way for more mature screen treatment of sexuality. On the other hand, there is a refreshing refusal to linger on the scenes of violence; while two gladiators are fighting to the death, the camera does not pornographically dwell on the violence, but instead focuses on the faces of the two men who will fight next, as they study each other's eyes. Most important, though, *Spartacus* offered a virtual blueprint for what would take place in America during the Sixties. Douglas is the rebel figure, opposing an unfair system and finding himself crucified for his ef-forts; Olivier is the strong conservative ruler, who would destroy all rebellions, no matter how legitimate, and even attempts to do away with the democratic system of government in order to help his country survive; Laughton is the liberal senator, who tries to aid the rebellion for reasons of his own, though he is unable to understand it and ultimately seems sadly impotent when compared to the more strong-willed Olivier; Gavin is the political animal, manipulative and quick to leave his early liberal ideals behind when he is exposed to the corruptive influence of total political power; and Ustinov is the apolitical character, hoping only to survive by flattering both sides of the political spectrum. The story of *Spartacus* would, before the decade's end, be lived out in modern American history.

Rebellion on horseback: By decade's end, the politics of *Spartacus* provided a blueprint for the insurrections we experienced in the Sixties.

Four scenes from *Spartacus:* (1) Kirk Douglas and Peter Ustinov; (2) Kirk Douglas and Charles McGraw; (3) Peter Ustinov and Jean Simmons; (4) Kirk Douglas and Jean Simmons.

The Magnificent Seven: Yul Brynner, Steve McQueen, Horst Buchholz, Charles Bronson, Robert Vaughn, Brad Dexter, and James Coburn.

THE MAGNIFICENT SEVEN

UNITED ARTISTS/MIRISCH-ALPHA

Produced by John Sturges; screenplay by William Roberts, based on a Japanese film by Akira Kurosawa; directed by John Sturges.

CAST

Chris (Yul Brynner); *Calvera* (Eli Wallach); *Vin* (Steve McQueen); *Chico* (Horst Buchholz); *Harry* (Brad Dexter); *O'Reilly* (Charles Bronson); *Lee* (Robert Vaughn); *Britt* (James Coburn); *Old Man* (Vladimir Sokoloff); *Petra* (Rosenda Monteros)

For many years, a gifted Japanese director named Akira Kurosawa dreamed of making an oriental equivalent to his favorite films: American westerns. Digging back into the history and myths of his country, Kurosawa eventually discovered the figure of the "samurai," a wandering knight as quick to draw his sword in defense of the weak as the legendary westerner had been to draw his gun. Freely interpreting the Japanese folk hero in light of cowboy films Kurosawa came up with the samurai movie, in which the main character embodied a strange combination of oriental philosophies and frontier values. The greatest of all such epics was *The Seven Samurai*, which also marked Kurosawa's clearest attempt to transplant the morality of an American western to an ancient eastern setting. When released in America, the film led to an interesting, unexpected event: Hollywood filmmaker John Sturges immediately seized on the idea of remaking it as a western.

The new non-hero: Yul Brynner as an oriental cowboy. *(The Magnificent Seven)*

The Magnificent Seven roughly follows the same plot as its predecessor: Calvera (Eli Wallach), a neurotic bandit leader, terrorizes a small isolated Mexican town with his army of outlaws. One of the elders of the village (Vladimir Sokoloff) determines to protect his community by journeying to a Rio Grande border town and hiring some professional gunmen. He meets Chris (Yul Brynner), a cynical, dark-garbed gunfighter, who agrees to help—for reasons never made clear. First, though, Chris must organize a small company of henchmen, and in a ritualistic recruitment ceremony, he chooses Vin (Steve McQueen), a recent acquaintance who stood by him in an earlier confrontation with killers; Harry (Brad Dexter), a boisterous old buddy convinced Chris is actually after some fabulous fortune; O'Reilly (Charles Bronson), a strong, quiet man who loves small children; Lee (Robert Vaughn), a one-time fast draw who has turned gunshy; and Britt (James Coburn), an expert knife fighter. Eventually joining their ranks is Chico (Horst Buchholz), an arrogant youth out to become a man by making his reputation as a fast gun.

Many critics assumed a standoffish attitude toward the film, comparing it with (and finding it inferior to) its Japanese forerunner: in fact, *The Magnificent Seven* established the tone and themes of the upcoming decade's westerns as clearly as *The Gunfighter* did, one decade earlier, for the Fifties. First, *Seven* gave us an offbeat, articulate westerner in Yul Brynner. His articulate, existential de-

In the Sixties, the Mexican influence grew ever more pronounced in westerns. Eli Wallach and friends sport huge sombreros in *The Magnificent Seven*.

The Professionals meet the peasants: Yul Brynner, Charles Bronson, and Brad Dexter coach farmers in the art of fighting in *The Magnificent Seven.*

meanor suggested a clear departure from tight-lipped westerners of the past. Even Brynner's black outfit was an innovation; previously, dark clothes had been most often associated with villains. But in the complex world of the Sixties, the distinction between hero and villain would grow tenuous.

But there were other innovations as well. Previously, westerns had been shot either on studio sets or actual locations in the American west, most notably Monument Valley. *Magnificent Seven* was the first of many major westerns shot in Mexico, Italy, and Spain, giving the audience a new visual experience as background for such a story while beginning a trend toward international westerns. Importantly, the protagonists are all professionals at their jobs, and establishing such characters as pop-culture heroes would lead to the most significant Sixties idol, James Bond, as well as the characters in the ultimate Sixties western titled, appropriately enough, *The Professionals.* A sense of cynicism runs through the film, as the gunfighters risk their lives for the townspeople, only to learn these simple folk hate and fear them. Also noteworthy is that the film introduced a number of relative newcomers (McQueen, Vaughn, Buchholz, Coburn, Bronson); the film can be viewed as a showcasing of the decade's upcoming stars. Elmer Bernstein's strong musical score, with heavy Spanish and Mexican influence, broke entirely with the traditional concept of soundtracks for previous westerns. In the first year of the new decade, *The Magnificent Seven* set a style which revitalized and revamped the oldest of American film genres for an emerging era.

THE TIME MACHINE
METRO-GOLDWYN-MAYER

Produced by George Pal; screenplay by David Duncan, based on the novel by H. G. Wells; directed by George Pal.

CAST

George (Rod Taylor); *David Filby* (Alan Young); *Weena* (Yvette Mimieux); *Dr. Hillyer* (Sebastian Cabot); *Anthony Bridewell* (Tom Helmore); *Walter Kemp* (Whit Bissell); *Mrs. Watchett* (Doris Lloyd)

In the Fifties, American filmmakers—reflecting the mood of the American public—created a variety of pictures dealing with atomic annihilation: they included melodramas (*Split Second*), monster movies (*Them!*), pseudo-documentaries (*The Beginning or the End?*), science fiction (*The Day the Earth Stood Still*), and finally full-scale tragedy (*On the Beach*). In the Sixties, as fear of nuclear holocaust gradually began to seem less an immediate threat—as we learned to "stop worrying and love the bomb," as filmmaker Stanley Kubrick would eventually put it—moviemakers dealt less often with atomic annihilation and more with the concept of survival—man's ability to adjust, in some form or other, to the changes, however catastrophic, created by modern science. At the beginning of a new movie decade, special effects wizard George Pal created such a fable by bringing to the screen H. G. Wells' science fantasy classic of 1895, *The Time Machine.*

In Pal's film version, the essential premises of the Wells novel are kept intact, though the author's cynical notion of man's devastation of his own planet is played down in favor of an optimistic sense of our ability to overcome our own mistakes. The story begins in Victorian England on December 31, 1899—the end of one era, the eve of another—as George (Rod Taylor), a young scientist, completes his new invention: a time traveling device. Strapping himself into the apparatus in the privacy of his lab, George hurtles himself into the future at high speed, passing first the events which did transpire during the first half of the twentieth century (the filmmakers wisely chose to sacrifice Wells' imaginative projection of events in favor of actuality), stopping in 1966—an upcoming, and therefore frightful year, for the film's viewers.

Picking up on fears left over from the Fifties, Pal dropped his time traveller down in the middle of the

45

In *The Time Machine*, Rod Taylor whacks a Morlock.

Yvette Mimieux and Rod Taylor in *The Time Machine:* Eons in the future, a turn-of-the-century scientist meets a precursor of the Sixties' flower children.

Yvette Mimieux is abducted by a Morlock in *The Time Machine*.

then-expected atomic war. George pauses long enough to watch our society go up in the smoke of a mushroom shaped cloud, then swiftly pilots himself 800 millennia into the future to discover whether mankind could possibly have survived. Surprisingly enough, it has. The people—or, rather, descendents of people—living in 800,000 A.D. have divided into two distinct tribes. First, there are the Eloi, gentle,

46

The Eloi: Pacifists and hippies, they presaged one aspect of the youth culture that would appear by the end of the decade. *(The Time Machine)*

blonde creatures who have been reduced to human vegetables; they mill around in the sunlight, eating fruit and laughing with one another. Also, there are the Morlocks, a monstrous tribe of mutants who dwell in the hugh, machine-filled caverns under the earth's surface, preying on the surface dwellers like farmers butchering so many animals for their dinner tables. To do this, the Morlocks sound the ancient air raid sirens, left over from the great atomic holocaust; whenever they do, the surface dwellers unquestioningly, unthinkingly walk into the shelters, where they are at the mercy of the Morlocks. George finds himself changing from a casual observer of the future to an active participant in it, when he falls in love with Weena (Yvette Mimieux), a lovely surface dweller, and fights to make her, and her people, struggle to survive as humans rather than go on as creatures bred for consumption.

In all of this, H. G. Wells had found a terrible possibility for the future; for George Pal, it became the basis of a most entertaining, if slightly superficial, science fiction film. Unlike so many entries in this genre, turned out on a small budget and at a quick pace, *The Time Machine* was a most ambitious, elegant product; as in his previous pictures, including *Destination Moon* and *War of the Worlds,* Pal created elaborate sets and stunning special effects. The evocation of Victorian London in the last days of the nineteenth century is charming—a Christmas card cutout version—while the world of the future is imaginatively created in unrealistic but irresistible colors, looking not so much like the future scientists expect as a combination of Munchkinland and Shangri-La. But the fantasy elements fit in nicely with Pal's conception for this story; his *Time Machine* is, after all, not sci-fi melodrama so much as it is a sci-fi fairy tale. The film's impressive production values would have been appreciated by sci-fi fans at any time, but the tone with which Pal told his story—the sense that the threat of an atomic holocaust did not necessarily imply the total annihilation of mankind—broke clearly with Fifties thinking, and heralded the approach of the sci-fi films of the Sixties.

NEVER ON SUNDAY

UNITED ARTISTS

Produced, written, and directed by Jules Dassin.

CAST

Ilya (Melina Mercouri); *Homer* (Jules Dassin); *Tonio* (Georges Foundas); *Jorgo* (Titos Vandis); *The Captain* (Mitsos Liguisos); *Despo* (Despo Diamantidou); *Sailor* (Dimitri Papamikail)

Jules Dassin's career would receive nothing more than a minor footnote in film history, had he not journeyed to Europe—where his highly individualistic style of movie-making was more appreciated—to do a film he had long been considering but knew was impossible to produce within the Hollywood studio system. By happy accident, he came upon Melina Mercouri, a robust Greek actress previously wasted because of the unconventionality of her appeal. Mercouri projected precisely what Dassin had in mind for the female lead in his most personal picture, while Dassin gave Mercouri the role that carried immediate stardom with it.

Never on Sunday opens as Homer (Dassin), an overly serious American tourist with more than a touch of the professor about him, travels to the port of Piraeus in Greece. The people he meets there are grubby, hardworking peasants who cannot comprehend this fellow with the sad eyes and beaming smile. Homer hopes to discover the Truth in life, since his studies indicate the great Greek civilization of the past had the corner on everything important about reality and art. Almost immediately, he comes in contact with Ilya (Mercouri), the good-natured prostitute who services the sailors all week long, saving only Sunday for her great love: the classic Greek theater. Amazed to learn this earthy, energetic woman is, in her spare time, a student of literature, Homer decides on the spot to reform her, to cultivate her tastes in the classics and help her rise socially, morally, and spiritually in the world.

Much of the film's humor emerges from the conflict between their ways of approaching reality, as well as theater. He is aghast to learn she sees in the plays of the past what she wants to see. Instead of a terrible tragedy Oedipus is, for Ilya, a charming story of a man who truly loves his mother; Medea, the monstrous female butcher, is interpreted as a sympathetic creature who has been badly used by the men in her life and does not really kill her chil-

Never on Sunday: The new frankness of the screen was in ample evidence as Melina Mercouri went happily about her business in *Never on Sunday.*

48

The lusty, unforgettable dance sequence that helped make an inexpensive European import, *Never on Sunday,* one of the surprise hits of the early sixties.

Surrounded by a group of admirers, Melina Mercouri demonstrates the hard stare and proud posture that would be her hallmark as a star of the sixties. *(Never on Sunday)*

dren at the end: after all, the scene does not occur onstage. At first, this quality is—like everything else about Ilya—exasperating for Homer. As time wears on, though, he falls under her spell, his desire to reform her crumbling as he, in turn, mellows. Ilya shouldn't, of course, be reformed, just as her way of seeing shouldn't be changed. She is truly an innocent: despite all her experience, her mind is virginal. In fact, it is Homer who must be educated, uplifted, changed. He must learn to ignore the fact that Ilya is a prostitute or, rather, accept it: to take her for what she is. By the end, Homer has discovered The Truth, though it a far cry from what he came looking for. Instead of learning about the meaning of life by studying ancient civilizations, he learns by truly living for the first time.

Today, *Never on Sunday* may seem an easygoing, acceptable film which could be shown on prime time, family hour TV with little, if any, editing. In 1960, it was more than a little risqué and controversial. Dealing with the subject of prostitution was, by this time, acceptable in American films—the subject had already been broached in major pictures like *Elmer Gantry*—but the flippant, casual attitude toward prostitution, which is at the heart of *Sunday,* was deemed immoral by American censors. Ilya is another example of that significant Sixties creation, the professional; she doesn't worry much about the morality of her job, but only cares about being good at it—and keeping the customers satisfied. Even the attitude conveyed at the ending, when Homer—the symbol of traditional virtue and the joys of the intellect over the pleasures of the flesh—is captivated by Ilya's spirit, would have then been impossible in an American studio film. The surprising popularity of the film during its American release proved that the mass audience could be coaxed into an art house, if the material was strong enough; that an inexpensively produced European effort could satisfy an audience accustomed to the slick Hollywood product; that audience tastes in the Sixties would shift drastically enough to accept films with an unconventional morality which did not obey, or even try to fit in with, the collapsing concepts of the Production Code.

The Earth Mother versus the Intellectual: Melina Mercouri and Jules Dassin in the tempestuous moment when his head gives way to his heart. *(Never on Sunday)*

1961

ONE, TWO, THREE

UNITED ARTISTS

Produced by Billy Wilder; screenplay by Billy Wilder and I. A. L. Diamond, based on a play by Ferenc Molnar; directed by Billy Wilder.

CAST

MacNamara (James Cagney); *Otto* (Horst Buchholz); *Scarlett* (Pamela Tiffin); *Phyllis* (Arlene Francis); *Ingeborg* (Lilo Pulver); *Hazeltine* (Howard St. John); *M. P. Sgt.* (Red Buttons); *Schlemmer* (Hanns Lothar)

One significant characteristic of the early Sixties was an ability to poke fun at current situations which had appeared fit for nothing less than serious drama only a year or two before. No world problem loomed more ominously than the division of Berlin into the East and West sectors following the war, and the creation of the Berlin Wall to separate capitalists from communists. But among our most important artists are the satirists, those amazing creators of comedy who can make us laugh at even the least funny of occurrences, in so doing saving us from becoming overly morbid about our problems. Few American filmmakers have created as striking examples of such humor as I. A. L. Diamond and Billy Wilder, the writer/director team responsible for such classics of black humor as *Sunset Boulevard* and *Some Like It Hot*. In *One, Two, Three,* they took an old idea from that master of the farce, Ferenc Molnar, and turned it into a broad, freewheeling film that poked fun at the eccentricities of life on both sides of the Iron Curtain.

C. R. MacNamara (James Cagney) serves as the representative for Coca-Cola in East Berlin and he takes his position seriously, realizing Coke is, after all, synonymous with America itself. MacNamara is a self-made man, but he hasn't yet achieved what he really wants in life. In fact, he's working very hard now for the promotion that will carry him and his wife Phyllis (Arlene Francis) back to the States. Complicating matters is young Scarlett Hazeltine (Pamela Tiffin), a pretty, empty-headed daughter of an important Coca-Cola bigwig. The young woman arrives for a visit in Berlin while making the grand tour of Europe. While Mac hopes his treatment of the young lady will earn him his long-awaited Vice-Presidency, she falls in love with a young Communist, Otto Ludwig Piffl (Horst Buchholz). MacNamara is astounded to learn of the affair, more astounded still to learn the two are secretly married. With orders that everyone move quickly—"one, two, three!" as he puts it, with a jaunty snap of the fingers—MacNamara leads a wild, desperate diplomatic move to manipulate an annulment to this unwanted relationship between the dewy-eyed Georgia belle and the propaganda-spouting radical. No sooner has this been accomplished, though, than MacNamara learns the girl is pregnant, necessitating an even wilder attempt to rescue the estranged boy from the Eastern sector and somehow turn him into an acceptable son-in-law for the arriving American businessman (Howard St. John).

Like his non-hero, MacNamara, Wilder was an all-American in every respect—a charming, conniving manipulator of the public's emotions, able to conceive of unlikely gags and somehow pull them off. Diamond's script is peppered full of genuinely satiric lines that poke anarchistic fun at various sacred cows, including the values of both communists and capitalists. Wilder is apolitical in his approach, and no one escapes the barbs of his wit. At the heart of the film's success stands James Cagney—the scrappy but well-scrubbed little Irish tough guy from three decades earlier has developed into an amoral, ruthless, but charming American businessman, able to sell anyone his bill of goods. What's best for Coca-Cola and for R. MacNamara is, in his book, good for America and good for the world. Through the presence of Cagney, Wilder was able to shoot humorous holes in any number of subjects, from such universal themes as the short-lived sincerity of young love to the very modern problem of the sincerity of one's political commitment to East or West. At the end, MacNamara and his less than fond wife are headed home, toward that position he always planned on and played for. The one-time Bolshevik boy has himself changed into an eager young capitalist businessman. Wilder's movie provided Cagney with his last screen role to date; for, after the film's release, the aging star announced his intentions to retire and become a gentleman farmer. *One, Two, Three* provided a fitting conclusion to the canon of his performances, suggesting that the kind of character who, as a young man during the Thirties, might have been a street punk would now, in the context of the Sixties, have matured into a respectable executive in a major American industry.

One, Two, Three: Horst Buchholz gets coaching from James Cagney in the art of capitalism.

The Americanization of a communist: Pamela Tiffin takes Horst Buchholz for a visit to Coca-Cola in One, Two, Three.

In One, Two, Three, James Cagney scrutinizes Pamela Tiffin's portrait of her boyfriend, whose features are hidden behind a Khrushchev poster.

The Cold War cools off: James Cagney, Horst Buchholz, and Pamela Tiffin in One, Two, Three.

THE MISFITS

UNITED ARTISTS

Produced by Frank E. Taylor; original screenplay by Arthur Miller; directed by John Huston.

CAST

Gay Langland (Clark Gable); Roslyn Taber (Marilyn Monroe); Perce Howland (Montgomery Clift); Isabelle Steers (Thelma Ritter); Guido (Eli Wallach); Church Lady (Estelle Winwood); Ray Taber (Kevin McCarthy); Charlie Steers (Philip Mitchell).

In the Sixties, the popular concept of the Hollywood product would experience the most drastic changes in its history. The studio system, which had flourished in the Thirties and Forties, then survived the troubled Fifties, would at last break down and be replaced by small production companies and independent distributors. With the studio system would go the idea of the great movie star—a public commodity and popular idol. Throughout the early Sixties, the few old-time movie stars who had passed through the drastic changes of the Fifties would now pass away or retire. And, in 1961, three of the greatest came together for the first time, to make what would prove to be the last major star vehicle for each of their impressive talents. Clark Gable, Marilyn Monroe, and Montgomery Clift were featured in a film titled, appropriately enough, The Misfits.

Between two generations: Clark Cable, in a telling pose. (*The Misfits*)

Three doomed superstars: Montgomery Clift, Marilyn Monroe, and Clark Gable in *The Misfits*.

Marilyn Monroe entertains Clark Gable, Thelma Ritter, Eli Wallach, and Montgomery Clift in *The Misfits*.

The macho male: Montgomery Clift and Clark Gable rope wild horses in *The Misfits*.

The story, written by Arthur Miller as a special project for his then-wife, is often self-indulgent material, soggy in its ideas and sophomoric in its psychoanalyzing of the characters. Yet even while it lacks the objectivity of Miller's best work, there is still a great poetry to the film. If it is uneven and sometimes downright awkward, it at least displays one of America's finest writers dealing with a subject that was too close to him for comfortable, casual scrutiny; if the emotions sometimes seemed forced and the themes imposed on the material, *The Misfits* is undeniably an original; so unlike anything else Miller ever wrote, John Huston ever directed, or the stars ever appeared in as to make it of more than passing interest, if not necessarily the highest quality. *The Misfits* is a failed film, but there is more life in it than in many more synthetically successful pictures. While watching *The Misfits,* one is constantly aware of its weaknesses; in retrospect, the film's strengths glow in the memory.

Gay Langland (Gable) and his sidekick Guido (Eli Wallach) are a pair of itinerant saddle bums, traveling through the modern west in search of jobs. A stopover in Reno, Nevada, brings the boys in contact with a young divorcee, Roslyn Taber (Marilyn Monroe), who has left her successful executive husband after discovering she cannot communicate with him about the things that trouble her deeply. Immediately, Roslyn is attracted to the gruff, cynical Gay, but another man enters the picture: a sensitive rodeo cowboy named Perce Howland (Clift), who purposefully drives himself into the arena where he is physically battered about, in a neurotic attempt to rid himself of his obsessive loneliness for his distant mother. In the film's second half, they journey to the plains and capture a herd of wild ponies. The action in the sequence is overpowering, especially the one-on-one confrontation between Gay and the leader of the herd. (The physical exertion on Gable during this sequence may partially explain his death shortly after filming was completed.) But the small community of outcasts explodes when Roslyn realizes the animals are not to be sold to a ranch but rather to a dog food factory. The loving woman desperately attempts to free the creatures they have finally caught, while the men choose up sides: who will help her and who will stand in her way as she tries to free the creatures that are as clearly misfits as themselves.

The actors, as well as the characters and the ponies, were misfits too. And at least part of the picture's power derives from the fact that the stars were inseparable from the characters they were playing. Gable, as the ironically named Gay, tries to prove he is as masculine as ever, despite the oncoming of age; Monroe portrays a sensitive woman regarded, by the men in her life, as a sex object; Clift is the alienated loner, looking for something to commit himself to, while never escaping from the shadow of his domineering mother. In each case, the description fits the star as well as it does the character; though the setting and details of the story were fictional, there is a terrible beauty in watching these figures go through the motions of dramatizing their own unique plights. *The misfits* was their swan song; one of the first unforgettable films of the sixties served as a farewell to three superstars of the past.

THE HUSTLER
20TH CENTURY–FOX

Produced by Robert Rossen; screenplay by Robert Rossen, from the novel by Walter Tevis; directed by Robert Rossen.

CAST

Fast Eddie Felson (Paul Newman); *Sarah Packard* (Piper Laurie); *Bert Gordon* (George C. Scott); *Minnesota Fats* (Jackie Gleason); *Charlie Burns* (Myron McCormick); *James Findlay* (Murray Hamilton); *Big John* (Michael Constantine); *Bartender* (Vincent Gardenia); *Waitress* (Carolyn Coates)

Sometimes a single part can turn a moderately popular screen actor into a major star. That was the case with Paul Newman. His first film, *The Silver Chalice* (1954), was so bad Newman temporarily retreated from Hollywood, and moved back to the Broadway stage for a period of two years. When he again attempted the Hollywood trip, he found himself stuck in tepid potboilers and forgettable comedies. On occasion, he found a good role in an interesting film, playing Billy the Kid in *The Left Handed Gun* and Brick in *Cat on a Hot Tin Roof.* But after five years of a film career, Newman had made no more impact than any of a number of other handsome leading young men—Jeffrey Hunter, Robert Wagner, Edmund Purdom—and hardly seemed likely to rise above the status he shared with them. Then came the Sixties and, with them, a new style of moviemaking. In *Exodus,* Newman took his first stab at playing the cool, cynical char-

55

The punk as hero: Paul Newman as Fast Eddie, a desperate man in a shadow world of hostile forces, in *The Hustler*.

acter he would embody. But it was Fast Eddie Felson in *The Hustler* that established him as the reigning superstar of the Sixties.

Fast Eddie is a pool shark—a charming, frustrated young man who travels the backroads of America with his partner, Charlie Burns (Myron McCormick), fleecing local yokels and travelling salesmen out of a few bucks at every roadside bar that boasts a pool table in the backroom with his boyish grin and casual demeanor. But Eddie has one great ambition in life: to someday beat Minnesota Fats (Jackie Gleason), renowned king of the pool halls, in a marathon match.

Though originally written for *Playhouse 90* back in the late Fifties, *The Hustler* functioned as a morality play for the early Sixties.

Eddie is the first full-blown non-hero, and a character quite different from the anti-heroes of the previous decade. In the Fifties, such characters were best symbolized by Montgomery Clift in *From Here to Eternity,* Marlon Brando in *The Wild One,* and James Dean in *Rebel Without a Cause*—troubled, sincere men who suffer much anguish at the hands of an unfair system, but fight to remain true to their own moralities in spite of the world's general amorality. In the Sixties, Newman eclipsed these three superstars: his Fast Eddie is amoral, anguished, and alienated from the world. He is not true to a code of

his own—and therefore superior to the mainstream—but only unable to reach out to others. In their films, Brando, Dean, and Clift all longed for a sincere woman with whom they could share a separate peace; in *The Hustler,* Newman is unable to accept such commitment and communication with Sarah (Piper Laurie). When Eddie allows his girl to be mauled by Bert Gordon (George C. Scott), she kills herself; only then does Eddie realize what he has destroyed and—empty after wasting what might have been the first meaningful relationship in his life—can challenge Minnesota with no fear of losing. Any human fallibility is long since gone.

The anti-hero of the Fifties experiences victory in defeat, cleaning up a lousy system while sacrificing himself in the process; the Sixties non-hero undergoes defeat in victory, winning what he wanted and finding it without value. Newman's demeanor—his intense nervous energy and cool, casual cynicism—found its perfect embodiment in this role, making him the pop-culture idol for a new generation, the star of a new kind of cinema. Robert Rossen's sparse, effective screenplay (written in collaboration with Sidney Carroll) and his stark, shadowy scenes set the proper pace for this downbeat tale. But it was Newman's electrifying performance that made *The Hustler* such a smashing experience for viewers.

56

"My thumbs—they broke my *thumbs!*" Paul Newman and Piper Laurie in *The Hustler.*

The Hustler: Robert Rossen's stark imagery lent a sense of heightened realism to the encounters between Paul Newman and Myron McCormick.

BREAKFAST AT TIFFANY'S

PARAMOUNT

Produced by Martin Jurow and Richard Shepherd; screenplay by George Axelrod, from the novel by Truman Capote; directed by Blake Edwards.

CAST

Holly Golightly (Audrey Hepburn); *Paul Varjak* (George Peppard); *2E* (Patricia Neal); *Doc Golightly* (Buddy Ebsen); *O. J. Berman* (Martin Balsam); *Jose* (Vilallonga); *Mr. Yunioshi* (Mickey Rooney); *Stripteaser* (Miss Beverly Hills); *Salesman at Tiffany's* (John McGiver); *Sally Tomato* (Alan Reed, Sr.)

Even as Paul Newman was creating a male archetype for the Sixties in *The Hustler,* so was Audrey Hepburn doing the same for the female of the species in *Breakfast at Tiffany's.* She was, of course, already a major star, but in the Fifties Hepburn had established a sense of aristocratic innocence, of fawn-like vulnerability, of pixieish charm blended with a vixenish soul. By that decade's end, it was clear Ms. Hepburn would soon be too old to play such ingenuous parts and, wisely, she started searching for something different. Hepburn needed a vehicle which would provide the proper transition into more mature, sophisticated roles without ever turning her back on her old screen image. Luckily, she happened on Holly Golightly, the unforgettable female created by Truman Capote in his delightful novella.

In the opening sequence, Holly—to the tune of the Henry Mancini song, "Moon River," which would quickly become a pop standard—leaves a handsome limousine on a deserted early morning in Manhattan, and walks to Tiffany's window, where she eats a sandwich while quietly contemplating the array of jewels on display. Holly was to Truman Capote what Sally Bowles was to Christopher Isherwood: an image of the sophisticated but amoral modern woman, who by accident encounters a young writer (a thinly disguised version of the author himself) and becomes the focus of both his art and his life. Paul Varjak (George Peppard) soon discovers Holly is a contradiction in terms: at one moment the life of the party, throwing all-night bashes for her dozens of friends, then turning without warning into an isolated, lonely, neurotic hermit. She seems loyal to Paul after a fashion, but never

57

A classic shot that demonstrates the unglamorous but provocative sexual attitudes of *The Hustler.*

stops visiting her mysterious "benefactor" in Sing Sing, a ganglord named Sally Tomato (Alan Reed, Sr.), or slipping into nightclub powder rooms with young men and returning with a fast fifty dollars in cash. She appears elegant in her fashionable clothes, sporting a sophisticated foot-long cigarette holder, though Paul eventually discovers her real name is Lulumae Barnes, that she hails from rural Texas, and even has a farmerish husband (Buddy Ebsen) who at one point journeys to New York in hopes of retrieving his wayward wife.

O. J. Berman (Martin Balsam), Holly's agent and friend, offers a significant description of her half-way through the film: "She's a phony, alright," he insists, "but a *real* phony!" Holly puts on a show for everyone; she has recreated herself in the image of the way she believes people should live. Yet, for all the artificiality, one senses something honest and deep under the surface. Holly is not superficial any more than she is forgettable. She captivates all the characters in the film, which is why parties continuously form around her presence. Even "2E" (Patricia Neal), the attractive older woman who keeps Paul in his apartment, and Mr. Yunioshi (Mickey Rooney), the no-nonsense Japanese photographer who lives in an adjoining flat, sense something magical about Holly. For audiences, she captured something of the spirit of the times: Holly is as amoral as Paul Newman's Fast Eddie Felson and, in fact, complements him as the first significant female role of the new decade. Holly stands as a precursor to the liberated woman who would appear in the films of the late Sixties, insisting on living her own way yet deeply in need of a man's love and companionship. Holly, one realizes at the end, is not as tough, or independent, as she would have us believe.

The conclusion marks the only major departure from Capote's book, and while it did provide audiences with the happy ending Hollywood producers insisted audiences still desired, it nonetheless detracted from the story's power. Other than that one weak moment, though, George Axelrod's screenplay captured the ambience of Manhattan's East Side with an array of effectively satirized character types, while Blake Edwards established his reputation as a director of sophisticated comedies with his handling of the varied confrontations between actors. Most important of all, a new kind of woman made her first significant appearance on the screen.

Opposite page: Audrey Hepburn as Holly Golightly in *Breakfast at Tiffany's.*

Martin Balsam beats George Peppard to the light for chic Audrey Hepburn in *Breakfast at Tiffany's.*

A mellow moment in *Breakfast at Tiffany's:* John McGiver helps the sophisticated couple (Audrey Hepburn and George Peppard) shop for jewelry.

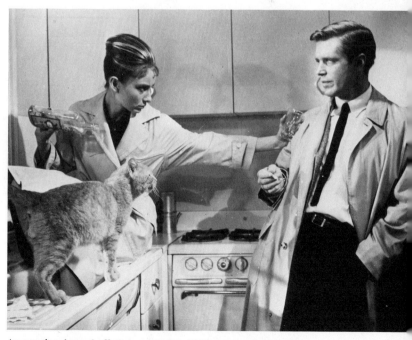
An emotional stand-off: Cat and Audrey Hepburn square off with George Peppard, in a scene that nicely demonstrates filmmaker Blake Edwards's talent for composing his image with the directness of line and careful balance that might be found in a fine painting. *(Breakfast at Tiffany's)*

TWO WOMEN
EMBASSY PICTURES

Produced by Carlo Ponti; screenplay by Cesare Zavattini, based on the novel by Alberto Moravia; directed by Vittorio de Sica.

CAST

Cesira (Sophia Loren); *Michele* (Jean-Paul Belmondo); *Rosetta* (Eleanora Brown); *Giovanni* (Raf Vallone); *Florindo* (Renato Salvatori)

After the fall: Sophia Loren mourns the lost innocence of her daughter in *Two Women*.

In Italy, during the days following World War II, screenwriter Cesare Zavattini developed a set of principles for what would emerge as the most important school of filmmaking ever conceived in that country. He called for a type of film that would tell fictional stories in a documentary style, ennobling common men and women in all their pain and suffering, dealing with the attempts between such people to communicate with one another despite the machine-like world around them, which constantly threatens to destroy the simplest, and most beautiful, of human emotions. In the late 1940s, Zavattini's philosophies were followed by numerous directors, including Roberto Rossellini and the young Federico Fellini. But the filmmaker who most effectively brought the Neorealist ideas to the screen was Vittorio De Sica. In such pictures as *Shoeshine* and *The Bicycle Thief,* Zavattini and De Sica collaborated on projects that glorified, without ever romanticizing, the working class of Italy. With the passing of years, though, the Neorealist school began to fade, as some filmmakers—like Fellini—defined unique styles of their own, while others—such as De Sica—journeyed to Hollywood and made forgettable films. Finally, in 1961, De Sica returned to Italy and created what was, in essence, both a revival and a reminiscence of the Neorealist technique.

Two Women also represented a significant step for its female star. Sofia Villani Scicolone had grown up a penniless child in Rome and, as a teenager during the war, suffered greatly. As Sophia Loren, she managed to create a niche for herself in the movie industry, first in the least prestigious kinds of Italian skin flicks, then in acceptable but run-of-the-mill pictures, finally winning the leads in major movies and attracting the attention of the American movie public in the mid-Fifties. She had respectability and money, but was smart enough to realize only full acceptance as a serious actress would make her a true star. Returning to her homeland, she agreed to work, with De Sica, at playing a decidedly unglamorous role—an image of the kind of woman of poverty she had worked so hard to escape from being herself.

Two Women takes place during the last days of World War II, and begins in Rome, where Cesira (Sophia Loren), a young widow, lives with her tender, pre-teen daughter Rosetta (Eleanora Brown). The terrible bombing raids of 1943 cause the woman to decide it would be a wise move to flee the city; since the death of her husband, Cesira's most important concern is the safety of her child—psychologically as well as physically. So Cesira leads the girl off to the isolated town of La Ciociara, where Cesira spent her own youth. There, the war causes few problems, except for a slight shortage of food. But as Rosetta begins to mature, Cesira grows ever happier about her decision to leave the large city. Protecting her daughter's innocence becomes a kind of obsession, even as the atrocities mount. Then, finally, the war is over and, like so many other Italians, mother and daughter follow the Allied troops back to Rome. But just as Cesira believes the danger is past, and her self-appointed mission has been accomplished, they are assaulted and raped on the road by a gang of off-duty Moroccan soldiers.

A time out from war: Jean-Paul Belmondo and Sophia Loren comfort each other amid the ruins of Italy. *(Two Women)*

Two desperate women: Sophia Loren finds herself unable to protect the innocence of her daughter, Eleanora Brown. *(Two Women)*

Loren's handling of the final scene—her attempt to communicate with the battered child who has for so long a time been sheltered from ugliness only to be now dragged down into it—provided the film's towering moment of truth. For the girl, we feel pathos; what has been done to her is horrible indeed. But for the mother, we feel something more: an emotion that can only be termed tragic. Some critics interpreted the story as a symbolic statement about (and condemnation of) Italy's attempts to avoid a direct involvement during the war, which led to their position as a "ravaged" country afterwards. But the great power of *Two Women* remains on the human level: the tale of one person's ultimate realization that all her efforts at positive work are in vain, owing to an indifferent universe that dwarfs her every action. With this role, Loren forever changed the public's notion of her from sex object to mature actress.

The last breath of innocence: Sophia Loren comforts Eleanora Brown in a tender interlude in *Two Women*.

Sophia Loren: a sex symbol turned marvelous actress in *Two Women*.

Vincent Price wields the pendulum over John Kerr in *The Pit and the Pendulum*. The real star of the scene is the expressionistic set.

THE PIT AND THE PENDULUM

AMERICAN-INTERNATIONAL PICTURES

Produced by Roger Corman; screenplay by Richard Matheson, from the story by Edgar Allan Poe; directed by Roger Corman.

CAST

Nicholas Medina (Vincent Price); *Francis Barnard* (John Kerr); *Elizabeth Barnard Medina* (Barbara Steele); *Catherine Medina* (Luana Anders); *Dr. Leon* (Anthony Carbone)

In 1960, American-International Pictures—then known mainly for its rock bottom, double bill, B-budget films—attempted to upgrade their product by producing something a bit more original and ambitious. The film was *House of Usher,* based on a story by the estimable Edgar Allen Poe. It featured a well-known star, Vincent Price, who had already established himself as a possible successor to Bela Lugosi and Boris Karloff with his fine Fifties horror film, *House of Wax.* Even more important, *Usher* was produced on a respectable enough budget to allow for some eerie special effects and an impressive gothic atmosphere. The public responded enthusiastically, setting off a cycle of pictures loosely derived from the works of Poe, most of them starring Price. By far, the best was the second in the series: a tingling, taut little thriller called *The Pit and the Pendulum.*

Poe's original conception, in which a political prisoner of the Spanish Inquisition is mercilessly tortured in a house of horrors, was too slight for a full-length feature, and so an elaborate introductory episode was invented. Richard Matheson, a writer well known for his science fiction novels (including a classic of the genre, *I Am Legend*) which owed at least a bit of their inspiration to Poe's style and themes, concocted a tale about young Francis Barnard (John Kerr), who journeys to the strange haunted castle of his brother-in-law, Nicholas Medina (Price), in order to inquire about the death of Medina's wife, Elizabeth. But Barnard and Medina's sister (Luana Anders) quickly discover the man is on the edge of madness, for he hears the voice of his deceased wife (Barbara Steele) calling to him from the grave. In fact, she is not dead at all: only working at driving him insane so she can continue her adulterous affair with the family doctor (Anthony Carbone).

The infamous pit and pendulum torture system was reserved for the film's final moments, when the crazed Medina straps the innocent Barnard down and forces the man to watch a descending scythe. The film's exceptional qualities were in large part due to the brilliant set design created for this moody, atmospheric sequence. Likewise, the earlier scenes in the castle are more effective because of the frightening tone of decadence they create. The color design—rich, flamboyant, suggestive—caused this and future films in the series to be acknowledged by serious film critics as noteworthy works which demonstrated experimentation in terms of film style. The sheer visceral experience of

watching one of these Poe pictures is an exciting one for anyone able to overlook the oftentimes routine plot and concentrate on the visual quality. Also, the camera movement helps create a dream-like atmosphere, with its constant dolly shots, while the soundtrack features a cacophony of creatively scary music. Constantly, the cameras track down macabre hallways toward nightmare doors and, if none of it makes much sense, the effect is still moody, menacing, mysterious.

The appeal of Vincent Price in such films was noteworthy. Neither a subtle actor like Mr. Karloff nor an out-and-out entertaining ham like Mr. Lugosi, Price worked a middle ground between the two: it was often near impossible to decide whether his performances were flamboyantly dramatic or floridly overdone, so perfectly were they suited to these Grand Guignol products. In *Pit,* though, he was matched by a memorable villainess. Barbara Steele looked like one of those seductive vampire women in Hammer horror films without even putting on any makeup; as much a natural for the horror genre as Mr. Price, she here incarnated a lustful creature who, at the end, gets her just deserts by being locked in an iron maiden until she dies of starvation. It was a fitting end for her character; unfortunately, though, Ms. Steele never received the classic roles in creepy films, and her obvious talents at terrifying viewers with a scariness combined with sexuality was sadly wasted.

Magnificent Barbara Steele, queen of the horror films, menaces Vincent Price in *The Pit and the Pendulum.*

In *The Pit and the Pendulum,* Vincent Price descends into madness—and hammy acting.

Paula Prentiss, Dolores Hart, Yvette Mimieux, and Connie Francis in *Where the Boys Are.*

Yvette Mimieux succumbs to the attentions of an overamorous beach boy and soon finds herself "in trouble," in *Where the Boys Are.*

WHERE THE BOYS ARE
METRO-GOLDWYN-MAYER

Produced by Joe Pasternak; screenplay by George Wells, based on the novel by Glendon Swarthout; directed by Henry Levin.

CAST

Merritt Andrews (Dolores Hart); *Ryder Smith* (George Hamilton); *Melanie* (Yvette Mimieux); *TV Thompson* (Jim Hutton); *Lola* (Barbara Nichols); *Tuggie Carpenter* (Paula Prentiss); *Angie* (Connie Francis); *Police Captain* (Chill Wills); *Basil* (Frank Gorshin)

During the early Sixties, college students embarked on an annual odyssey only slightly less fascinating than the self-destructive trek of the lemmings. Each year, kids from all over the country—from the high status Ivy League schools to the unpretentious state university campuses—journeyed during spring vacation to Florida, where even the most nominally prudish among them would live for one week in a state of wild abandon, joining in a non-stop brawl on the beaches that ended only when they finally returned to their individual colleges and to their usual, sensible, clean-cut lifestyles. Though the syndrome now seems tame enough in comparison to the long hair, drugs, radical politics and free love that would be the hallmark of the Youth Movement a mere five years later, those Easter vacation jaunts were, in their time, eyebrow-raising. Fort Lauderdale, for no particular reason, became the single city that attracted most of the college students, and the place that Glendon Swarthout used as the subject for a synthetic mélange of drama, comedy, and romance in the novel *Where the Boys Are.* It was a clear indication of the changing times that the relatively racy film version of that book could open at the once sacrosanct Radio City Music Hall.

The plot centers on four college girls who travel together, by car, to the land of sun, surf, and sex, and the film served to introduce each of the actresses as a possible star for the upcoming decade. Merritt, the most intelligent member of the group and the girl who wants to meet an authentic Ivy League man while still (somehow) remaining pure, was played by Dolores Hart, a fascinating young actress who appeared ready to emerge as the logical successor to Grace Kelly, then abruptly left Hollywood and entered a strict, cloistered religious order. Tuggie, the kook of the group, was played by Paula Prentiss, and her performance was so well received that she found herself typed as an arch-kook in films through the decade; her equally kookie boyfriend, portrayed by Jim Hutton, seemed so well suited to her that they would be paired often in other pictures. Melanie, the "easy" girl of the group, was Yvette Mimieux, who looked so dazzling as the bikini-clad beauty that she would portray surfer girls for years; there was an engagingly simple quality about her that would very often cause her to be cast as a sweetly sexy but slightly retarded young woman, whether it was in *The Time Machine* the year before or *The Light in the Piazza* one year later. Finally, Angie, the pleasant but nondescript sidekick to the others, was enacted by Connie Francis, a popular singer turned actress who appeared in a few other "boy" oriented films (*Follow the Boys* and *When the Boys Meet the Girls*), all pallid spin-offs of her only celluloid success.

The film suffers from the same kind of Hollywood moralizing that infected the Elvis Presley musicals or the *Beach Party* flicks, which in fact harkens back to Cecil B. DeMille's religious epics: while exploiting the wild life of sexual freedom for the film's running time, the movie finally condemns that life in the final reel, thereby setting itself apart from the "decadence" it has dealt with and promoting itself as a morally upstanding picture. By resisting the advances of Ivy Leaguer George Hamilton, Dolores Hart proves herself worthy of winning him permanently in the end, and of course does; by giving in quickly to the advances of Ivy Leaguer Rory Harrity, Yvette Mimieux sets herself up for total destruction and suffers a mental collapse after her "boyfriend" treats all his fraternity brothers to her favors. The picture reeks of a kind of grass roots provincialism of attitude: the girls from the State University campus are portrayed in an extremely positive light, while the boys from the Upper Class Ivy League campus are all fickle and superficial. Yet for all that, the film delightfully represented a Hollywood fabrication of the lives of college students in those last calm days before radicalization set in.

WEST SIDE STORY

UNITED ARTISTS

Produced by Robert Wise; screenplay by Ernest Lehman, based on the stage play by Arthur Laurents from an

Romeo and Juliet in the slums: Richard Beymer and Natalie Wood in *West Side Story*.

idea by Jerome Robbins, inspired by a play by William Shakespeare; directed by Robert Wise and Jerome Robbins.

CAST

Maria (Natalie Wood); *Tony* (Richard Beymer); *Riff* (Russ Tamblyn); *Anita* (Rita Moreno); *Bernardo* (George Chakiris); *The Jets* (Tucker Smith, Tony Mordente, Eliot Feld, David Winters, Burt Michaels, Robert Banas, Scooter Teague, Tommy Abbott, Harvey Hornecker, David Bean); *Jet Girls* (Sue Oakes, Gina Trikonis, Carole D'Andrea); *The Sharks* (Joe De Vega, Jay Norman, Gus Trikonis, Robert Thompson, Lary Roquemore, Jaime Rogers, Eddie Verso); *Shark Girls* (Jo Anne Miya, Suzie Kaye, Yvonne Othon); *Social Worker* (John Astin); *Doc* (Ned Glass); *Officer Krupke* (William Bramley); *Lt. Schrank* (Simon Oakland)

When *West Side Story* opened on Broadway in the late Fifties, it changed popular ideas about the stage musical; when it made the transition to motion picture screens in the early Sixties, it similarly altered the nation's notion of what a movie musical ought to be.

The film, like the play, is a retelling of *Romeo and Juliet*, modernized into a fable of the American urban slums: the Capulets and Montagues are now a pair of street gangs, the Jets (a "club" composed of

"When you're a Jet, you're a Jet all the way. . . ." *(West Side Story)*

The dance at the gym: Natalie Wood, George Chakiris, and Richard Beymer in *West Side Story*.

white youths) and the Sharks (newly arrived Puerto Ricans). Mercutio's metamorphosed into Riff (Russ Tamblyn, a young veteran of the last great M-G-M musicals), the white gang leader intent on establishing the Jets' supremacy over their turf; Tybalt has been transformed into the tough but dignified Bernardo (George Chakiris), eager to win respectability and power for his people. But the conflict is heightened when a pair of modern star-crossed lovers attempt to ignore racial barriers: Jet Tony (Richard Beymer) is torn between loyalty to his best friend Riff, and love for a recently arrived girl, Maria (Natalie Wood).

Numerous talents combined to make *West Side Story* a unique achievement. First, there was the script by Arthur Laurents and Ernest Lehman, which effectively captured much of the street jargon of teenage gangs. Then there was Leonard Bernstein's magnificent musical score, which added a symphonic sense of importance to a tale that could have come directly from an evening paper's headlines. Stephen Sondheim's lyrics gave a simple but classic stature to many of the individual numbers, including "Tonight!" and "Maria."

Jerome Robbins' choreography changed the style of dance in musical films, thanks to the sequences featuring the teenage gangs menacing tenement streets, then flying into the air with grand jumps expressing their youth, energy, and exuberance; such stylized actions were effectively offset against realistic backgrounds. Rita Moreno brought her considerable talents as an actress, singer, and dancer to the secondary but scene-stealing role of Anita, Bernardo's sultry mistress. Even Saul Bass, famed creator of unique and original title sequences, found a suitable style for the material at hand fashioning the credits as graffiti.

Ultimately, though, the overall effect of *West Side Story* was due to the work of director Robert Wise. His first shot was a shocker: New York City, viewed through a telephoto lens on an aerial camera miles from the subject. All at once, the camera eye zoomed in, at a tremendous rate of speed, toward the street where most of the action was to take place. Meanwhile, the musical overture appeared on the soundtrack in a stereophonic system, as elaborate and exciting as the images onscreen. *West Side Story* was clearly a breakthrough film in terms of technological achievement as well as social concerns, with its overpowering sensation of visual and aural grandness.

But *West Side Story* was not without its faults. The screenplay fails in precisely the places where it should be strongest: the love scenes, which are written (and played) in the most stereotypical manner. Some of the acting is weak, notably the performance by Richard Beymer, who seems too softheaded and weakhearted to ever have been a hoodlum. Natalie Wood is respectable as Maria, but the need to create a synthetic perfomance (dubbing in another woman's voice for the songs) detracts from the total effect. Finally, there is an awkward shift from the actual street locations of the opening to what are clearly studio sets. In 1961, though, few people found those objections very important. In addition to sweeping the Oscars (including Best Picture of the Year), the film proved a box office bonanza and gained rave reviews from most critics. Bosley Crowther of the New York *Times* hailed it as a "cinematic masterpiece," Arthur Knight of the *Saturday Review* called the film a "triumphant work of art," and Stanley Kauffmann, writing in the *New Republic,* exclaimed that *West Side* was "the best musical ever made." In retrospect, such praise sounds excessive, but it serves as an effective reminder of the impact *West Side Story* exerted. The movie musical was no longer in a state of innocence.

66

The Rumble: Friends restrain Richard Beymer, while George Chakiris and Russ Tamblyn fight. (*West Side Story*)

Rita Moreno, in her Academy Award–winning performance as Anita in *West Side Story*.

Walking through a dream: Richard Beymer and Natalie Wood in *West Side Story*.

A new maturity in love scenes: Warren Beatty and Natalie Wood in *Splendor in the Grass*.

The Generation Gap: Father Pat Hingle berates son Warren Beatty. *(Splendor in the Grass)*

SPLENDOR IN THE GRASS
WARNER BROTHERS

Produced by William Inge and Charles H. Maguire; screenplay by William Inge; directed by Elia Kazan.

CAST

Wilma Dean Loomis (Natalie Wood); *Bud Stamper* (Warren Beatty); *Ace Stamper* (Pat Hingle); *Mrs. Loomis* (Audrey Christie); *Ginny Stamper* (Barbara Loden); *Angelina* (Zohra Lampert); *Del Loomis* (Fred Stewart); *Mrs. Stamper* (Joanna Roos); *Toots* (Gary Lockwood); *Kay* (Sandy Dennis); *Carolyn* (Lynn Loring); *Minister* (William Inge)

The tragic problems of two young lovers owing to well-meaning "families" had already provided the basis for one of the year's most successful films, the innovative musical *West Side Story*. In that picture, Natalie Wood portrayed a sweet young woman of today who loses her boyfriend during a switchblade fight. In *Splendor in the Grass*, Natalie Wood again created an image of a young woman who loses the great love of her life. This time, though, there were different circumstances at work, for she played a high school girl living in Kansas, circa 1925.

Wilma Dean Loomis (Ms. Wood) is happy enough at school, dating one of the most popular boys, Bud Stamper (Warren Beatty), and winning generally good grades in her classes. But their relationship is controversial with both sets of parents; neither Bud's father, Ace (Pat Hingle), a wealthy oil driller, nor Wilma's mother (Audrey Christie) is absolutely sure the young people are either ready, or right, for such a match and interfere. The kids are separated when Bud's father sends him to another city. Ace's plan backfires: Bud, seemingly readying himself for an important job with his father's business, becomes embroiled in an affair with a pizza waitress (Zohra Lampert), gets the girl pregnant, and ends up married; Wilma suffers a nervous breakdown from the experience.

The material may have sounded like the makings of yet another youth exploitation film. But it is the treatment of the material that saved it from such a fate. William Inge's original screenplay (and his first attempt to write directly for the movie medium) dealt with the frustrations and anxieties of middle America as effectively as his earlier plays— *Picnic, Bus Stop,* and *Come Back, Little Sheba*— had, in their time, done. Director Elia Kazan

No Generation Gap: Mother Audrey Christie comforts daughter Natalie Wood. *(Splendor in the Grass)*

avoided all the usual youth-cult clichés. The love-making scenes in parked cars were played for neither for overtly comic nor melodramatic effect, but portrayed with a stunning sense of realism: anxiety and guilt clash with lust and romance.

The title was a letdown for many audiences, who hoped for a lascivious concentration on sex. Nothing could have been further from Inge and Kazan's intentions: the concept of "Splendor in the Grass" actually derives from the English romantic, Wordsworth:

Though nothing can bring back the hour
of splendor in the grass, of glory in the flower:
We will grieve not,
But rather find strength in what remains behind. . . .

When we first encounter the teenagers they are in their last giddy days of high school, unable to take seriously the poetry their teacher attempts to ex-

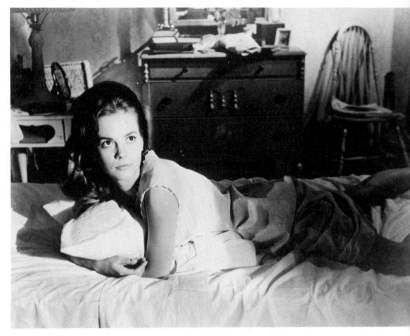

In the early Sixties, Natalie Wood emerged as a former child actress who had become a full-fledged superstar. *(Splendor in the Grass)*

Natalie Wood, in her finest emotional sequence in *Splendor in the Grass*.

plain. At the film's end, though, the mature, sophisticated Wilma visits her one-time boyfriend, finding he has not grown—he is still the silly, good-natured high school hero—though now he is saddled with an ever-pregnant wife with whom he shares a seedy apartment. Wilma's fear was that, seeing him again, she might discover she is still in love with Bud. But Wilma discovers she feels only warmth and affection for what once was but can never be again. As she leaves, the words of her schoolteacher come back—only now, she fully understands them.

There have always been conflicts between the generations, and they have always found their way into the great drama of various times and places—from *Antigone* to *Hamlet*. But in the Sixties, this friction would grow to unheard of dimensions, and the emotional battle between youth and their parents would eventually become so heated that a new term would be added to the popular vocabulary in order to explain it: the Generation Gap. Though the movement would not be fully felt until later in the decade, the forces that caused it were already at work. Set in the past, *Splendor in the Grass* was nonetheless the first major film of the decade to deal with what would become one of the most overriding issues of this era.

1962

RIDE THE HIGH COUNTRY

METRO-GOLDWYN-MAYER

Produced by Richard E. Lyons; screenplay by N. B. Stone, Jr.; directed by Sam Peckinpah.

CAST

Steve Judd (Joel McCrea); *Gil Westrum* (Randolph Scott); *Elsa Knudsen* (Mariette Hartley); *Heck Longtree* (Ron Starr); *Joshua Knudsen* (R. G. Armstrong); *Billy Hammond* (James Drury); *Elder Hammond* (John Anderson); *Sylvus Hammond* (L. Q. Jones); *Henry Hammond* (Warren Oates); *Judge Toliver* (Edgar Buchanan)

One important factor in the early Sixties was the rise of bright young directors who were able to understand the problems of America in an era of transition, and offered us images of the confused times. Equally noteworthy was the passing of the great old stars, some into retirement and others as a result of their deaths. One particular picture offered a combination of these two significant trends, a little sleeper of a film called *Ride the High Country*.

In the film's opening sequence, a turn-of-the-century western town full of roughnecks awaits the beginning of a big race between their fastest horse and an army supply camel, when an aged, dust-covered lawman named Steve Judd (Joel McCrea) rides his tired horse down the main street. Angered at the intrusion of this tramplike figure, the people wave him to move out of the way. Judd, however, mistakes their gesture for a welcome greeting; in a point of view shot, we see the crowd as he sees them, a group of admirers who turned out to pay tribute to the man who helped win the West. He tips his hat politely, delighted he has not been forgotten. Then, objective and subjective truths collide; Judd at last realizes the reactions are hostile and, swallowing what is left of his pride, moves out of the way. Early automobiles glide by and, gazing around at the general chaos, Steve Judd realizes he has become an anachronism: a man who has clung to old values in a new, modern world that no longer respects them.

An old friend and former deputy has gone another route. Gil Westrum (Randolph Scott) now makes his living by playing off their myth. A kind of bargain basement Buffalo Bill, Westrum dons a wig and challenges all comers to beat him at target shooting. Westrum is a survivor; he has trans-

The vanishing Westerner: Randolph Scott and Joel McCrea in *Ride the High Country*.

Randolph Scott and Mariette Hartley in *Ride the High Country*.

71

formed himself into a clown-like creation and, in so doing, corrupted everything he once stood for. There is one chance for his salvation, however. Judd takes on a job guiding a gold shipment from an isolated mountain town back down to the city, needs a deputy, and hires his one-time sidekick, never realizing that Gil plans to take the money—by force, if necessary—and abandon him in the wilds.

Sam Peckinpah had already earned a reputation as a strong hand at the western genre and, conceivably, a possible successor to John Ford, thanks to his work on numerous TV westerns. With *Ride the High Country,* Peckinpah established as his major theme the closing of the American frontier and, with it, the final glow of American innocence. In the classic westerns of the past, filmmakers usually concerned themselves with the golden days of the West; in the Sixties, the focus would shift to the end of the era, perfectly reflecting the transitional mood of this turbulent decade.

If the film served as a fitting introduction for its director, it likewise closed the book for both its stars. Randolph Scott and Joel McCrea had, for three decades apiece, starred in minor westerns which captured the imaginations of young boys everywhere. Scott was a cut-rate Gary Cooper, McCrea a second string Henry Fonda. But each had his own unique charms, and a sense of authenticity which he brought to his portrayal of cowboy heroes. There was something charmingly sentimental about seeing them do their swan song together, especially since their exit proved so graceful. At the conclusion, the two lawmen—finally reunited after their skirmish with each other—march to a gun duel with the Hammond boys and, as they do, the legendary status of both the characters and actors is momentarily restored.

Randolph Scott, Ron Starr, and Joel McCrea in *Ride the High Country.*

LONELY ARE THE BRAVE
UNIVERSAL-INTERNATIONAL

Produced by Edward Lewis; screenplay by Dalton Trumbo, based on the novel *The Brave Cowboy* by Edward Abbey; directed by David Miller.

CAST

John W. "Jack" Burns (Kirk Douglas); *Sheriff Johnson* (Walter Matthau); *Jerri Bondi* (Gena Rowlands); *Paul Bondi* (Michael Kane); *Hinton, the Truck Driver* (Carroll O'Connor); *Angry Lawman* (George Kennedy); *Softspoken Deputy* (William Schallert); *Man in Helicopter* (Bill Bixby)

In *Spartacus,* Kirk Douglas proved he could take the formula for a super spectacular and use it to convey a new, radical theme; in *Lonely Are the Brave,* he carried that theme a step further, this time forsaking the big, expensive format and instead opting for a small, highly personal picture. Once again, Dogulas—an avid reader—based his project on a book which had captured his imagination, this time a cult classic by Edward Abbey called *The Brave Cowboy;* once again, he chose Dalton Trumbo to pen a script. In this case, however, he experienced little cooperation from his studio. When *Lonely Are the Brave* garnered rave reviews, it had already appeared for a brief week and then disappeared. Over the years, however, it would gradually amass a reputation as one of the great "little films" of all time.

Like Sam Peckinpah's *Ride the High Country, Lonely Are the Brave* concerns an anachronism: John W. Burns, last of the old-time cowboys. Rather than the turn-of-the-century, though, this story takes place in the modern west. We first see Jack Burns on the prairie, sleeping beside a campfire, his horse hobbled nearby. Gradually, an unpleasant roaring sound appears, frightening the animal. Burns looks angrily at the sky, where supersonic jets roar overhead. The sequence symbolizes the central conception of the picture: the rugged individualist in conflict with the ever more mechanized modern society, which necessarily restricts his freedom and endangers his lifestyle. Shortly thereafter, Burns is seen cutting down a barbed wire fence, an act which exemplifies his antagonism toward the curtailment of individual freedom by the Establishment.

The story itself is a modern parable, in which Burns purposefully gets himself into a barroom

The last individualist: Kirk Douglas on Whiskey in *Lonely Are the Brave*.

fight so that he'll be thrown into jail, where his old buddy (Michael Kane) is interred; his idea is to break the both of them out and head for the hills. But the college-educated friend, who was imprisoned for hiding illegal aliens, has been beaten down by the system, and now only wants to serve his full time, then return to his wife (Gena Rowlands) and child. Burns breaks out by himself, certain no one will even bother to pursue a man whose only crime was drunk and disorderly conduct. What he doesn't know, as he makes his way over the mountain toward Mexico, is that an Air Force detachment is in the area on maneuvers; when the commander learns an escaped convict is nearby, he offers the services of his men to the local police and, before long, an amazed Burns finds that modern society is descending on him *en masse*.

An ever present sense of foreboding lends the film the aura of modern tragedy. Early in the story, a truck driver (Carroll O'Connor) is seen traveling down a highway, heading south with a load of toilets. Throughout the film, the camera continuously leaves Burns and cross-cuts back to the truck driver, though his connection with Burns is never made clear. Along the way, however, Burns' at-

An old cliché given a new twist: Modern cowboy Kirk Douglas kisses his best friend's wife (Gena Rowlands) goodbye before departing for the hills. *(Lonely Are the Brave)*

73

While fleeing the sheriff, Kirk Douglas disarms George Kennedy. *(Lonely Are the Brave)*

Lonely Are the Brave: Kirk Douglas enjoys a tranquil moment before his fight with the one-armed man, who would shortly cause David Janssen much trouble on TV's *The Fugitive.*

tachment to his horse, Whiskey—a frolicsome young colt—is clearly established. Burns could easily escape the encroaching forces of the law if he were only willing to leave the horse behind. But the cowboy's classic love for his steed ultimately proves to be his undoing. Burns manages to elude the immense posse pursuing him, but he has an appointment with fate. As Burns tries to cross the highway into Mexico, his horse panics—and the truck carrying the toilets crashes into them. The canvas here is noticeably smaller than in *Spartacus,* but the message is clear. The underlying theme of the Sixties would be rebellion against the established order of things and expression of personal individuality.

Much of the film's power derives from the excellent cast, deftly directed by David Miller. But the greatest triumph was Douglas' performance: richly textured, with a combination of physical strength and emotional softness, it proved to be the pinnacle of his career, and the last time he would be able to persuade a studio to bring one of his favorite literary works to the screen. For the next ten years, in fact, he would struggle to bring Ken Kesey's *One Flew Over the Cuckoo's Nest*—another story about a rebel battling the system—to the screen, without success. Years later, when Douglas had finally grown too old to effectively play the part, his son Michael finally managed to finance the project, and prove to the studios they had been incorrect in assuming that the book could not be turned into a financially successful motion picture.

WHAT EVER HAPPENED TO BABY JANE?

WARNER BROTHERS

Produced by Robert Aldrich; screenplay by Lukas Heller, from a novel by Henry Farrell; directed by Robert Aldrich

CAST

Blanche Hudson (Joan Crawford); *Jane Hudson* (Bette Davis); *Edwin Flagg* (Victor Buono); *Della Flagg* (Marjorie Bennett); *Elvira Stitt* (Maidie Norman); *Mrs. Bates* (Anna Lee); *Liza Bates* (Barbara Merrill); *Baby Jane* (Julie Allred); *Blanche as a Child* (Gina Gillespie); *Ray Hudson* (Dave Willock); *Cora* (Ann Barton)

One year after *The Misfits* provided the swan song for a trio of doomed superstars, another film of the early Sixties showed that two durable stars were quite able to cast off the old glamor in order to continue their careers.

Joan Crawford first arrived in Hollywood in the mid-Twenties. She had spent a miserable childhood in San Antonio, Texas, in a very poor family, and changed her name from Billie Cassin to Lucille Le Sueur when she went to work as a chorus girl in order to escape the deprivation of her early years. In many respects, she came to symbolize more than anyone else the old-fashioned notion of a "star"— that created entity, modelled for consumption by the mass audience. Even the name "Joan Crawford" came to her not from the studio bosses but as the winning entry in a fan magazine contest. During the last days of the Roaring Twenties, she had shared with Clara Bow the status of being filmdom's chief incarnation of the Flapper girl, thanks to roles in films like *Our Dancing Daughters*. But when the dark days of the Depression hit, and Bow's career slipped into oblivion, Crawford changed as quickly as a chameleon. Throughout the Thirties, she played strong-willed, independent young women in films as diverse as *Rain* (as a low-class prostitute) and *Mannequin* (as a high fashion model). In the Forties, she went on to create the role of an unloved female executive in such pictures as *Mildred Pierce* and *Daisy Kenyon*. Instead of, like Garbo, slipping out of sight so the public would not witness the disintegration of her beauty, she continued, in the Fifties, to work, playing middle-aged women menaced by young men in *Sudden*

Two who survived: Bette Davis and Joan Crawford forsook the old glamor and continued their careers at a time when other "mature" stars were swiftly fading. *(What Ever Happened to Baby Jane?)*

Bette Davis is menaced by Victor Buono, who emerged from the film a cult star. *(What Ever Happened to Baby Jane?)*

Fear and the appropriately titled *Autumn Leaves.*

Each studio had its uncrowned royalty and, while Joan Crawford was the undisputed Queen Bee of MGM throughout the Thirties and early Forties, Bette Davis occupied a similar position of prestige over at Warner Brothers. Yet if their careers ran in parallel courses, their personal lives were total opposites. Instead of a succession of created personas, Bette Davis kept the name she was born with; instead of abject poverty, she was brought up in a pleasant Massachusetts family that educated her in fine private schools and the John Murray Anderson school for drama in New York City. If people wondered, during the early years, if Crawford were a movie star only because of her beauty, they wondered, with Davis, if this immensely talented lady were beautiful enough to become a great star. Crawford was always at her best when playing slum women who scratch their way to the top: Davis played women who were born there, then desperately hang on to their positions of prominence despite various forces which threaten to drag them down; her great triumphs were as the doomed rich girl in *Dark Victory* and the spoiled southern belle in *Jezebel.* She forced Jack Warner—and Hollywood itself—to reconsider the notion of the ''star contract'' by refusing to appear in any part handed her and fighting a long, costly, and bitter court case. In the Forties, she played older, stronger women in *The Little Foxes* and *Watch on the Rhine;* in the Fifties, she admitted her age by portraying the neurotic aging star in *All About Eve,* one of the first great films of that decade.

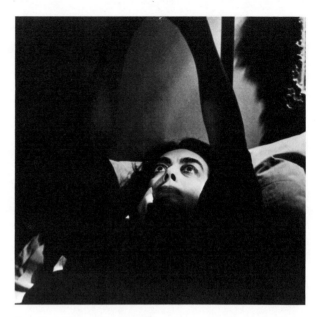

Joan Crawford as Blanche Hudson, in a scene that perfectly captures the paranoid lighting style that lent Robert Aldrich's *What Ever Happened to Baby Jane?* its psychological intensity.

A frantic moment in *What Ever Happened to Baby Jane?:* Blanche (Joan Crawford) tries to summon help, but the deranged Jane (Bette Davis) has spotted her.

In all their years as the queens of Hollywood, Davis and Crawford had never worked together in a film. Then, in 1962, writer-director Robert Aldrich gave them that opportunity. The same year that those two masterful old stars of the western, Randolph Scott and Joel McCrea, were at last united for the first time in *Ride the High Country,* Davis and Crawford teamed for *What Ever Happened to Baby Jane?* But instead of providing them with a fitting swan song, it rather redirected the careers of these two indomitable ladies. The film is to the Sixties what *Sunset Boulevard* was to the Fifties: a Grand Guignol, high camp melodrama about the Hollywood Babylon. Most of the action takes place in a decrepit house where the wheelchair-bound Blanche (Crawford) is tormented by Jane (Davis), who brings her dinner platters full of scalded rats and strangled canaries. The enmity grows from a childhood occurrence: the ''accident'' which left Blanche in a wheelchair grew directly out of Jane's obsession that Blanche's stardom in motion pictures overshadowed Jane's own fame in vaudeville. At once, a new movie genre was created, in which two great ladies of the past would be matched against one another in just such a decadent situation. The parts were hardly in keeping with the sophisticated vehicles such women had known in the Thirties, but they nonetheless proved that certain superstars did possess the energy, ambition, and indomitability to go on seemingly forever.

THE MIRACLE WORKER

UNITED ARTISTS

Produced by Fred Coe; screenplay by William Gibson, based on Helen Keller's autobiography; directed by Arthur Penn.

CAST

Annie Sullivan (Anne Bancroft); *Helen Keller* (Patty Duke); *Captain Keller* (Victor Jory); *Kate Keller* (Inga Swenson); *James Keller* (Andrew Prine); *Aunt Ev* (Kathleen Comegys); *Viney* (Beah Richards); *Mr. Anagnos* (Jack Hollander); *Helen at 7* (Peggy Burke); *Helen at 5* (Mindy Sherwood)

At the same point in time when *What Ever Happened to Baby Jane?* reintroduced two great old Hollywood stars in the new kind of roles (and new kind of picture) they would play throughout the upcoming decade, another film simultaneously introduced two other women who would emerge as significant stars of the "New Hollywood." Both women repeated roles they had made famous onstage and both, coincidentally, had been born with the same name: Anna Marie. Other than that, they came from backgrounds as diverse as those of Davis and Crawford.

Anne Bancroft was born Anna Marie Italiano in 1931; her working class parents pushed her into acting at an early age and, years later, she still recalled singing and dancing for WPA workers on the streets of the East Bronx. Unlike most serious performers, who begin working in New York and eventually try to make the great leap to Hollywood, she was picked up at once by Twentieth Century–Fox, put under contract, and provided with a new name by Darryl F. Zanuck. But the fifteen films she made over the next five years were best exemplified by the title of one of them—*Gorilla at Large*—and she turned her back on the Hollywood rat race. In New York, she tried out for the part of Gittel Mosca, the Jewish beatnik, in *Two for the Seesaw*, for the serious-minded team of writer William Gibson, producer Fred Coe, and director Arthur Penn. Bancroft did not know how to walk across a stage, and was almost dropped from the project—but she learned so quickly, and was so well received, that when Coe, Gibson, and Penn later produced *The Miracle Worker*, they never considered any actress but Bancroft for the role of Annie Sullivan. When they planned the motion picture version, Bancroft

Patty Duke as Helen Keller in *The Miracle Worker*.

was at last able to return to movies—on her own terms.

Patty Duke, born in 1946, was raised by her mother after the woman's divorce from Anna's New York cabdriver father. The girl developed into a street-savvy child, and became an actress only through an interesting coincidence. Her older brother Raymond joined a boys' club where he performed in various plays, and was spotted by John and Ethel Ross, managers of child performers. When they met young Anna Marie, they re-christened her Patty and trained her for a stage career, spending long hours working on various accents— Italian, German, Southern United States, etc.—in order to rid the girl of her idiomatic New York speech patterns. Duke immediately proved a natural, and was soon appearing regularly on live TV, in everything from plays with Laurence Olivier and Helen Hayes, to early soap operas such as *Kitty Foyle* and *Brighter Day*. A few early film roles followed but it was the stage role of Helen Keller in

Success at communication: Anne Bancroft and Patty Duke in *The Miracle Worker*.

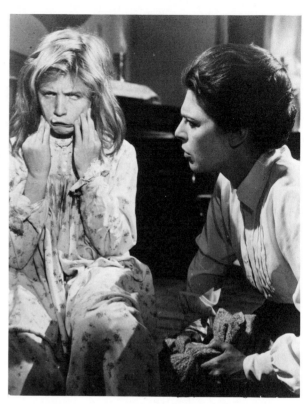

A failure to communicate: Patty Duke and Anne Bancroft in *The Miracle Worker*.

Inga Swenson protects Patty Duke from Anne Bancroft, while Andrew Prine looks on. *(The Miracle Worker)*

The Miracle Worker that made her reputation, while repeating that role in the film version made her a star—and the youngest Oscar winner ever in a regular category.

The film tells the story of the conflict between the dedicated teacher Annie Sullivan, who works with handicapped children, and her pupil Helen Keller, a blind, mute, and deaf child. As Duke sullenly exploded like a miniature time bomb, Bancroft calmly but enduringly attempted to break through the shell and reach the girl's mind. Two significant themes of Sixties films were clearly in evidence. First was the concept of "communication" as Annie fights to convey a single word to the vegetable-like child. Second, there was the notion of the Generation Gap—a term that would be on everybody's tongue shortly, as the young fought to free themselves from an earlier generation's form of knowledge. Though *The Miracle Worker* presented such a notion in only the most broadly symbolic of terms, it nonetheless provided the first powerful image of two generations locked in a heated fight, gradually learning from one another and finally finding themselves in a state of exhausted reconciliation.

Opposite page: The moment of triumph. Clockwise, from left: Anne Bancroft, Patty Duke, Victor Jory, and Inga Swenson. *(The Miracle Worker)*

Keir Dullea and Janet Margolin in the title roles of *David and Lisa.*

DAVID AND LISA
CONTINENTAL

Produced by Paul M. Heller; screenplay by Eleanor Perry, from a book by Theodore Isaac Rubin; directed by Frank Perry.

CAST

David (Keir Dullea); *Lisa* (Janet Margolin); *Dr. Swinford* (Howard Da Silva); *Mrs. Clemens* (Neva Patterson); *John* (Clifton James); *Mr. Clemens* (Richard McMurray); *Carlos* (Jaime Sanchez); *Josette* (Karen Gorney)

David and Lisa was a little picture that caught on in a big way, an offbeat love story exploring an unpleasant situation in a sensitive style. Though the film was not the type usually associated with important "breakthroughs" in the commercial film industry—it featured no smashingly modern techniques, no controversial theme—it did manage to assert that there was a growing audience for films made without the look of a typical Hollywood product; that American moviemakers could handle small, touchy subjects as well as their European counterparts could; and that medium-budget pictures of intelligence and quality might be expected to do well in places other than New York City and some college campus film societies. The American cinema was coming of age, and *David and Lisa* represented one aspect of its new maturity.

The film was the product of Eleanor and Frank Perry who, based on this movie's reputation, were for a while the darlings of those people who championed the cause of films made without the usual tinsel approach. Screenwriter Eleanor based her story on an actual case history that had been fictionalized by Dr. Theodore Isaac Rubin; it concerns young David (Keir Dullea), a psychoneurotic boy living at a private school for disturbed young adolescents, and his gradual growth of affection for Lisa (Janet Margolin), a schizophrenic girl at the same institution. David is unable to make friendships, due largely to his strange, unexplainable phobia about being touched by anyone; he harbors an antagonistic, mistrustful attitude toward both his seemingly loving and concerned parents, and also toward all parental figures including the well-meaning Dr. Swinford (Howard Da Silva), the enlightened head of the school. Lisa is far less connected with the realities of her present situation. She speaks in deeply involved rhymes, and removes herself al-

Janet Margolin as Lisa, the disturbed young woman. *(David and Lisa)*

most entirely from the everyday world by burrowing ever deeper into her shell. Despite their problems, David and Lisa gradually learn to love one another—so much so that, eventually, she is able to physically touch him without his being upset by the contact, while he can speak to her of their present feelings without her needing to withdraw from the conversation or disguise her true emotions.

In essence, David and Lisa are able to achieve some good for one another thanks to their mutual love. If this was an extremely simple message, and if director Frank Perry communicated it in an uninspired movie style, it still packed a punch. At approximately the same time, other filmmakers were moving in similar directions. An English-made movie, *The Mark,* dealt with the love affair between a man (Stuart Whitman) formerly convicted of child molesting and a young woman (Maria Schell) who must, through love, help him escape from the obsession; in *A Patch of Blue,* Sidney Poitier played a gentle black man who befriends Elizabeth Hartman, as a blind white girl.

Each is an offbeat love story and, more significantly for the time in which they were made, each deals with a handicapped person brought out of his/her shell through honest affection from another human being. Mentally disturbed people are no longer seen as monsters (as in the Fifties classic, *The Bad Seed*) or pathetically twisted subjects of case studies *(The Three Faces of Eve)* but as people, capable of emotional relationships despite their problems. In the early Sixties, films about mental patients, as seen from this new and liberated point of view, would suddenly dominate the screen. John Huston's *Freud* featured Montgomery Clift as the father of modern psychology, attempting to cure a beautiful young woman (Susannah York); *The Slender Thread* presented Anne Bancroft as a woman on the edge of suicide, who is brought back to reality by Sidney Poitier, a concerned social worker; and even cheapjack melodramas *(The Caretakers)* and trashy thrillers *(Shock Corridor, Shock Treatment)* continued the trend. On Broadway, there was Kirk Douglas in an adaptation of Ken Kesey's novel about life in an institution, *One Flew Over the Cuckoo's Nest.*

But no film gave this theme a more believable yet lyrical treatment than *David and Lisa.* These were strange times for the country, and for Hollywood too. The psychological films of the early Sixties represent an attempt at enlightenment that may appear sentimental today, but which in its time characterized the American consciousness and was reflected in its films.

A Happy Ending: Janet Margolin and Keir Dullea in *David and Lisa.*

Toward communication: Keir Dullea and Howard Da Silva in *David and Lisa.*

Alienated Youth: David (Keir Dullea) rejects the lifestyle of his parents. *(David and Lisa)*

Hanging from a church steeple, Red Buttons witnesses the destruction of his squad. *(The Longest Day)*

THE LONGEST DAY
20TH CENTURY–FOX

Produced by Darryl F. Zanuck; screenplay by Cornelius Ryan, from his book, with additional episodes written by Romain Gary, James Jones, David Pursall, and Jack Seddon; directed by Andrew Marton (American episodes), Ken Annakin (British episodes), and Bernhard Wicki (German episodes).

CAST

Lt. Colonel Benjamin Vandervoort (John Wayne); *Brig. General Norman Cota* (Robert Mitchum); *Brig. General Theodore Roosevelt* (Henry Fonda); *Brig. General James M. Gavin* (Robert Ryan); *Destroyer Commander* (Rod Steiger); *U. S. Rangers* (Robert Wagner, Paul Anka, Fabian, and Tommy Sands); *Private "Dutch" Schultz* (Richard Beymer); *Maj. General Robert Haines* (Mel Ferrer); *Sgt. Fuller* (Jeff Hunter); *Pvt. Martini* (Sal Mineo); *Pvt. Morris* (Roddy McDowall); *Col. Newton* (Eddie Albert); *General Barton* (Edmond O'Brien); *Pvt. Steele* (Red Buttons); *Lt. Wilson* (Tom Tryon); *Maj. General Walter Bedell Smith* (Alexander Knox); *General Eisenhower* (Henry Grace); *General Omar Bradley* (Nicholas Stuart); *R.A.F. Pilot* (Richard Burton); *Lord Lovat* (Peter Lawford); *Major Howard* (Richard Todd); *General Parker* (Leo Genn); *Pvt. Flanagan* (Sean Connery); *Janine Boitard* (Irina Demick); *Mayor of Colleville* (Bourvil); *Commander Kieffer* (Christian Marquand); *General Blumentritt* (Curt Jurgens); *Lt. Ocker* (Peter Van Eyck); *Sgt. Kaffeeklatsch* (Gerd Froebe)

The great producers of the Thirties and Forties were suddenly all gone, save one: Darryl F. Zanuck stood as a final reminder of the uniquely gifted people, from David O. Selznick to Louis B. Mayer, who had conceived of great projects and then carried them through in spite of constant setbacks: assembling the teams of directors, writers, and stars they wanted, then inducing them into delivering on screen the very picture which the producer had had in mind from the beginning. The Sixties would see an upsurge of "little" films like *David and Lisa.* But Zanuck flamboyantly continued to supply the public with an updated version of the movie genre which was quickly slipping from favor: all-star superspectaculars. *The Longest Day,* his stirring, occasionally stunning tribute to the men who fought during the Normandy invasion, proved to be one of the last great examples of this costly type of American movie.

The picture begins on the morning of the D-Day invasion, and introduces us to the various people who will take part: the Americans and English, waiting on their boats for a combined air-sea invasion; the Germans, realizing that occupied France must be the next target of the Allies; the French resistance, hurriedly working to make the path of attack as safe as possible for the oncoming troops. Previous war films merely used such massive confrontations as a backdrop for melodrama between fictional characters. Zanuck insisted on closely following Cornelius Ryan's book, which was a study of the battle itself: the strategies as they were elucidated by the officers in charge and then carried out by the fighting men on the battlefields. Essentially, Zanuck called for a dramatized documentary, alternating a concentration on the technical side of modern warfare with choice human moments of emotion as illustrated in brief cameo sequences.

Therefore, the main thrust of the action alternates between two sets of two men: the officers, Colonel Vandervoort (John Wayne) of the 82nd Airborne Division, assigned to infiltrate the enemy outposts by a parachute attack, and General Cota (Robert Mitchum) whose 29th Division spearheads the assault onto the Omaha Beachhead; and the privates, John Steele (Red Buttons), whose parachute

Irina Demich proves understandably distracting to the German guards in *The Longest Day*.

Darryl F. Zanuck re-created the Normandy Invasion in all its epic "glory" for *The Longest Day*.

Robert Wagner as a U.S. Ranger in *The Longest Day*.

becomes caught on a church steeple of the town square, forcing him to hang helplessly and watch the slaughter of his fellows by the Nazis, and "Dutch" Schultz (Richard Beymer), who loses contact with his outfit shortly after the first attack on the beach and spends the entire film trying desperately to find them. In both these latter episodes, there is an element of humor drawn from the absurdity of war. But the film's total effect is epic in nature, and these four characters remain the important threads which, again and again—after countless other characters have appeared and reappeared—serve to give us the sensation of constant elements.

In the tradition of the great producers of the past, Mr. Zanuck permitted himself the luxury of casting the current leading lady in his personal life—a pretty but talentless girl named Irina Demick—in a major role as a pretty French resistance fighter who peddles her bicycle past Nazi lines in order to deliver important messages to the Allies; Zanuck was insistent that she wear an anachronistic dress in order to show off her marvelous legs. Otherwise, the cast was made up almost entirely of name stars. Some critics argued that having the roles of the officers and enlisted men played by movie stars damaged the film's sense of realism, since, for example, we were always aware it was Henry Fonda, not really General Roosevelt, we were watching.

On the other hand, the star system casting had its benefits. Without such well known faces, it would be nearly impossible for anyone in the audience to remember, from one scene to the next, who was who. And despite the claims of commercialism, Zanuck did make some impressive demands on his

audience. The film was shot in the authentic languages of the French and German, with subtitles provided during those sections of the story. The film is artistically innovative, featuring one unforgettable traveling camera shot which whisks us over a vast terrain of battle, slowing down in order to allow us momentary glimpses of the fighting, then moving on again to another area of interest; how the sequence was accomplished without a single edit is still a wonder to film students. All in all, *The Longest Day* offers an impressive combination of old-fashioned commercialism and, for its time, groundbreaking technical achievements.

LAWRENCE OF ARABIA
COLUMBIA

Produced by Sam Spiegel; screenplay by Robert Bolt; directed by David Lean.

CAST

T. E. Lawrence (Peter O'Toole); *Sherif Ali* (Omar Sharif); *Prince Faisal* (Alec Guinness); *Auda Abu Tayi* (Anthony Quinn); *General Allenby* (Jack Hawkins); *Dryden* (Claude Rains); *Colonel Harry Brighton* (Anthony Quayle); *Jackson Bentley* (Arthur Kennedy); *The Bey* (Jose Ferrer); *General Murray* (Donald Wolfit); *Tafas* (Zia Mohyeddin); *Farraj* (Michel Ray); *Daud* (John Dimech)

T. E. Lawrence was one of those enigmatic figures who capture the imagination of the entire world: the man had charisma enough to charm massive nations of primitive people with his golden mien; intelligence enough to manipulate tribes of nomadic Arabs into guerrilla warriors working for the British; and talent enough to capture a kind of mystical poetry in his writings. Also, there was a touch of cruelty that made him appear dangerous and frightening, as well as mysterious. What terrible demons were at work under the surface calm of this amazing fellow? How he might have changed the future of the world had he not died in a freak motorcycle accident—but would he have changed it for good or for evil? These were some of the questions producer Sam Spiegel hoped to raise in his multi-million dollar movie epic about Lawrence. Realizing the immense spectacles that had emerged during the Fifties were no longer selling tickets, Spiegel decided to try a new style for oversized

84

movies. Instead of the ordinary ploy—casting Charlton Heston in any role that featured a historical setting and large scope—Spiegel decided to have Lawrence portrayed by an unknown young British performer who had recently dazzled the London stage with his interpretation of Hamlet. Overnight, Peter O'Toole became a star—and the entire world's conception of T. E. Lawrence.

Unfortunately, the film was not as successful as Spiegel hoped. At well over three hours running time, even the most interesting material can easily turn tedious, and the script provided by playwright Robert Bolt didn't always keep that from happening. The actual impetus to do the story in the first place—studying enigmatic qualities of Lawrence's personality, and presenting this to the audience within the content of a popular entertainment film—was precisely what the production missed. Bolt told the story of Lawrence's life: his entrance into the Arabian desert as a representative of England during World War I; his ability to win over the skeptical Arab forces to the belief that their future rested with Britain; his effectiveness at organizing the tribesmen into a lightning strike force that could attack as a guerrilla army; his conception of a United Arab State to be augmented at some time in the future; his waning interest in the entire situation once the fighting was over and the professional politicians began moving in. What was unintentionally omitted were the most important things of all: Lawrence's motivations for what he did. As Bosley Crowther rightly complained in his New York *Times* review, *Lawrence* reduced "a legendary figure to conventional movie hero size amidst magnificent and exotic scenery . . . We know little more about this strange man when it is over than we did when it began."

Still, *Lawrence* won a large number of Academy

Peter O'Toole and Anthony Quinn map out their strategy for a brutal attack. *(Lawrence of Arabia)*

Lawrence of Arabia: Lawrence's raiders await the approach of a train . . .

. . . and then attack with ferocity.

86

Award nominations for what it did have to offer. First, there was the exquisite cast, which featured such major names as Anthony Quinn (hiding behind a putty nose as an Arab chieftain), Jack Hawkins (a British general), Alec Guinness (a Machiavellian desert prince) and Arthur Kennedy (an American journalist attempting to capture the riddle of Lawrence for his newspaper, and proving just as ineffectual at that job as this movie). *Lawrence* offered an eyeful on the level of sheer spectacle: the great vistas, the caravans of camels, the tribesmen in their cloaks and hoods, crossing and re-crossing the desert sands. Mostly, though, what stands out in the mind years later are the action sequences, especially one notable moment when a group of tribesmen, inspired by Lawrence, ambush a train in the desert. As captured on film by director David Lean,

the spectacle affects us as much as Lawrence did those around him: we are caught up in the tremendous rush of excitement, almost hypnotized by the image of Lawrence rising, Christ-like, in his white robes out of the ranks of his men, then strolling down a hillside with his shouting disciples circling him on all sides.

Much of this magical quality came from Peter O'Toole's presence in the title role. Some critics suggested this would prove a one-shot for him, that the role of Lawrence would be as deadly for his career as the role of Christ had already turned out to be for so many actors. That did not happen to be the case. Shortly thereafter, O'Toole co-starred with Richard Burton in *Becket,* and was totally acceptable in that very different historical role.

The first plane attacks on the desert kingdom in *Lawrence of Arabia.*

"How did they *ever* make a movie out of *Lolita*?" Sue Lyon and James Mason.

LOLITA

METRO-GOLDWYN-MAYER

Produced by James B. Harris; screenplay by Vladimir Nabokov, based on his novel of the same name; directed by Stanley Kubrick.

CAST

Humbert Humbert (James Mason); *Charlotte Haze* (Shelley Winters); *Clare Quilty* (Peter Sellers); *Lolita Haze* (Sue Lyon); *Vivian Darkbloom* (Marianne Stone); *Jean Farlow* (Diane Decker); *John Farlow* (Jerry Stovin); *Dick* (Gary Cockrell); *Lorna* (Roberta Shore); *Nurse Lore* (Lois Maxwell)

In an era of unforgettable advertising ploys, it was, perhaps, the ultimate: "How did they *ever*," the billboards asked, "make a movie out of *Lo-*

lita?" For those people who had actually waded through Vladimir Nabokov's immense, perversely entertaining novel, the answer was simple: they didn't. The most controversial aspect of the book had been the hero's uncontrollable passion for a child—a "nymphet," as Nabokov labelled her. In 1962, the mass audience was not yet ready (or so MGM believed) for such a subject to appear on film; the impact was watered down somewhat when the role of Lolita Haze was handed to a teenage actress, and the story became an older man's tragic but understandable lust for an attractive younger woman. Despite this and certain other compromises, *Lolita* still turned out to be one of the year's better pictures, and an important step toward the gradual maturity of the mass-audience film.

The picture opens at the point where the book ends: Humbert Humbert (James Mason) enters a mansion-like house which is in a state of total disrepair. Curled up on a couch drunk is Clare Quilty

(Peter Sellers), the man Humbert holds responsible for the gradual loss of affection from the young woman he loves. Humbert wakes Quilty, talks to him calmly, and cajoles the man into a desperate game of table tennis. Gradually, Quilty realizes Humbert's actual reason for being there: the intruder pulls out a pistol and quietly explains he's about to have his revenge. Quilty begs for his life—at first desperately, then hysterically—while Humbert continues to serve ping pong balls, putting Quilty (and to a degree the viewer as well) through excruciating humiliation until he at last pulls the trigger and ends the cad's life. As the scene fades to dark, we are whisked back to the series of events that led directly to this incident: beginning on the fateful day when Humbert, a pseudo-celebrity and frequent guest on the dinner lecture circuit, allowed himself to be swept into a relationship with the nouveau riche, overweight matron Charlotte Haze (Shelley Winters) in order that he might pursue the woman's flirtatious daughter, Lolita (Sue Lyon).

The casting of Ms. Lyon in the title role was the film's only major flaw. Though she looked right for the part—thin enough so that she appeared not yet a woman, but with big, eager eyes peering over her famous heart-shaped plastic sunglasses—her acting was awkward. Though Tuesday Weld was by that time a young woman, she probably should have played the role anyway. Otherwise, the casting was perfect: as Clare Quilty, Peter Sellers had the chance to don a series of disguises, which fit in well with the similar multi-character roles he had been playing in English comedies. Shelley Winters, onetime glamor girl who had been steadily gaining weight—along with a formidable reputation as a character actress—added another of her comically pathetic portraits as the well-intentioned but pretentious mother. Best of all, though, was James Mason, employing his subtle voice to add levels of sardonic dimensions to Humbert.

Fortunately, Nabokov was himself employed to write the screenplay, which helped keep *Lolita* from slipping into the exercise in sensationalism it might, very easily, have become. But *Lolita* the film is more a work of personal expression for its director, Stanley Kubrick. His great theme—classical art, and its relationship to our lives—permeates *Lolita,* as it does his later works including *A Clockwork Orange,* in which the protaganist beats a woman to death with a statue of Beethoven while listening to the Fifth Symphony. Even in his earlier work, Kubrick was defining his statement about the humanities: they do little to make us more human.

The infernal triangle: James Mason, Shelley Winters, and Sue Lyon providing a bizarre image of an American "family" in *Lolita*.

Enter Clare Quilty: Peter Sellers dances with Marianne Stone, but his mind is clearly elsewhere. *(Lolita)*

End as beginning: Humbert (James Mason) murders Quilty (Peter Sellers) in *Lolita*.

The gigolo and the dilettante: James Mason and Shelley Winters, caught in the act. (*Lolita*)

The generals in *Paths of Glory* enjoy excellent painting and fine music, even as they order the shooting of three innocent men; when Humbert kills Clare Quilty in the mansion, immense paintings stare down. *Lolita* may not have offered a film version of what was most fascinating in the book it was based on, but it did provide audiences with yet another work of sophisticated entertainment that would have been impossible to make only a few years earlier.

THE INTERNS

COLUMBIA

Produced by Robert Cohn; screenplay by Walter Newman and David Swift, from the novel by Richard Frede, directed by David Swift.

CAST

Dr. Considine (Michael Callan); *Dr. John Paul Otis* (Cliff Robertson); *Dr. Lew Worship* (James MacArthur); *Dr. Sid Lackland* (Nick Adams); *Lisa Cardigan* (Suzy Parker); *Mado* (Haya Harareet); *Mildred* (Anne Helm); *Gloria* (Stefanie Powers); *Dr. Sidney Wohl* (Buddy Ebsen); *Dr. Riccio* (Telly Savalas); *Loara* (Ellen Davalos); *Didi Loomis* (Kay Stevens); *Nurse Flynn* (Katharine Bard)

Doctors are sex symbols and objects of fantasy for almost any woman who doesn't happen to be married to one. Lew Ayres and Van Johnson provided heartthrobs aplenty throughout the Thirties and Forties as young interns. But in the Fifties, doctors were noticeably absent from the screen, except for one large scale melodrama, *Not as a Stranger,* with Robert Mitchum and Frank Sinatra. In the Sixties, though, sexy young doctors would return—in droves. First, television-industry executives finally cancelled most of the long-running western series and put doctors on in prime time in their place: Richard Chamberlain provided a clean-cut interpretation of *Young Doctor Kildaire,* while Vince Edwards offered a surly surgeon named *Ben Casey.* The ratings on both shows were high, and moviemakers revived the doctors, too.

Based on a best-selling book by Richard Frede, *The Interns* followed four young medical practitioners during their first year of internship at New North Hospital, concentrating more on their melodramatic love lives than on their growing expertise as surgeons. Dr. John Otis (Cliff Robertson), an extremely serious older student, thinks of nothing except the great work he will one day accomplish until, by accident, he meets and falls in love with a sophisticated New York model, Lisa (Suzy Parker), who desperately needs some drugs in order to abort a baby she does not want; Lew Worship (James MacArthur) falls for a student nurse (Stefanie Powers) who is insistent she doesn't want to marry a doctor; Dr. Alec Considine (Michael Callan), the school's would-be manipulator of women, tries to live a double sex life with both a pretty socialite (Anne Helm) he eventually plans to marry and with Nurse Flynn (Katharine Bard) who has important connections that can further his career; Sid Lackland (Nick Adams) is a wise guy whose big mouth actually covers a wealth of sincerity and vulnerability, which becomes clear when he falls for one of the patients, Loara (Ellen Davalos), a Eurasian woman suffering a slow death from an incurable disease.

But the most fascinating element in the entire film actually had nothing to do with any of them, involving instead a feminist plea which predated the Women's Movement by several years. A dedicated young woman, Mado (Haya Harareet) comes into conflict with the chauvinist in charge of residents, Dr. Riccio (Telly Savalas), who deeply believes it is a waste of time to educate women since so many of them leave practice in order to have families. Their problem is resolved in a surprisingly enlightened way for such a sensational sort of film, when Mado gradually convinces Riccio of her worth, and he requests she be allowed to work under him the following year. But the teenage audience that thronged to see *The Interns* was willing to tolerate such sensible happenings while waiting for the film's big scenes, including a well publicized wild party in which the obligatory dumb blonde nurse who has never taken a drink is induced into first downing half a bowlful of spiked punch, then gyrating in a lavish striptease.

The Interns served as a cinematic introduction to the four young actors being touted for future stardom. Cliff Robertson had of course already established himself as a serious performer in films *(Picnic, The Naked and the Dead)* and television work *(The Hustler, Days of Wine and Roses)* during the Fifties, without ever achieving full stardom; his role in *The Interns* was easily the finest acting among the young leads, although he still appeared to be slumming while waiting for better pictures. James MacArthur would find himself replaced by Dean Jones in the sequel, *The New Interns,* but found work as a private eye on TV's *Hawaii Five-O;* Mi-

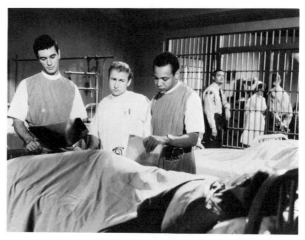

Nick Adams, star of TV's *The Rebel,* made an ill-fated bid for movie stardom as the young doctor whose girlfriend dies of an incurable disease in *The Interns.*

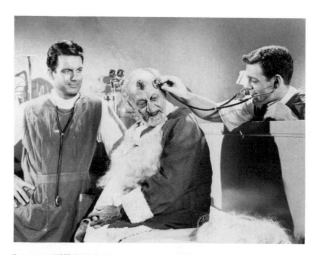

Interns Cliff Robertson and James MacArthur treat a drunken street-corner Santa Claus. *(The Interns)*

Women's liberation received a boost when uncompromising doctor Telly Savalas recognized the talents of female intern Haya Harareet. *(The Interns)*

A less than merry Christmas: James MacArthur looks on as Cliff Robertson proposes to Suzy Parker in *The Interns*.

In the brainwashing sequence of *The Manchurian Candidate*, the communists make their captives (Frank Sinatra, Laurence Harvey, and an unbilled player) believe they are attending a tea party.

chael Callan, a graduate of teenage exploitation flicks (*Because They're Young, Gidget Goes Hawaiian*), tried to establish himself as a combination Tony Curtis–Jack Lemmon, but his career never took off. Nick Adams was soon lost in Japanese horror films and never fulfilled the promise of his hit TV series, *The Rebel*. Essentially, for all the young leads except Cliff Robertson, *The Interns* proved to be only a momentary success that offered youthful audiences two hours of escapism on hot summer evenings.

THE MANCHURIAN CANDIDATE

UNITED ARTISTS

Produced by George Axelrod and John Frankenheimer; screenplay by George Axelrod, from the novel by Richard Condon; directed by John Frankenheimer.

CAST

Bennett Marco (Frank Sinatra); *Raymond Shaw* (Laurence Harvey); *Rosie* (Janet Leigh); *Raymond's Mother* (Angela Lansbury); *Chunjin* (Henry Silva); *Senator Iselin* (James Gregory); *Jocie Jordan* (Leslie Parrish); *Senator Jordan* (John McGiver); *Cpl. Melvin* (James Edwards); *Yen Lo* (Knigh Dhiegh); *Berezovo* (Madame Spivy)

Could it have been mere coincidence that only one year before the assassination of President Kennedy by a man who seemed, from all outward indications, the least likely person to embark on such an undertaking, that a motion picture would not only predict a major political killing but also explain how any man might be twisted into an assassin by various world powers? John Frankenheimer's *The Manchurian Candidate* contained its share of prophecy, even as it analyzed a situation that would soon become an unpleasant but regular element in our lives. In essence, the moviemaker reacted to the quality of life shaping up in the America of the Sixties, and projected a view of what would inevitably follow.

The Manchurian Candidate begins with a nightmare vision, as a young Korean war vet, former Corporal Melvin (James Edwards), wakes with terrible memories of that point in his life when he was confined in an enemy P.O.W. camp. Other one-time squad members have similar dreams, including

Frank Sinatra watches as Laurence Harvey deals the cards and, unwittingly, unlocks the key to his brainwashed mind. (*The Manchurian Candidate*)

Bennett Marco (Frank Sinatra), who cannot comprehend why he constantly tells everyone Raymond Shaw (Laurence Harvey) is his best friend—seeing as he never particularly liked Shaw. Despite the fact that these men are now living apparently normal lives, they were all brainwashed by their captors, and Shaw's state is the most frightening of all—because he has been carefully programmed as an assassin who would without hesitation kill the moment he comes into contact with the code developed to set him off. Shaw is now in love with the daughter (Leslie Parrish) of a likable liberal senator (John McGiver) but eliminates them both when his psychological-kill mechanism is activated. Ultimately, he becomes the pawn in a monstrous assassination attempt, when he is manipulated by his own mother (Angela Lansbury) and her red-baiting, Joe McCarthy-ish senator-husband (James Gregory). Fighting against time to stop the assassination is his old war-buddy Marco, who combats his own brainwashed mind—programmed to respect and protect Shaw, above all else—in order to stop the travesty about to take place.

John Frankenheimer's direction combined the slick thriller quality of an Alfred Hitchcock suspense story with the arty camerawork of Orson Welles' early classics like *Citizen Kane*. The public appeared ready to accept the interestingly awkward camera angles Welles had attempted to introduce two decades earlier and which, at that time, seemed confusing and unnerving to the mass audience. In one famous sequence, a staging of the actual brainwashing incident, Frankenheimer juxtaposed a "realistic" image of the American P.O.W.'s under the influence of their Communist captors with scenes illustrating the experience as it appears in the minds of the men. The commercial cinema was, in the Sixties, embracing surrealism: that significant trend in modern art which had first captured modern painting and then the avant garde cinema with its exaggerated lines and distorted shapes mirroring a world gone mad. Importantly, all this was achieved in *Candidate* without any loss of dramatic tension, while even a conventional romantic subplot (improbable, but nonetheless involving) was introduced between Marco and an attractive young woman (Janet Leigh) who falls in love with the man.

At the time of its release, *Candidate* proved controversial. Richard Condon's novel had been written for the screen by George Axelrod, a well-known humorist *(The Seven Year Itch),* and he infused the project with a quality of black comedy; people were uncertain as to whether they should take this as a tale of psychological horror or a dark farce.

Frank Sinatra and Laurence Harvey clown on the set of *The Manchurian Candidate*.

The Manchurian Candidate changed Hollywood's notion of what audiences would accept in both the style and subject of a mass market film, blending a savage satire of politics in particular and America in general with suspense and romance. Within a year of the film's release, the country would begin to explode: the assassinations, the race riots, the peace demonstrations would all follow in time. In the final days of peace and tranquility, *The Manchurian Candidate* hinted at what was just around the corner.

James Gregory, as a Joe McCarthy-ish U.S. Senator, in *The Manchurian Candidate*.

A troubled Frank Sinatra is comforted by Janet Leigh, who helps him understand the psychological trap he is in. *(The Manchurian Candidate)*

1963

AMERICA AMERICA

WARNER BROTHERS

Produced, directed, and written for the screen by Elia Kazan.

CAST

Stavros Topouzoglou (Stathis Giallelis); *Vartan Damadian* (Frank Wolff); *Isaac Topouzoglou* (Harry Davis); *Vasso* (Elena Karam); *Grandmother* (Estelle Hemsley); *Hohanness Gardashian* (Gregory Rozakis); *Abdul* (Lou Antonio); *Odysseus* (Salem Ludwig); *Garabet* (John Marley); *Vartuhi* (Johanna Frank); *Aleko Sinnikoglou* (Paul Mann); *Thomna* (Linda Marsh); *Sophia* (Katherine Balfour)

America America: Young Stathis Giallelis is exuberant at the thought of reaching America.

The films of Elia Kazan are all concerned with one great subject: America. In *A Tree Grows in Brooklyn,* his premiere motion picture, Kazan dealt with the sentiments of a large family trying to hang on to their old values in the changing world of a modern city; in *Gentleman's Agreement* and *Pinky,* he treated anti-Semitism and racism, revealing how they infect every aspect of our society; in *Panic in the Streets,* he intruded on the low life of New Orleans and, in *On the Waterfront,* the working class of New York; in *East of Eden* and *Splendor in the Grass,* the director focused on the rebelliousness of American youth. Even his later, far less successful films display a scrutiny of the American success ethic, and its corruptive influence on creative people: *The Arrangement* (based on his own popular novel) and *The Last Tycoon* (taken from an unfinished work by Scott Fitzgerald) prove Kazan's themes, if not the quality of his work, remained constant. But nowhere was Kazan's feeling for America so strong and sincere as in *America America.*

That was in part due to the fact Kazan based this picture on a book he had himself written a few years previously, about his own uncle—a man who traveled to America from Turkey and eventually made his way through Ellis Island into the melting pot of early twentieth-century America. Kazan's story thus foreshadowed the incredibly popular *Roots,* with its tracing of a single family's heritage; at the same time, it predated *The Godfather, Part II* with its powerful vision of modern America as a place shaped by the faceless immigrants who survive in the big city jungles of the new world. Kazan, who usually employed the biggest movie stars for his projects, was wise enough to realize unknowns were necessary for this story. He chose a young Greek actor, Stathis Giallelis, for the difficult, demanding role of his uncle Stavros, then followed the man on an uncertain odyssey from Anatolia to America. Vividly, and very often brilliantly, Kazan chronicled the brutality of the Turkish regime in the boy's homeland, clearly communicating to viewers the motivation for leaving. Then, Stavros' singular trek is followed from this outpost in Asia Minor, across a ravaged landscape where he is at first befriended, then betrayed, by a wily Turk, Abdul (Lou Antonio), who leaves the lad with literally no possessions to carry to America with him.

All of this is conveyed in stunningly stark black-and-white cinematography by Haskell Wexler. Just as significant to the effect is the ethnic music of Manos Hadjidakis, which flavors the film with a feeling for Greek culture. As the young hero arrives in Constantinople, he is waylaid by an attractive young woman, Thomna (Linda Marsh), to whom he is temporarily engaged—and almost married. But he leaves in order to pursue his dream and, after many adventures culminating with a long ocean voyage, finally arrives in America. Kazan dared to make this a two-hour, 45-minute film in length, almost as long as an all-star epic like *The Longest Day* or *Cleopatra.* But while his film is epic in length, the absence of big name stars suggests it is, after all, a personal epic, restrained in its outlook

95

A dramatic moment in the old country. *(America America)*

Mounted horsemen give the villagers reason to want to emigrate. *(America America)*

A joyous, exuberant moment relieves the heavy drama of *America America.*

and without any of those qualities—grand passions or elaborate action scenes—that usually distinguish motion pictures of such size.

Instead, Kazan combined the known facts of his family's history with some subdued fictionalized episodes employed to fill in the unknown stretches of Stavros' life, producing a masterful study of the kind of spirit that created the vast number of families which formed the backbone of our country in the early years of this century. Significantly, it is a film which could only have been made in the first half of this decade. By the late Sixties, the Youth Movement and the campus revolution would create a growing cynicism with the American Dream, and that feeling would manifest itself in the already mentioned *Godfather* films of the Seventies, in which the immigrants would be portrayed as a corrupting influence on the country that embraced them. Kazan's critically, if not commercially, successful picture stands as the last great example not only of the serious black-and-white socially oriented melodrama that had come to popularity in the Fifties, but also as one of the final films to treat the country's origins with respect and dignity.

THE BIRDS
UNIVERSAL

Produced by Alfred Hitchcock; screenplay by Evan Hunter, from the story by Daphne du Maurier; directed by Alfred Hitchcock.

CAST

Mitch Brenner (Rod Taylor); *Melanie Daniels* (Tippi Hedren); *Lydia Brenner* (Jessica Tandy); *Annie Hayworth* (Suzanne Pleshette); *Cathy Brenner* (Veronica Cartwright); *Mrs. Bundy* (Ethel Griffies); *Sebastian Sholes* (Charles McGraw); *Mrs. MacGruder* (Ruth McDevitt); *Salesman* (Joe Mantell); *Fisherman* (Doodles Weaver); *Man in Elevator* (Richard Deacon); *Man in Front of Pet Shop with White Poodles* (Alfred Hitchcock)

96

An ecological doomsday: Tippi Hedren, Rod Taylor, and Jessica Tandy attacked by *The Birds*.

Every Hitchcock film has a MacGuffin: the key that unlocks a logical explanation for all the apparently insane things occurring throughout the story. Always, we enjoy the eerie elements of suspense: strange things are happening! Always, though, the mystery is ultimately cleared up, and motivations are made to seem quite rational—if less than likely. That is the basis of the successful Hitchcock formula, and it worked well for over 30 years. But in 1963, Hitchcock gave his audience the greatest shock of all: a film without a MacGuffin.

It was *The Birds,* a beautifully controlled nightmare-come-to-life that begins with a tantalizingly pleasant, deceptively relaxed confrontation in a pet store between an attractive young man, Mitch Brenner (Rod Taylor) and a beautiful woman, Melanie Daniels (Tippi Hedren). As in a typical Hitchcock outing, the two take an immediate dislike (or is that only to cover up their mutual attraction?) to one another. The only hint of anything unnatural brewing is the large number of birds, circling in the distant skies over Southern California; interestingly, no one seems to notice or pay them much attention. The heroine, acting mischievous, plays a practical joke on the man and then, being a creature of impulse, decides to drive to the fishing village some miles south of San Francisco where he lives—carrying along with her, as a present, a pair of love birds—to make up for their bad start. Upon arrival, Melanie meets Annie Hayworth (Suzanne Pleshette), a local teacher and former girlfriend of Mitch's, who warns the newcomer about the man's obsessively domineering mother (Jessica Tandy).

For some time, the film unravels as a strange romantic melodrama, until the sound of the birds in

Rod Taylor and Suzanne Pleshette rescue a downed child, while Tippi Hedren runs to join them, in *The Birds*.

Children are menaced by *The Birds*.

the sky grows louder. The schoolteacher is killed in the first wave of an onslaught by the thousands of winged creatures who sweep down while Melanie, Mitch, Mrs. Brenner and Mitch's young sister, Cathy (Veronica Cartwright), take refuge in the Brenner family's house. It quickly becomes apparent the birds are concentrating their attack on this place—but why? Could it be the presence of a web of passions at work between the people that is carrying over to nature? Is Hitchcock trying to realistically show how the balance of nature can be dangerously thrown off, or is this his view of Armageddon? The special effects are fascinating and frightening, but the most amazing thing about the film is that those questions are never answered.

In the Thirties, Forties, and Fifties, Hitchcock complied with the audience's desire for everything to be tied up neatly at the end. But first with *Psycho* and then with *The Birds,* he stepped carefully away from his successful format and began experiment-

ing with more demanding approaches to his material. And while many viewers complained about the confusing ending, the film's box-office success proved that viewers would accept an entertainment picture even if it refused to satisfy them in the way they were used to being satisfied. The film's only great weakness, in fact, was not the ambiguous ending but the presence of Tippi Hedren, whom Hitchcock hoped would emerge as his new Grace Kelly. Though Ms. Hedren had the high cheekbones, classic beauty and classy aura, she proved rather zombie-like onscreen—without any of the charm and depth of personality that Ms. Kelly had brought to her roles.

In terms of its theme, *The Birds* predated the ecology movement which would, in the latter half of the decade, emerge as one of the great social causes—as more and more citizens became concerned over the possibility that our technological-industrial way of life was throwing off the balance of nature, a mistake for which we would eventually have to pay a price. In terms of its technique, *The Birds* emphasized—by virtue of its omitting the MacGuffin—the notion that, in the Sixties, there would no longer be simple answers. Part of the reason Hitchcock was able to survive as a popular film-maker must be attributed to the fact that, unlike many of his contemporaries, he could sense the changing times and artistically adjust to them. *The Birds* displays his uncanny intuitive understanding of the new Sixties sensibility.

BEACH PARTY

AMERICAN-INTERNATIONAL PICTURES

Produced by James H. Nicholson and Lou Rusoff; screenplay by Lou Rusoff; directed by William Asher.

CAST

Professor Sutwell (Bob Cummings); *Marianne* (Dorothy Malone); *Frankie* (Frankie Avalon); *Dolores* (Annette Funicello); *Eric Von Zipper* (Harvey Lembeck); *Deadhead* (Jody McCrea); *Kenny* (John Ashley); *Cappy* (Morey Amsterdam); *Ava* (Eva Six); *Miss Perpetual Motion* (Candy Johnson); *Dick Dale and the Del Tones* (Themselves)

In the late Fifties, filmmakers had discovered, to their delight, the new potential of the youth market as an important box-office possibility, and such items as the Elvis Presley pictures (*Jailhouse Rock*), ludicrously conceived and exasperatingly executed youth dramas (*High School Confidential*), and rock 'n' roll exploitation vehicles (*Rock Around the Clock*) at once flooded the market. Quickly, however, a backlash from church, school, civic and parental groups set in against the ill-kempt looking heroes of such epics, which offered impressionable adolescents their own set of idols who looked suspiciously like those juvenile delinquents the newspapers continuously warned us against. Thus, in the early Sixties, rock 'n' roll was cleaned up, even as it experienced a major transition—moving from the East Coast to the West, where teenage styles were soon to be established by such surfer groups as the Beach Boys and Jan and Dean. The first film to acknowledge this major shift in musical styles and popular thinking was *Gidget,* in 1959. But the one that caught the feel of that transition most perfectly was *Beach Party.* The picture was originally con-

Annette Funicello strikes up a matronly pose (and is noticeably well covered) while surrounded by bikini-clad California girls. (*Beach Party*)

The *Beach Party* kids break into an impromptu twist session.

Frankie Avalon watches out for Annette while fending off the attentions of an overanxious surfer in *Beach Party*.

ceived as a one-shot exploitation quickie flick from American-International Pictures, the company that had long since established itself as a leading purveyor of cinematic schlock. The producer, James Nicholson, was considered a connoisseur of the genre, a man with a keen eye and quick, unfailing knowledgeability for what the kids would buy next year. Legend has it the screenplay for *Beach Party* was written on the back of a book of matches, over a luncheon engagement in a Hollywood restaurant. The film was rushed into production and, within a week of its release, proved so popular that first a sequel, then a cycle, soon followed. In truth, the Beach Party pictures represented the Sixties equivalent to the "flaming youth" films made during the flapper era, with Joan Crawford and Clara Bow; they were also the only original movie musicals (as opposed to Broadway musical plays being adapted for the screen) produced regularly during the decade, save for the Presley pictures; and they represented the only successful cycle of films other than the spy series to appear during the Sixties. Crude, primitive, sloppy and yet oftentimes thoroughly entertaining despite all that, the Beach Party pictures were a significant staple of Sixties moviemaking: on the one hand dependable moneymakers, on the other amazing representations of youthful fantasies before the tumultuous Youth Movement of 1968 made such images look irrelevant, causing the bikini epics to quickly disappear.

The first of the beach pictures differed to a degree from the others in the series, in that two well-known older stars (Robert Cummings and Dorothy Malone) received top billing. Cummings played an anthropologist studying the sex habits of California teenagers, while Malone was his attractive assistant. Introduced as the young leads were the characters who would dominate the future films in the series, Frankie Avalon—an already over-the-hill crooner from the late Fifties whose career was salvaged by the unexpected success of these films—and Annette Funicello—a recycled Mouseketeer who traded her ears for a bathing suit. Interestingly, Annette never once wore a bikini in the series—her top-heavy figure and poor waistline, along with her personal sense of modesty, would not permit it, and she always looked rather matronly, sitting in a one-piece or conservative two-piece suit like a quiet queen of the beach, while dozens of lithe, slim, blonde surfer girls danced, nearly nude, around her. Harvey Lembeck appeared as Eric Von Zipper, an effectively corny takeoff on Marlon Brando's classic characterization from *The Wild One*. And the plot continuously provided plenty of situations for pajama parties, young love presented in a highly moralistic but thoroughly leering and suggestive manner, and much raucous dancing to the music of Dick Dale and the Del Tones.

TOM JONES
WOODFALL PRODUCTIONS/LOPERT PICTURES CORPORATION

Produced by Tony Richardson; screenplay by John Osborne, from the novel by Henry Fielding; directed by Tony Richardson.

CAST

Tom Jones (Albert Finney); *Sophie Western* (Susannah York); *Squire Western* (Hugh Griffith); *Miss Western* (Dame Edith Evans); *Lady Bellaston* (Joan Greenwood); *Molly* (Diane Cilento); *Mrs. Waters* (Joyce Redman); *Squire Allworthy* (George Devine); *Lord Fellamar* (David Tomlinson); *Blifil* (David Warner); *Thwackum* (Peter Bull); *Partridge* (Jack McGowran)

Henry Fielding's classic eighteenth-century novel *Tom Jones* still makes for fine reading thanks to the deceptively sly comic tone of the narrator, the luscious descriptions of rural England, the multitude of cleverly drawn characterizations, and the perceptively witty outlook on life itself. But the notion that this ancient picaresque, with its immense length and old-fashioned story of a young rogue's travels across Britain over two hundred years ago, could provide the material for a motion picture that would dramatically change the current style of moviemaking was unthinkable—until the English-made *Tom Jones* opened to rave reviews, which were at once followed by box-office success and, in the end, an Oscar for Best Picture of the Year.

The non-hero himself marked a radical departure from what American audiences were used to seeing, as Tom—played with zest and vigor by Albert Finney—combined a naive innocence with a rigorous amorality. Finney's face always looked brash, boyish, full of puckish charm; at the same time, there was a glint of the devil in his eyes. To a degree he is truly honest, ingenuous, and innocent; at other moments, though, he is quite capable of guile. The two blend together beautifully to make this a real, flesh and blood, multi-dimensional and believably self-contradictory character. The willingness of the

Tom Jones: Albert Finney and Diane Cilento share one of the film's many sexually charged moments, which contributed to a new maturity of the screen.

mass audience to accept such an ambiguous person as the protagonist of a major motion picture further dispelled the conventions and clichés of the old Hollywood.

Equally important was the contribution of screenwriter John Osborne. Known primarily as the author of such plays as *Look Back in Anger,* the social protest, working class treatises that earned him a reputation as one of England's most outspoken and articulate Angry Young Men, Osborne seemed an unlikely choice to whittle down a mammoth book by one of England's old masters, especially seeing as it was a work of comic intentions and high spirits. But by 1963, the era of social protest Osborne had been a part of was on the wane, and he found a new outlet for his social consciousness while proving his versatility and adaptability as a writer. For all the fun that this bawdy novel offered, Henry Fielding was also interested in social satire—his clever portrait of the hypocritical, lustful Squire Western and other such types repre-

sented various aspects of the British class system. Always a critic of that system, Osborne allowed a wonderful old tale to emerge in his screenplay as a wild, rollicking comedy which also contained a substantial amount of serious implications.

Ultimately, though, the success of *Tom Jones* rested with the film's director, Tony Richardson. As a means of cinematically conveying a two-century-old tale in a style that would be palatable for modern audiences, he chose to revive visual conventions from the earliest days of filmmaking. Thus, the opening sequence, in which the baby Tom is first discovered, was played as a flickering silent film, complete with title cards; the great deer hunt through the woods and over the fields was speeded up to give it the "undercranked" quality of a Keystone comedy; the wipes—that long since abandoned style of changing scenes and making transitions—was reinstituted to replace one screen image with another. Rather than make the film appear dated, these stylistic devices instead lent it a sophis-

Hugh Griffith, in one of the exuberant moments of *Tom Jones*.

Albert Finney (left), in one of the more dramatic sequences of *Tom Jones*.

tication enjoyed by viewers who had come to regard the old movies with admiration and respect. Combined with these techniques were other tricks, some from the stage—Tom often speaks directly to the viewers in "asides"—and from nouvelle vague cinema, as when a hand-held camera is used to convey rushes of movement in a manner similar to the technique recently developed by Jean Luc Godard in France. The unforgettable eating sequence, in which Tom and Mrs. Waters (Joyce Redman) lustfully down a multi-course meal as a prelude to sex, was delightfully scandalous, though at the last moment Tom places his hat over the camera so he can continue his amorous adventures unseen by us. The final result proved to be an enthusiastically accepted work of popular entertainment which adapted the ambitious innovations of offbeat filmmakers to the commercial film.

102

Lovely Susannah York, as young Sophie Western, in *Tom Jones*.

THE VICTORS

COLUMBIA

Produced by Carl Foreman; written for the screen by Carl Foreman, from a book by Alexander Baron; directed by Carl Foreman

CAST

Trower (George Hamilton); *Chase* (George Peppard); *Craig* (Eli Wallach); *Baker* (Vincent Edwards); *Maria* (Rosanna Schiaffino); *Grogan* (James Mitchum); *French Lieutenant* (Maurice Ronet); *Jean-Pierre* (Joel Flateau); *Frightened French Woman* (Jeanne Moreau); *Regine* (Romy Schneider); *Eldridge* (Michael Callan); *Weaver* (Peter Fonda); *Madga* (Melina Mercouri); *Trudi* (Senta Berger); *Helga* (Elke Sommer); *Russian Soldier* (Albert Finney)

George Peppard and Vince Edwards face the grim reality of war. (*The Victors*)

In the history of the cinema there are the tragically mistreated masterpieces—great films which were brutalized beyond repair, cut by producers and distributors overanxious to turn them into more conventional looking films, finally reduced to a shadow of what some gifted director had achieved. In the Sixties, the most irresponsible mishandling of a potentially brilliant film came with *The Victors*, Carl Foreman's mammoth attempt to make a new kind of anti-war movie. But when the initial box-office returns failed to substantiate the major investment, Columbia Pictures quickly cut the film down in hopes of turning it into precisely what Foreman had tried to avoid: a routine World War II blockbuster.

Writer-director Foreman adapted a technique that had been employed years before by the great American novelist John Dos Passos in his masterwork *U.S.A.* Instead of telling a linear story in a matter-of-fact way, Dos Passos had alternated incidents in the lives of several characters whose paths crisscross, tying them together with newsreels that ironically comment on the stories we see. Foreman believed this approach could be carried over to the film: the idea for his picture was to follow a squad of American infantrymen from the moment they land in Europe to the end of the war. The film emerged as a series of episodes and, in each separate vignette, a different member of the squad provides the point of focus, with the others temporarily slipping into the background. At the same time, Foreman wanted to directly convey to his audience the

To the victors go the spoils. Senta Berger and George Hamilton in *The Victors*.

Vince Edwards finds himself alienated from his fellow soldiers in *The Victors*.

Melina Mercouri and George Peppard: a time out from war. *(The Victors)*

sensation of actually being a member of such a squad as it had been articulated by many veterans, who remembered that certain soldiers disappeared, without anyone knowing for certain if they had been killed, wounded and replaced, or deserted. In order to capture this quality, Foreman purposefully picked one character, Baker (Vincent Edwards), for the center of interest during the film's opening sequence. About twenty minutes into the picture, he is suddenly gone—and no one ever mentions the man again. Other characters fall by the wayside, some turning up again, some not. Always, though, between any two episodes in the tale there is an ac-

tual 1940s newsreel sequence, showing the war as it was presented to the folks back home, the surface of life as captured by the camera—then presenting the essence of war, via the next dramatic sketch, in such a way that it clashes drastically with the popular image.

Most of the characters in the story are defined by the women they relate to during the course of the war. One oft-voiced complaint was Foreman had been unwise in choosing popular young international starlets to play the roles of the women, as they were simply too beautiful to be fully believed, thus giving the film an aura of artificiality.

106

Still, *The Victors* was more authentic than any other American movie made on the subject of World War II, especially since it covered the kinds of incidents usually ignored by conventional, commercial moviemakers. One incident depicts the execution of an American serviceman (closely modelled after the Eddie Slovik case) shot in the snow by a firing squad. Foreman filmed the scene in gritty black-and-white, then dubbed in a recording of Frank Sinatra singing "Have Yourself a Merry Little Christmas" followed by a resounding "Hallelujah Chorus." Finally, though, the picture insisted on the futility of war—the notion that there are no victors—when, after the fighting has subsided, the only surviving American member of the squad (George Hamilton) meets a Russian ally (Albert Finney) in the streets of Berlin and, during a drunken brawl, the two men kill each other.

The last sequence served as a symbol for the Cold War of the Fifties and Sixties, with its notion of America and Russia destroying each other in the remnants of the Europe they have both suffered to save from Hitler. Unfortunately, the public was not quite ready for so cynical a vision.

The execution staged to the tune of "Have Yourself a Merry Little Christmas." *(The Victors)*

THE GREAT ESCAPE

UNITED ARTISTS

Produced by John Sturges; screenplay by James Clavell and W. R. Burnett, from the book by Paul Brickhill; directed by John Sturges.

CAST

"Cooler King" Hilts (Steve McQueen); *"The Scrounger" Hendley* (James Garner); *"Big X" Bartlett* (Richard Attenborough); *Senior Officer Ramsey* (James Donald); *Danny Velinski* (Charles Bronson); *"The Forger" Blythe* (Donald Pleasence); *"The Manufacturer" Sedgwick* (James Coburn); *Ashley-Pitt* (David McCallum); *Mac-Donald* (Gordon Jackson); *Willie* (John Leyton); *"The Mole" Ives* (Angus Lennie); *Goff* (Jud Taylor)

The Great Escape: Steve McQueen, during his famous motorcycle stunt . . .

Ever since Jean Renoir's *Grand Illusion* in 1937, tales of prisoners of war escaping from high security camps have been measured against the yardstick of that unforgettable yarn, and few were able to involve audiences in the adventure of digging a tunnel to freedom as effectively as the classic French film. Then, in 1963, John Sturges created a classic escape picture—and, at the same time, a variation on the superspectacular production. Unlike Darryl F. Zanuck's *The Longest Day,* with its all-star cast in cameo roles, Sturges focused on an even dozen men, all played by relatively unknown performers who were destined for future stardom. Most importantly, continuing his liaison with Steve McQueen, the ingratiating young actor whose screen personality Sturges had been so instrumental in shaping a few years earlier with *The Magnificent Seven,* Sturges came up with one of the era's most popular "group" pictures.

The script by James Clavell and W. R. Burnett follows closely the mechanics of an actual prison break—"great" in the sense that it involved more allies breaking for freedom at one time than any other such incident in the course of World War II— as elucidated in Paul Brickhill's 1950 book of the same name. However, the writers were also willing to take dramatic liberties with the plot and characterizations in order to make their film a successful work of entertainment. The end result was a perfectly balanced combination of the two elements: historically accurate to the degree that it communicated the actual techniques of the massive escape, thoroughly entertaining in its ability to hold viewers

with some highly engaging protagonists. Balding, softspoken Donald Pleasence was introduced as the brains behind the operation, but a man going blind and unable to join in the actual escape—until befriended by an unlikely ally, con man James Garner. Charles Bronson portrayed the man respected for his ability to dig perfect tunnels, though he becomes claustrophobic halfway through the project. But most memorable of all was Steve McQueen's mole-like non-hero, who remains apart from most of the other men throughout the story's running time. A loner, he can usually be seen pitching his baseball into a mitt (McQueen represents an idealized image of the all-American boy from back home) and, at a crucial moment following the escape, stealing a Nazi motorcycle in a desperate attempt to reach free Europe.

That single sequence, which was extended during the shooting of the film in order to allow McQueen to show his prowess on a bike, turned out to be the essential ingredient for the film's box-office success. McQueen was already emerging as an important young star, but desperately needed the proper role: one which would demonstrate his comic as well as dramatic abilities, while simultaneously allowing him to establish his screen image once and for all. A kind of updated James Dean with a sense of humor, McQueen found what he'd been searching for with the role of "Hilts," and introduced a new kind of non-hero for the Sixties: isolated without being alienated like those Fifties anti-heroes

... and after!

from whom he derived his character. His film presence fit in well with the film's aura of fun: not since *Stalag 17* had a P.O.W. picture provided audiences with so many effective gags, such good dramatic bits, such non-stop tension. Though *The Great Escape* runs for almost three full hours, it holds viewers the entire time and its suspense is never for a moment diffused. The excellent English cast had the opportunity to prove their subtle talents at acting while their American counterparts were given equal time to prove their abilities as broad entertainers. There was a complex chemistry of elements but, amazingly enough, they worked. The *Great Escape* had nothing new to say about the futility of war, but it did employ its recycled statement for some irresistible filmmaking.

James Garner and Donald Pleasence as unlikely allies: a charming con man and a nearly blind intellectual. *(The Great Escape)*

Steve McQueen (right) and James Garner (left) lead their fellow prisoners on a protest march in *The Great Escape*.

A crazed soldier makes a desperate bid for freedom. *(The Great Escape)*

Paul Newman and Patricia Neal: the new non-hero meets a committed woman. *(Hud)*

HUD
PARAMOUNT

Produced by Martin Ritt and Irving Ravetch; screenplay by Irving Ravetch and Harriet Frank, Jr., from the novel *Horseman, Pass By* by Larry McMurtry; directed by Martin Ritt.

CAST

Hud Bannon (Paul Newman); *Homer Bannon* (Melvyn Douglas); *Alma Brown* (Patricia Neal); *Lon Bannon* (Brandon de Wilde); *Burris* (Whit Bissell); *Hermy* (John Ashley); *Joe Scanlon* (George Petrie); *Kirby* (Carl Low); *Truman* (Curt Conway); *Myra* (Sharyn Hillyer); *Lily Peters* (Yvette Vickers)

"Why *Hud*?"

So asked the full-page newspaper ads which prefaced the distribution of *Hud*. Certainly, audiences needed some preparation: the title character, played by Paul Newman, was described by *Time* Magazine as an "unregenerate heel"; the language broke barriers for the commercial American cinema, including many words previously unspoken in a Hollywood movie; the shocking scenes included a terrifying attempted rape of the heroine, by the protagonist; and the entire affair might have appeared to a casual observer as an exercise in sensationalism.

But *Hud* offered more than that. First, it insisted on a re-examination of the legendary character of the Westerner. Few movie genres are as deeply entrenched in ritual and tradition as the classic westerns, set in the mid-nineteenth-century and concerning upstanding heroes who protect womankind by wiping out the forces of disorder. *Hud* offered an anti-traditional "modern" western: a view of the unromantic twentieth-century west, served up in brilliant but unromantic black-and-white photography. In order to express their desire to re-evaluate not only the west but the movie mythology of "the western," the filmmakers shrewdly let us see *Hud* through the point of view of Brandon de Wilde—the same young man who harbored a case of hero worship for *Shane* in 1953.

At the end of that film, Shane rode off into the sunset, leaving the boy tearfully to deal with his remembrance of the straight, strong hero; at the end of *Hud,* it is the boy who walks off into the sunrise, this time tearfully attempting to handle his rejection of everything Hud stands for. "There's so much *crap* in this world," the deserted Hud calls after him. "You're going to wallow in it sooner or later, like it or not!" Even in the Fifties, the wild ones and the rebels without causes never left us, in the final moments of a film, so steeped in *nada*—nothingness and emptiness. *Hud* provided the first expression of the Sixties psychology, which started as a strain in movies and became, by the decade's end, the popular image of the world that movies offered.

In Larry McMurtry's excellent novel, *Horseman, Pass By,* the focus remained on young Lon Bannon's growth toward maturity. Thus, another actor might have played Hud as a character role; as portrayed by Newman, Hud emerged as the latest instalment of that actor's particular brand of nonhero, and a worthwhile successor to Fast Eddie Felson of *The Hustler.* Thus, Hud's modern west appears as a twentieth-century equivalent to the "poisoned city" of ancient mythology, and director Martin Ritt staged a stunning sequence in which The Bannons' entire herd of cattle, suffering from a communicable disease, is led into a gully and shot down by the men who have spent their lives perfecting the breed. The experience proves too much for old Homer (Melvyn Douglas), a symbol of the admirable but decaying values; shortly after the cattle have been slaughtered, he collapses and dies—clearly a man who belongs to the past history of the west, and one who cannot survive in the brutal, meaningless west of the present. The ranch, and by process of abstraction the country it stands for, is infected: while killing the cattle may stop the spread of disease, it does not eradicate the problem.

In the 1960s, rape scenes would emerge as a basic staple of films; that trend began with *Hud,* when a drunken, hysterical Hud Bannon breaks down the doors of the building where Alma (Patricia Neal), the flirtatious but high-minded housekeeper, lives. It is only the intervention of Lon—who has also lusted after Alma in his innocent, boyish way—that stops the rape from transpiring. The scene is filled with complex emotions, for Alma is clearly attracted to Hud, and with different treatment would certainly respond to him.

At the end of *Hud,* Homer and the frontier qualities he stands for have died off; Alma, who could have put passion and humanity into the ranch, has been literally driven away; young Lon, the hope of the future, walks off to search for another world. Hud stands alone—alienated, abandoned, and as amoral as ever—laughing sarcastically, yet undeniably lonely. The character, and the man who played him, would set the pace for the non-heroes of the Sixties.

Patricia Neal, in the role in *Hud* for which she won an Academy Award.

After the attempted rape, Alma (Patricia Neal) leaves the ranch. (*Hud*)

Hud in action: Brandon de Wilde (in car) observes Paul Newman conning a cowboy.

Paul Newman and Brandon de Wilde join a barroom brawl in *Hud*.

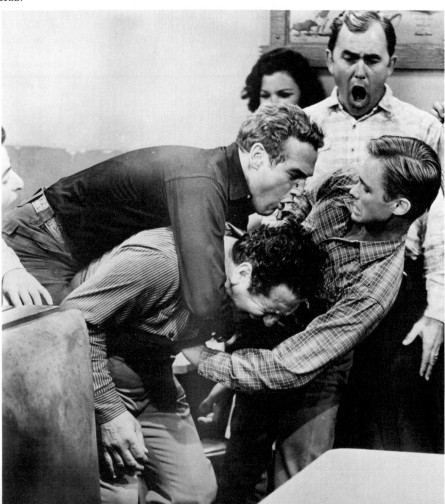

CLEOPATRA

20TH CENTURY–FOX

Produced by Walter Wanger; screenplay by Joseph L. Mankiewicz, Ranald MacDougall, and Sidney Buchman from histories by Plutarch, Suetonius, Appian, as well as *The Life and Times of Cleopatra* by C. M. Franzero; directed by Joseph L. Mankiewicz.

CAST

Cleopatra (Elizabeth Taylor); *Mark Antony* (Richard Burton); *Julius Caesar* (Rex Harrison); *High Priestess* (Pamela Brown); *Flavius* (George Cole); *Sosigenes* (Hume Cronyn); *Apollodorus* (Cesare Danova); *Brutus* (Kenneth Haigh); *Agrippa* (Andrew Keir); *Rufio* (Martin Landau); *Octavian* (Roddy McDowall); *Cassius* (John Hoyt); *Casca* (Carroll O'Connor); *Metullus Cimber* (Michael Gwynne); *Ptolemy* (Richard O'Sullivan)

The eternal triangle, ancient version: Richard Burton, Rex Harrison, and Elizabeth Taylor in *Cleopatra*.

Long before this film's release, the advance publicity had pre-sold *Cleopatra*. There was, after all, the chemistry of the two stars—Elizabeth Taylor and Richard Burton—who, while playing the passionate lovers Cleopatra and Mark Antony, had themselves become passionate lovers, much to the scandal and delight of everyone in the world except Eddie Fisher and Sybil Burton. Thanks to the stars slipping off together, production costs rose—and what was supposed to be just another of the waning superspectacular films became legendary since potential viewers anticipated that, when they watched the film, the love scenes would provide at least a glimmer of what had really taken place. As the stars dallied in each other's arms instead of working in front of the cameras, *Cleopatra* went so far over budget that it could never possibly bring back its costs at the box office. What a situation for 20th Century–Fox! Knowing, on the one hand, that their film would prove one of the most popular releases of the year and, on the other, that it would very likely put their studio into a state of bankruptcy. Significantly, after *Cleopatra* the costume spectacle disappeared from American screens.

But at least the genre went out in style: writer-director Joseph L. Mankiewicz, noted for such handsome productions of the past as *Dragonwyck, All About Eve,* and *Julius Caesar,* thoroughly researched Plutarch, Suetonius, Appian, and other ancient sources. There was also an influence from both Shakespeare and Shaw as he began penning his drama about love and politics in Rome and Egypt.

Thus, audiences who approached the picture believing they'd encounter the ultimate in sensationalism were surprised—perhaps even disappointed!—to discover something else entirely. At a running length of well over four hours, the production often proved as tedious as it was long, detailing carefully not only the love affair between Cleopatra and Antony but also the workings of the political systems, both in Rome and on the Mediterranean. Mr. Mankiewicz's modern films such as *Eve* offer brittle, sophisticated character studies with biting dialogue and fascinatingly devious people embroiling themselves deeply in difficult situations, and the filmmaker viewed the material of *Cleopatra* as more of the same—only in a different setting. Therefore, his conception of the romantic triangle involving Cleopatra, Antony, and Julius Caesar was not offered as an episode from the past, between stuffy figures whose motivations are beyond our comprehension. For Mankiewicz, people are the same, several thousand years ago or today—only the costumes change—and these figures emerge not so much as legendary giants from times gone by but as interesting people.

If the film has a fault, it's that Mankiewicz did not maintain a proper tone throughout. At moments, the characters are provided with modern equivalents for expressions they might have used informally—"Hey, man, hand me that spear!" type of talk. In other scenes, however, they speak in elevated language, hinting at Shakespearean poetry. Either approach might have been highly effective but the two don't jell when mixed. As for such other

Caesar (Rex Harrison) approaches Cleopatra, Queen of the Nile (Elizabeth Taylor).

The sparks onscreen mirrored the real-life situation. Elizabeth Taylor and Richard Burton in *Cleopatra*.

114

elements as the costumes and setting, no such problem emerged. Mankiewicz and his designers managed to effectively combine what information they were able to lay their hands on about the sights and scenes of the ancient world with a modern approach to fashion and styles, giving us a unique world that belongs totally to this film—neither pure history nor pure speculation, but rather an imaginative combination of the two.

An interesting footnote: Richard Burton was not the original choice for Antony. Another actor, Stephen Boyd, had been set for the role. But when various problems began to slow down production, Boyd left to fulfill other commitments and Burton, widely considered a has-been, was brought in. As the chemistry between the two leads grew uncontrollable, the public's conception of the film changed. Without such a draw, this grotesquely expensive product might have been an even more costly failure than it turned out to be—despite the ironic fact it was also one of the year's biggest box-office grossers.

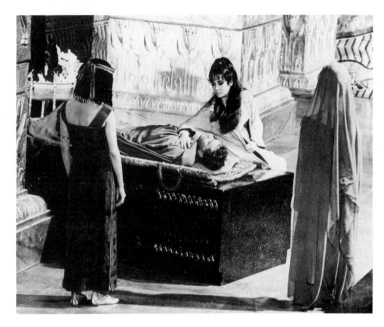

The death of Antony: Richard Burton and Elizabeth Taylor in *Cleopatra*.

In addition to spectacular romance, *Cleopatra* also featured spectacular battle sequences.

Jack Lemmon and Lee Remick momentarily forget their troubles as they rediscover romance in the country, far from the modern lifestyle that has contributed to their alcoholism. (*Days of Wine and Roses*)

DAYS OF WINE AND ROSES

WARNER BROTHERS

Produced by Martin Manulis; screenplay by J. P. Miller; directed by Blake Edwards.

CAST

Joe Clay (Jack Lemmon); *Kirsten Arnesen* (Lee Remick); *Ellis Arnesen* (Charles Bickford); *Jim Hungerford* (Jack Klugman); *Radford Leland* (Alan Hewitt); *Debbie Clay* (Debbie Megowan); *Mrs. Nolan* (Katherine Squire); *Dottie* (Maxine Stuart); *Party Guest* (Charlene Holt)

The Lost Weekend stood, for years, as the classic cinematic treatment of alcoholism—the most powerful and upsetting film ever undertaken on the subject. Invariably, all other films created on this theme were compared, and found inferior, to it—so much so that some filmmakers found it safer to avoid the issue altogether. With *Days of Wine and Roses, Lost Weekend* finally met its equal. For in this taut, memorable, oftentimes excruciatingly upsetting movie, the problems of alcoholism were portrayed in the most modern of moviemaking techniques, and illustrated with far more charming and, at least initially, likable characters than had been the case with Billy Wilder's earlier film. In that 1945

picture, the protagonist (Ray Milland) was portrayed as a desperate, frustrated writer—a compassionate character, but hardly one most viewers could closely associate with; therefore, no matter how much punch and authenticity the film conveyed, a sense of universality was clearly lacking. *Weekend* remains a film about a particular, peculiar kind of man, and his unique problem; it can be interpreted not so much as a warning about alcoholism as about the dangers of writing as an occupation. In *Wine and Roses,* the focus is on two extremely normal people—an average couple, the alcoholics next door—and the force of the film was increased through audiences' awareness that this was indeed a typical, rather than extreme, experience.

J. P. Miller's drama had originally been presented on television's highly respected live-drama anthology, *Playhouse 90,* in the late Fifties, and the superb actor (though only nominal star name) Cliff Robertson enacted the male lead. He also appeared in the TV version of *The Hustler,* but when such projects were eventually turned into films, bigger box-office stars were sought after. Paul Newman, thusly, made the hero of *The Hustler* a prototype of the anxious loner he would incarnate throughout the upcoming decade, while Jack Lemmon created a richly comic-dramatic characterization for *Wine and Roses.* The picture opens as the young advertising-executive, Joe Clay (Jack Lemmon), meets an attractive, formidable young woman, Kirsten

Arnesen (Lee Remick), and wins her affection despite the objections of her stern father, Ellis (Charles Bickford). The tone, up to this point, is reminiscent of something like *The Apartment,* and one might easily expect the picture to unfold as a brittle comedy-drama. Then, a difficult but believable transition takes place. This typical happy couple is married and soon after, the wife discovers her husband is under great and constant pressure at work. When he comes home frustrated and beaten, there is nothing for him to do but drink; to demonstrate her companionship and commitment to him, she begins drinking with him. Ultimately, they become slaves to the bottle, unable to control their urge for ever greater quantities of alcohol. Realizing the extremity of their situation, the husband joins Alcoholics Anonymous and is slowly, painfully taught self-control by an understanding member of the organization, Jim Hungerford (Jack Klugman).

Days of Wine and Roses: Jack Lemmon shows the prim Lee Remick how much fun drinking can be.

But Lemmon finds that drinking isn't fun when it leads to incarceration in a mental ward! *(Days of Wine and Roses)*

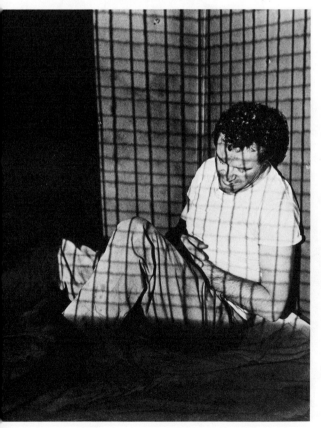

The wife is not so fortunate; she is unable to break with the bottle and finally, her husband—though he still loves her dearly—must walk out on the woman in order to maintain his newly discovered, but still precarious, self-control.

The film was noticeably free of any zealous moralizing; in fact, *Days of Wine and Roses* is not nearly so much an attack on alcohol or even the disease of alcoholism as it is a scathing indictment of the modern lifestyle of the Sixties which, in the film's context, is seen as the cause of the couple's dependence on booze. They are portrayed as a modern Everyman and Everywoman, trapped in the high level executive suite, where the ruthlessness of the success ethic can crush the values of the weak and alter the outlook of ordinary people. The film is an unpleasantly powerful one to watch, simply because we might easily see something of ourselves in either the pseudo-hip junior executive or his patient, well-meaning, devoted wife.

Jack Lemmon has begun to put his life back together, but now he despairs for his wife (Lee Remick), who is losing the battle of the bottle. *(Days of Wine and Roses)*

1964

Flashy trash: Carroll Baker struts her stuff for George Peppard in *The Carpetbaggers*.

Good-bye, Shane! Alan Ladd as Nevada Smith, his last screen role. (*The Carpetbaggers*)

THE CARPETBAGGERS

PARAMOUNT

Produced by Joseph E. Levine; screenplay by John Michael Hayes, based on the novel by Harold Robbins; directed by Edward Dmytryk.

CAST

Jonas Cord, Jr. (George Peppard); *Nevada Smith* (Alan Ladd); *Dan Pierce* (Bob Cummings); *Jennie Denton* (Martha Hyer); *Rina Marlowe* (Carroll Baker); *Monica Winthrop* (Elizabeth Ashley); *McAllister* (Lew Ayres); *Bernard Norman* (Martin Balsam); *Buzz Dalton* (Ralph Taeger); *Jedediah* (Archie Moore); *Jonas Cord, Sr.* (Leif Erickson); *Bellboy* (Frankie Darro); *Woman Reporter* (Ann Doran)

Great-bad movies are fun because they're so fatuous; it's impossible to tell whether the filmmakers themselves realized they were creating trash—and decided to make it as beautifully sordid as trash can be—or if they truly thought they were turning out a serious picture, and were totally surprised when audiences laughed in all the wrong places. Great-bad movies are entertaining because they're so bad, they're good; everything in them is so extreme, so arch, so overdone that instead of just run-of-the-mill, respectably mediocre failures, they turn out to be, in their own way, unforgettable—impressive in the extent of their awfulness. In the first half of the decade, one film towered above all others as the era's most enjoyably terrible film, and that was *The Carpetbaggers*.

Producer Joseph E. Levine first bought the screen rights to Harold Robbins' novel—which had become a popular best-seller with over 5,000,000 copies in print—then realized he had a potential disaster on his hands. What made the book such a phenomenal hit with readers was not its epic scope (covering several decades of time during the early portion of the century, while centering on the development of such significant industries as aviation and moviemaking), or even the roman-à-clef qualities (Jonas Cord, Jr., was clearly modeled after Howard Hughes, while Nevada Smith was a combination of William S. Hart and Bill Boyd, Rina Marlowe a Jean Harlow model, and Jennie Denton a carbon copy of Jane Russell); *The Carpetbaggers* was read and talked about due to the abundance of four letter words (a breakthrough, of sorts, for popular fiction) and its lavish, unsparing descriptions of the bedroom antics of the characters. In his earlier work, Robbins was best known for tough, embittered novels like *A Stone for Danny Fisher* and *Never Love a Stranger*, James T. Farrell-ish books filled with as much raw emotion as sex. From *The Carpetbaggers* on, he would be thought of as a prime manufacturer of stylish but synthetic sex novels, always based on some real life situation that was thoroughly fantasized for the fictionalized account. Here was Mr. Levine's dilemma; now that he had the rights to the book, how would he ever film it? The old Producton Code was still in effect (though its days were numbered and its power waning), and everything that made the novel such a hit in the first place would necessarily be lost in translation to the screen.

Levine decided on a blockbuster approach: he picked a rising young star, George Peppard, to play Jonas Cord, then lined up an army of big name Hollywood durables—Alan Ladd, Bob Cummings, Lew Ayres, Martin Balsam among them—for an all-star cast. He also developed a publicity build-up around Carroll Baker who, as Rina, had one of the film's showiest roles; despite the vast amount of money poured into the effort, though, the public absolutely refused to accept Ms. Baker as a new love goddess. Still, she and the film's other attractive young women—Elizabeth Ashley and Martha

Hyer—were featured in as many cheesecake shots as a commercial American film would allow, at times coming very close to total nudity without ever quite revealing what was then still unrevealable. Director Edward Dmytryk created his images in gross, gauche, grotesque color.

The Carpetbaggers emerged as a kind of off-color comic book for adults, with ugly undercurrents of drama that meant nothing and led nowhere. Worst of all was the decision to make Jonas, the heel of a non-hero, repentant at the finale, as compared to the far more realistic and meaningful situation of that very believable Sixties heel, Hud Bannon, who appeared more alienated at the end than at the beginning of that film. *The Carpetbaggers* delivered none of the scintillating sparks between characters its heavy advertising campaign promised, but it did provide viewers with some astonished chuckles at the seriousness with which these ridiculous (but entertaining, if you were in the mood to go slumming) antics were carried on.

Robert Cummings suavely tries to sweet-talk Martha Hyer . . .

. . . but finds liquor is quicker! *(The Carpetbaggers)*

The Beatles relax. *(A Hard Day's Night)*

A HARD DAY'S NIGHT

UNITED ARTISTS

Produced by Walter Shenson: screenplay by Alun Owen; directed by Richard Lester.

CAST

John (John Lennon); *Paul* (Paul McCartney); *George* (George Harrison); *Ringo* (Ringo Starr); *Grandfather* (Wilfred Brambell); *Norm* (Norman Rossington); *TV Director* (Victor Spinetti); *Shake* (John Junkin); *Millie* (Anna Quayle); *Man on Train* (Richard Vernon)

Without warning, the British suddenly emerged as the trend setters of popular culture. There were the films, like *Tom Jones* and *Billy Liar,* which caught something of the spirit of the times in which we lived as no American movies were doing; there were the newly acknowledged stars, such as Richard Burton and Peter O'Toole, who only a decade earlier would have appeared too intellectual to ever be accepted as male sex symbols; there were the young English 'birds,' best represented by Julie Christie, who apparently lived a freewheeling, modern lifestyle, and the models, including Twiggy, who revolutionized fashions, putting an emphasis

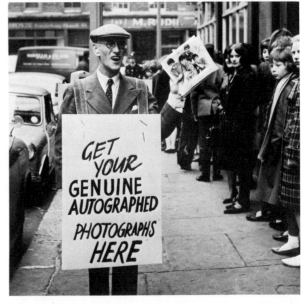

Grandpa (Wilfred Brambell) cashes in on the boys' popularity in *A Hard Day's Night.*

Ringo finds himself in trouble. *(A Hard Day's Night)*

122

on thinness and self-indulgent styles; and, finally, there were the Beatles, popping up on *The Ed Sullivan Show* and causing the greatest explosion to hit popular music since Elvis Presley's television debut in 1957. Beatlemania swept across America, as young people adapted the hairstyles and speech mannerisms of the four English lads. Naturally, an exploitation film was rushed into production for saturation release during the summer of 1964. Amazingly, it proved to be one of the best films of the year, establishing its four stars as not only temporary fad-celebrities but significant forces in chic fashion and modern art.

Instead of shooting *A Hard Day's Night* in the conventional style of previous rock 'n' roll movies, director Lester lured adults, as well as adolescents, into theaters by providing a fresh, lively, and in many respects surrealistic conception for his film. The picture generated an aura of Sixties-style sophistication, thanks to an editing scheme borrowed from TV commercials (a field Lester, a former creator of advertisements, was knowledgeable in) and an anarchistic sense of humor that served to remind many older viewers of the Marx Brothers. Rarely were the Beatles allowed to sing any of their hit songs "straight": instead, they were captured in the style of cinema verité camerawork, giving the spontaneous sensibility of a documentary to sequences depicting their recording sessions and live performances. Also, they acted out absurdist cameos to the tunes of some of their songs, allowing Beatle fans to hear a number in its entirety while seeing something other than four young men singing into the camera: the boys run around a park, and the incident is fragmented into a series of wildly cut bits of film that, in their final edited order, convey a certain quality the audience was already inclined to believe represented the essence, rather than the surface, of the Beatles' lifestyle: free, fast, and fun.

Doubtless, many of the United Artists' distributors would, initially, have preferred a more matter of fact approach to the material. After all, would American teenagers respond to something as offbeat as this, or would they be completely turned off and instead head for the nearest drive in where *Muscle Beach Party* was playing? To everyone's surprise, they responded, in droves: and suddenly the entire phenomenon known as rock 'n' roll was no longer the great divider in the ultimate breach of tastes. The complexity of the poetry in many Beatle lyrics, along with the sophistication of the filmmaking in their screen vehicles, lent an aura of respectability, and acceptance, to rock 'n' roll, allowing its

pop idols to enter the mainstream of American—and world—culture for the first time.

A Hard Day's Night was the first youth oriented film to openly spoof its subject matter, celebrating Beatlemania while simultaneously kidding it. The storyline offers nothing more than the responsibility these four lads assume in caring for the aged grandfather (Wilfred Brambell) of one ("He's a *clean* old man," they all agree) while at the same time preparing for a TV special, along with a subplot concerning the loneliness of one of the boys, Ringo, when he tries to flee from the pop-media-music world. Lester created a stock company of players (most notable among them Victor Spinetti) who offered cameo roles as the various grotesque characters inhabiting the television and recording business. With its flashy camerawork and tricky editing, *A Hard Day's Night* emerged as a grand send-up of the plastic-pop world of the Sixties, while establishing four lower middle class lads from Liverpool, England, as not only transient pop idols for kids, but examples of a new kind of cultural phenomenon as well.

Paul goes incognito in *A Hard Day's Night.*

George Harrison and Victor Spinetti in *A Hard Day's Night.*

BECKET

PARAMOUNT

Produced by Hal Wallis; screenplay by Edward Anhalt, based on the play by Jean Anouilh; directed by Peter Glenville.

CAST

Thomas Becket (Richard Burton); *King Henry II* (Peter O'Toole); *Bishop Folliot* (Donald Wolfit); *King Louis VII* (Sir John Gielgud); *Queen Matilda* (Martita Hunt); *Queen Eleanor* (Pamela Brown); *Gwendolen* (Sian Phillips); *Pope Alexander III* (Paolo Stoppa); *Cardinal Zambelli* (Gino Cervi); *Brother John* (David Weston); *Archbishop of Canterbury* (Felix Aylmer); *Pretty French Girl* (Veronique Vendell)

Richard Burton became a star with *Cleopatra,* after more than ten years of meandering through mediocre movie roles; Peter O'Toole found himself elevated to sudden superstardom after the success of just one film, *Lawrence of Arabia.* And the motion picture industry found itself with two relatively young, highly gifted English actors who were popular with both the intelligentsia and the mass audience. What better move than to bring them together for a film? Hal B. Wallis—the ever present, ever commercial producer of such diverse projects as *Little Caesar* with Edward G. Robinson, *Artists and Models* with Martin and Lewis, and *King Creole* with Elvis Presley—seized on the notion of facing off Burton and O'Toole in a film filled with conflict, confrontation, and high-class conversation. Surprisingly, the emphasis was to be on the latter. For instead of the usual man-to-man vehicle, which always proved perfect for the latest machismo team (be it Spencer Tracy and Clark Gable in the Thirties, Burt Lancaster and Kirk Douglas in the Fifties, or Paul Newman and Robert Redford in the Seventies), Wallis derived a tastefully literary adaptation of Jean Anouilh's intellectually ponderous, thematically philosophic play *Becket;* more surprising still, in bringing this story of a murder in the cathedral to the screen, Wallis entirely resisted the temptation to emphasize spectacle over ideology.

Anouilh had clearly followed, in his drama, the historical situation in which King Henry II (O'Toole) and his long-time friend Thomas Becket (Burton) turned against one another due to opposing points of view concerning the correct relation-ship between church and state. At the story's outset, Becket is the king's Chancellor, as well as his constant companion; the two men ride happily together in the dawn, gleefully gloating over their latest seduction of a country lass. Then, Becket is consecrated Archbishop of Canterbury, almost as a joke, by Henry, and the problems immediately begin. Henry assumed his old friend would make the King's job of putting the church under the yoke of the crown that much easier. Instead, Becket turns out to be a latent idealist who stands firm in his de-

Richard Burton and Peter O'Toole brought a new dimension to the concept of male teams in movies. *(Becket)*

sire to defend the church from any of Henry's attempts to seize authority and power over it. Naturally, this greatly affects the nature of the relationship between the two men. Henry grows ever more concerned, not so much about the political problems between the two of them as about the loss of their close friendship which, he realizes, was more important than he ever realized; at the same time, Becket grows ever more distant, aloof, internal, serious. Finally, the combination of personality and politics explodes. After a difficult reunion on a deserted beach, Henry arranges the murder of Becket.

Becket represents a masterful blending of sensible drama and visual splendor. Though there are the magnificent sets and lush backgrounds reconstructing the English Isles as they looked ages ago, they always remain backdrops to the ideas and the characterizations which are at the film's focus. At three hours running time, *Becket* proved a picture could be absorbing without, on the one extreme, turning too theatrical or, on the other, introducing superfluous

action sequences, as so many of the spectacles of the late Fifties and early Sixties had done. Perhaps most significant, *Becket* introduced a controversial theme and then handled it in a non-compromising manner. Though Becket and Henry are first seen sporting with willing women, their relationship borders on homosexuality—it is their dedicated love for one another that motivates them early in the story. Henry is rarely seen with his wife, Eleanor of Aquitaine (Pamela Brown), and then only when he is bantering a bit with her while preparing to run off and join Thomas.

While there is nothing so daring as a bedroom scene, or even a strong hint of physical attraction between the two, the Queen Mother, Matilda (Mar-

tita Hunt), admonishes the enraged Henry that his feelings for his friend are nothing short of "unnatural." It is, finally, the frustrated desire to possess Becket's love that causes Henry to convince himself he is acting out of political expediency in doing away with Becket—his true motivation being jealousy. By keeping these passions subtle enough so that they remain under the surface of the story (which never purports to be about anything except the division of church and state) and playing the film as a study of ideas, as well as men, locked in conflict, producer Wallis provided one of the decade's handsomest, most intelligent and important costume epics.

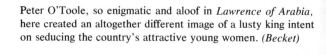

Peter O'Toole, so enigmatic and aloof in *Lawrence of Arabia,* here created an altogether different image of a lusty king intent on seducing the country's attractive young women. *(Becket)*

Richard Burton and Sir John Gielgud discuss morality, religion, politics, and most of all, King Henry. *(Becket)*

Peter O'Toole suggests the country would be better off with Becket (Burton) dead.

Becket: Richard Burton, dwarfed by the splendor of the church.

GOLDFINGER

UNITED ARTISTS

Produced by Harry Saltzman and Albert R. Broccoli; screenplay by Richard Maibaum and Paul Dehn, based on the novel by Ian Fleming; directed by Guy Hamilton.

CAST

James Bond (Sean Connery); *Goldfinger* (Gert Frobe); *Pussy Galore* (Honor Blackman); *Jill Masterson* (Shirley Eaton); *Tilly Masterson* (Tania Mallett); *Oddjob* (Harold Sakata); *"M"* (Bernard Lee); *Solo* (Martin Benson); *Felix Leiter* (Cec Linder); *Miss Moneypenny* (Lois Maxwell); *Bonita* (Nadja Regin); *"Q"* (Desmond Llewelyn)

The first James Bond adventure, *Dr. No.*, opened in the summer of 1962, introducing a relatively unknown actor named Sean Connery in the title role as Agent 007, a member of Her Majesty's Secret Service who is licensed to kill anyone, at any moment, with another virtual newcomer, Ursula Andress, as an Amazonian lovely he becomes involved with. The medium-budget film proved quite popular and at once launched both the leads toward stardom; Ms. Andress was not only the prototype for all Bond women, but also one of the first international movie stars to regularly pose in the nude for *Playboy*—setting a trend which other actresses would follow. Connery, meanwhile, played Bond again in a follow-up, *From Russia With Love.* Violence in our society was emerging as the most controversial issue of the time, and it seemed only appropriate that our new pop hero would be a man who dealt with death on a daily basis. In *Goldfinger,* the perfect formula was achieved, and James Bond became big business.

With its elaborate production qualities, *Goldfinger* was easily the biggest of the Bonds thus far, and all the latter films in the series were patterned after its successful format. First, there is the arch supervillain, Goldfinger himself (Gert Frobe), a self-possessed megalomaniac with vast reserves of power, money, and men. Goldfinger operates out of several secret headquarters located around the world and plans on depleting the world's gold supplies by ripping off the reserves at Fort Knox. Then there is his grotesque assistant, an oriental assassin named Oddjob (Harold Sakata), a colorful character who always dresses in formal wear and dispatches his victims with a lethal hat that decimates any object it's thrown at. Also in league with those comic book villains is a frigid

Sean Connery as James Bond in *Goldfinger*.

Shirley Eaton, before the gilding . . .

beauty, Pussy Galore (Honor Blackman), who operates a flying circus which is to be used for the raid on Fort Knox; she is spared the horrible fates of the other villains only because she has the good sense to let herself be seduced by Bond after a sado-masochistic judo match in which they try to kill (before making love to) one another.

The attitude of Bond toward his women would become a controversial topic a few years later, when feminists claimed he used them like so much Kleenex. Indeed, in *Goldfinger,* Bond makes his way through an array of pluperfect lovelies, including two blonde sisters, Jill (Shirley Eaton) and Tilly (Tania Mallett) Masterson, both of whom are killed by the baddies owing to their liaisons with Bond. James Bond, as portrayed by Connery, embodied the Sixties' image of what a male should aspire to, as outlined in the pages of the era's most popular men's magazine, *Playboy:* casual with women, and in fact

. . . and after! *(Goldfinger)*

129

Enter the villains: Harold Sakata as Oddjob and Gert Frobe as Goldfinger.

James Bond (Sean Connery) flips over Pussy Galore (Honor Blackman). *(Goldfinger)*

Bond (Sean Connery) and Jill Masterson (Shirley Eaton) enjoy a quiet moment together in *Goldfinger*. Such sexual explicitness was unheard of before the Sixties brought a new freedom to the screen.

far more interested in gadgets and items of technological sophistication. As a person, Bond displayed the two personality traits that would become essential to a Sixties hero: he was cynical and he was a total professional. Bond's companions in adventure proved almost as popular as the hero himself, and were on hand for each subsequent adventure: "M" (Bernard Lee), the arch serious commander who dispatches Bond on each new exploit; Miss Moneypenny (Lois Maxwell), the leggy lady receptionist who covers her jealousy over Bond's conquests with a bitchy sense of humor; and "Q" (Desmond Llewelyn), the little old gadget-maker who perfects Bond's ever more advanced weapons and defense mechanisms. Always on hand were his Aston Martin and black tuxedo, testifying to the urbanity of this deadly character. The settings ranged from Miami Beach to the Swiss Alps; the humor was sardonic and sadistic; the drama somewhere between pulp novels and the Marquis de Sade; the musical score by John Barry sufficiently brassy and the title song, as sung by Shirley Bassey, extremely classy. Best remembered were the impressive images, including the gilding of Shirley Eaton by the villains—which became an unforgettable moment not only in the film, but in film history. With its innuendos (and, at times, near explicitness) *Goldfinger* offered a deadly but liberated hero who was perfectly in tune with an era of growing violence and spreading sexual permissiveness.

Sterling Hayden and Peter Sellers join in the madness of *Dr. Strangelove.*

Peter Sellers as the beleaguered president in *Dr. Strangelove.*

DR. STRANGELOVE; OR, HOW I LEARNED TO STOP WORRYING AND LOVE THE BOMB

COLUMBIA

Produced by Stanley Kubrick; screenplay by Stanley Kubrick, Terry Southern, and Peter George, from the novel *Red Alert* by Peter George; directed by Stanley Kubrick

CAST

Captain Lionel Mandrake/President Muffley/Dr. Strangelove (Peter Sellers); *General "Buck" Turgidson* (George C. Scott); *General Jack D. Ripper* (Sterling Hayden); *Colonel "Bat" Guano* (Keenan Wynn); *Major T. J. "King" Kong* (Slim Pickens); *Ambassador de Sadesky* (Peter Bull); *Miss Scott* (Tracy Reed); *Lt. Lother Zogg* (James Earl Jones)

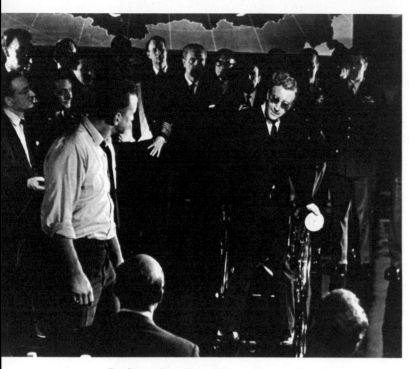

Dr. Strangelove (Peter Sellers) rises out of his wheelchair to confront the politicians and generals.

More than any other single filmmaker, Stanley Kubrick was propelled to a position of importance within the industry due to the drastic changes in the nature of commercial filmmaking. Kubrick's first major contribution came at mid-decade, with what was, in 1964, the most unlikely hit film of the year: the wildly titled *Dr. Strangelove; or, How I Learned to Stop Worrying and Love the Bomb*. Filmed on an extremely small budget (something Kubrick was no stranger to, thanks to his early days as a B-budget director of such sensational items as *The Killing* and *Killer's Kiss*), *Strangelove's* unexpected success convinced its studio, Columbia, that certain qualities once associated with the underground—anti-Establishment, counterculture, noncommercial filmmakers—were just then reaching the surface, being absorbed by the mainstream of moviemakers. *Strangelove* contained scathing satire of the United States government and military; dark comedy and sick humor; off-color language and an aura of intellectualism; a lack of major name stars but some impressive character actors; and a

Commander "King" Kong (Slim Pickens) mounts the atomic bomb cowboy-style, and prepares to launch a nuclear war with Russia. *(Dr. Strangelove)*

The President (Peter Sellers, far right) and his advisors listen to the top-ranking general (George C. Scott, center) warn of possible atomic war. (*Dr. Strangelove*)

pessimistic ending (the destruction of civilization as we know it) presented not as *On the Beach* type melodrama/tragedy but as Grand Guignol comedy. In short, *Strangelove* contained everything the mass audience would, supposedly, be offended by, and which was best left to the campus film societies or the art house circuit. Yet, for all that, *Stangelove* was embraced by the American public—a sign that long-existing distinctions between underground and commercial moviemaking were disappearing, and also that the public was growing more acceptant of ideas and images once thought of as exclusively for the avant garde.

Even the opening title sequence was a shocker, of sorts; a jet aircraft refuels from a mid-air station, photographed in such a way that it appears as a sexual act. Shortly thereafter, the viewer is introduced to General Jack D. Ripper (Sterling Hayden), a wild-eyed, old-time right-wing military man, who fervently believes a Communist conspiracy is polluting the body fluids of American citizens, under the guise of fluoridating our water supplies. In order to retaliate, he dispatches a fleet of jet bombers—equipped with missiles featuring nuclear warheads—toward Russia, led by the rootin', tootin', shootin' and salutin' Major T. J. "King" Kong (Slim Pickens), a Texas cowboy turned air force commander who wears his old Stetson on bombing missions and never misses a target. When General

133

Buck Turgidson (George C. Scott) learns what has happened, he quickly reports to the President of the United States (Peter Sellers) and, before long, President Muffley is embroiled in a heated debate over the hot line with the Russian premier—trying to explain that, at any moment, the man's country will be devastated by nuclear warheads, since there is no known way to recall the planes.

Such a situation was also the subject of a serious film that same year: *Fail Safe,* starring Henry Fonda as the President of the United States. But that more melodramatic treatment of the issue paled by comparison with Kubrick's strange mixture of avant garde techniques, comic book characterizations, burlesque humor and surrealistic style. The strikingly diffused lighting employed for the War Room confrontations helped make *Strangelove* as much a visual milestone as *Citizen Kane* had been almost 25 years earlier: viewers carried away with them the image of the President's special advisor, Dr. Strangelove (also played by Sellers), a former Nazi scientist whose mechanical arm constantly slips into an unintentional, uncontrollable "Sieg Heil" salute, and Major Kong, riding his nuclear warhead down to the target like an old-time cowboy straddling a bronc at a rodeo. Then too, there were the paranoid concepts comically treated in the film's scheme: World War III being fought to the tune of "We'll Meet Again, Some Sunny Day." Back in the late Fifties, when "sick humor" had been first introduced by such revolutionary nightclub comics as Lenny Bruce and Mort Sahl, such a point of view was thought of as representing their sick view of society and was, subsequently, rejected by the mainstream of people; by the mid-Sixties, sick humor had become a popular medium of expression to comment on what was now generally accepted as a sick society. With lacerating wit, *Dr. Strangelove* brought sick humor to the commercial cinema.

THE PINK PANTHER

UNITED ARTISTS

Produced by Martin Jurow; screenplay by Maurice Richlin and Blake Edwards; directed by Blake Edwards.

CAST

Sir Charles (David Niven); *Inspector Jacques Clouseau* (Peter Sellers); *George* (Robert Wagner); *Simone Clouseau* (Capucine); *Princess Dala* (Claudia Cardinale); *Angela Dunning* (Brenda De Banzie); *Greek "Cousin"* (Fran Jeffries); *Tucker* (Colin Gor-

don); *Defense Attorney* (John Le Mesurier); *Saloud* (James Lanphier); *Hollywood Starlet* (Meri Welles)

According to the script, "the pink panther" of the title referred only to a legendary gemstone containing one small imperfection which, when viewed in the proper light, looked a bit like a—well, like a pink panther. But rather than leave the title so intangible, Blake Edwards decided to give his film something new in the way of a title sequence, by having the pink panther come momentarily to life, via animation, and dance around the lettering—wreaking havoc with the words as they appear onscreen. Only problem was, audiences fell so in love with the cartoon conception for the creature that they were, understandably, disappointed when he disappeared after the credits. Shortly, though, he was back by popular demand—as the star of a series of Pink Panther cartoon shorts. But the panther was not the only character propelled, by this film's success, into the popular imagination. The redoubtable Inspector Jacques Clouseau, bumbling French detective, was so superbly played by Peter Sellers that he was soon the subject of a long-running series.

At the time, Blake Edwards was a young director in search of a style. He had already tried his hand at Billy Wilderish sophisticated comedy *(Breakfast at Tiffany's),* Hitchcockian psychological horror *(Experiment in Terror),* and Stanley Kramer-style message melodrama *(Days of Wine and Roses).* With *The Pink Panther,* he happened upon the approach that would make him highly popular with audiences of the Sixties: a sophisticated treatment of silly subjects and sexy situations. He set this film at Cortina d'Ampeozo, a classy winter resort community tucked away in a hidden corner of the Alps, where all the women wear Yves St. Laurent gowns and the men are under suspicion—one of them is, presumably, a notorious jewel thief who has been walking off with the finest gems in Europe. In fact, the thief is none other than the dashing Sir Charles (David Niven), an elegant gentleman con-artist whose attitude toward the ladies is as much inspired by his ambitions for their necklaces as his amatory interests; he finds himself particularly enamored of the Princess Dala (Claudia Cardinale) owing to her possession of the priceless "pink panther." But on the case is Inspector Clouseau (Sellers), who arrives with his bored, frustrated wife, Simone (Capucine), and makes the mistake of leaving her on her own in the luxurious setting, in order to pursue his case—though in no time at all, she has become the lover of the very thief her husband is hunting.

The Pink Panther: Peter Sellers as Inspector Jacques Clouseau.

Capucine and Peter Sellers dance, though her attention seems elsewhere . . .

. . . and in a short while, she seduces the very man her husband is out to catch, Sir Charles (David Niven). *(The Pink Panther)*

Though it is today unthinkable that any actor but Sellers could even attempt to play Clouseau (though it's worth noting Alan Arkin once gave the role a less than successful whirl), the part was originally designed with another performer—Peter Ustinov—in mind. From the outset of the filming, though, Edwards realized Ustinov was too cerebral a performer to play Clouseau, and happily replaced him with Sellers, who had established himself as an actor with a penchant for playing three different parts in each movie: *The Mouse That Roared, Lolita, Dr. Strangelove.* Sellers' earlier efforts caused him to become a cult *cause célèbre* with the art house audience; *The Pink Panther* helped establish his popularity with the broad moviegoing public. Sellers as Clouseau was a natural for a series, and Edwards would soon match him with the popular new sex kitten Elke Sommer for *A Shot in the Dark;* Sellers later returned to the character for a succession of Clouseau capers in the mid-Seventies.

The only problem with the first film in the series was that Clouseau did not happen to be the focus of the story. Nobody had any way of knowing how popular Sellers as Clouseau would become, and Edwards felt at the time that *The Pink Panther* would be more effective if the bumbling inspector shared screen time, as well as billing, with the debonair David Niven and the perennial all-American boy, Robert Wagner. Essentially, though, they only served to bog the movement of the film down; audiences responded to Sellers' Inspector as a direct descendant, and Sixties' version, of Chaplin's Little Tramp, and resented it whenever he was off-screen—which, in this initial picture, was quite often. In future instalments, Clouseau would find his faithless wife replaced by an oriental houseboy/karate expert named Kato, and all the other characters shifted into the background—in order that he might have more time for his sight gags and verbal shenanigans.

Inspector Clouseau (Peter Sellers) serenades his wife (Capucine) in *The Pink Panther*.

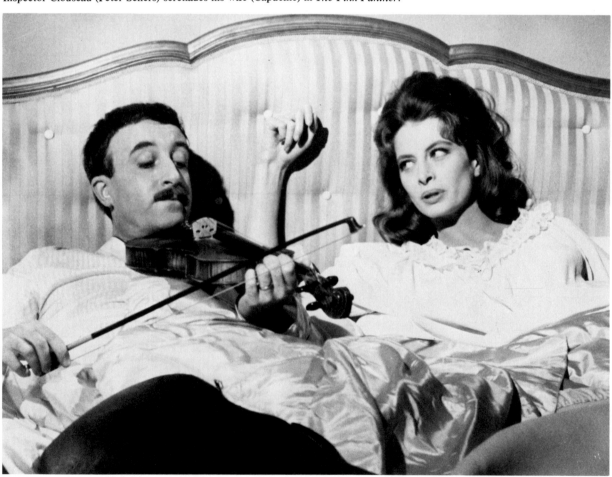

Colonel Pickering (Wilfrid Hyde-White) and Higgins (Rex Harrison) discover Eliza (Audrey Hepburn)
on the streets. *(My Fair Lady)*

MY FAIR LADY

WARNER BROTHERS

Produced by Jack L. Warner; screenplay by Alan Jay
Lerner, based on the musical play *My Fair Lady* by Alan
Jay Lerner and Frederick Loewe, in turn based on the
play *Pygmalion* by George Bernard Shaw; directed by
George Cukor.

CAST

Professor Henry Higgins (Rex Harrison); *Eliza
Doolittle* (Audrey Hepburn); *Alfred P. Doolittle*
(Stanley Holloway); *Colonel Hugh Pickering*
(Wilfrid Hyde-White); *Mrs. Higgins* (Gladys
Cooper); *Freddy Eynsford-Hill* (Jeremy Brett);
Zoltan Karpathy (Theodore Bikel); *Mrs. Eynsford-
Hill* (Isobel Elsom); *Prince Gregor* (Henry Daniell);
Ambassador (Alan Napier)

During the Sixties, Hollywood witnessed the near
extinction of one of the most beloved of movie

genres: the musical film, conceived and then created exclusively for the screen. Instead, filmmakers
turned their attention toward ever more elaborate—
and ever more expensive—screen versions of musical plays that had already proven their popularity
on Broadway. *The Music Man, Gypsy, Oliver* and
other long-run shows were all handsomely adapted,
but none made quite so pleasant a transition to the
screen as *My Fair Lady*.

Based on the renowned play *Pygmalion* by
George Bernard Shaw, *Lady* follows an audacious
experiment by Professor Henry Higgins (Rex Harrison), a linguistic expert who wagers with his good
friend Colonel Pickering (Wilfred Hyde-White) that
he can take an ordinary guttersnipe from off the
streets and, in a prearranged period of time, remove
her thick cockney accent and turn her into a lady so
aristocratic in bearing that no one will even suspect
her origins. The two men seize on poor Eliza Doolittle (Audrey Hepburn), a working class waif from
the slums, who is endlessly tutored (and in her esti-
mation, tortured) until she is, at last, able to repeat
Higgins' key phrase—"The rain—in Spain—stays

137

mainly in the plain . . ."—without so much as a touch of her ugly accent. Eliza's problem is that, having been transformed by Henry Higgins into his ideal image of womanhood, she has fallen in love with the man.

Shaw's wit and wisdom remained very much alive and well in the musicalized version, giving this light (but hardly lightweight) show a sly undercurrent of social satire on the English class system, as well as a coy analysis of man-woman relationships that runs through the author's work. Alan Jay Lerner and Frederick Loewe added to this an assortment of musical selections that rank among their best work—songs such as "I've Grown Accustomed to Her Face," "I Could Have Danced All Night," "On the Street Where You Live," and "Get Me to the Church on Time"—but the success of the film version finally rested with the director, George Cukor. Long hailed as the great "woman's director" of the 30s, 40s and 50s—turning out such female oriented vehicles as the appropriately named *Little Women, The Women,* and *Les Girls*—Cukor's kind of moviemaking was fast disappearing. He found one last, lovely project in this Edwardian costume piece. The elements of the story that could only be suggested onstage—the teeming street scenes, the crowded marketplace, the Ascot race track and the grand ballroom—proved perfect material for the recently improved Panavision widescreen process. The effectiveness of some musicals is diminished when they are "opened up" unnecessarily for the camera, since they lose the intimacy that made them so charming in the first place; *My Fair Lady* seemed to beg for a more spectacular set design than was ever possible in the legitimate theater, so the lusciously crafted film version fulfilled all its promises and possibilities.

The only shred of controversy concerned the casting. Early on, producer Jack L. Warner loudly announced the stars of the Broadway production—Rex Harrison and Julie Andrews—had been undeniably wonderful in their roles, but were hardly big enough names for his multi-million-dollar film. His first choices for Henry Higgins were either Rock Hudson or Cary Grant, both of whom wisely turned the man down. In fact, Grant went so far as to tell Jack Warner he wouldn't even go see the film if anyone but Harrison played the role. Warner relented, and Harrison's performance as Higgins won him a long overdue Oscar. But Andrews was ultimately passed over in favor of Audrey Hepburn. She sparkled as Eliza—even though her singing voice had to be dubbed in by Marni Nixon, who previously provided the voice for Natalie Wood in *West Side Story.* Since her performance was "synthetic," Hepburn was not allowed an Oscar nomination and when *My Fair Lady* swept the ceremonies that year, it received Oscars in every possible category save best actress—which, ironically enough, went to Julie Andrews for her role in *Mary Poppins.*

My Fair Lady: Audrey Hepburn as Eliza Doolittle, before . . .

A transformed Eliza (Audrey Hepburn) is introduced to royalty in *My Fair Lady*.

Eliza (Audrey Hepburn) charms Freddy (Jeremy Brett) and Higgins (Rex Harrison) in *My Fair Lady*.

. . . and after!

MARY POPPINS

BUENA VISTA

Produced by Walt Disney; written for the screen and co-produced by Bill Walsh, based on the "Mary Poppins" stories by P. L. Travers; directed by Robert Stevenson.

CAST

Mary Poppins (Julie Andrews); *Bert/Old Dawes* (Dick Van Dyke); *Mr. Banks* (David Tomlinson); *Mrs. Banks* (Glynis Johns); *Ellen* (Hermione Baddeley); *Jane Banks* (Karen Dotrice); *Michael Banks* (Matthew Garber); *Katie Nanna* (Elsa Lanchester); *Uncle Albert* (Ed Wynn); *Bird Woman* (Jane Darwell); *Constable Jones* (Arthur Treacher); *Admiral Boom* (Reginald Owen)

When Julie Andrews first learned she was not going to be allowed to play the role of Eliza Doolittle in the screen version of *My Fair Lady* she was, understandably, crushed. After all, the reviewers had praised her performance on the Broadway stage as one of the most impressive musical comedy creations in years, while audiences were enraptured by her combination of energy and craftsmanship. Though she hardly appeared a typical Hollywood star in any conventional definition of that term, Andrews had hoped that, given the chance to recreate Eliza onscreen, she might be able to redefine people's conception of a star in this decade when movies were clearly undergoing a transition. Weren't other English artists just then invading America, with spectacular results? But the role went to a tested box-office name, and Ms. Andrews had to satisfy herself with a role in a children's film—Walt Disney's screen treatment of some beloved stories by P. L. Travers. As it turned out, Julie had the last laugh. For *Mary Poppins* proved something other than a routine kiddie flick and, for the first time, an actress was awarded the Oscar for a role in a children's picture. On Academy Award night, when Julie Andrews shared the podium with Rex Harrison, the original Eliza and Higgins were, at least momentarily, reunited.

Released just two years before Walt's death, *Mary Poppins* was the last of the great Disney films, and the first impressive picture from that studio in several years. Just a short time before, their attempt to animate the great legends of King Arthur had produced nothing more than a ponderous disappointment, *The Sword and the Stone*. Mary Poppins was risky, in many respects. For one thing, the

Dick Van Dyke and Julie Andrews in *Mary Poppins*.

The dance of the chimney sweeps. *(Mary Poppins)*

141

Opposite page: Mary Poppins (Julie Andrews) arrives by umbrella.

Animation was combined with live-action sequences to create special scenes like this one for *Mary Poppins*.

ert B. Sherman that sounded slightly reminiscent of those Lerner and Loewe had created, and the original Eliza herself as the mysterious nanny who arrives by umbrella at the Banks household, soon having the two children (Karen Dotrice and Matthew Garber) dancing off to fantastic adventures. Mary slips up, rather than down, the bannister and, accompanied by her friend Bert (Dick Van Dyke), leads the children into a cartoon world where they enjoy an Irish fox hunt, a Derby horse race, and a barnyard songfest. The two most striking scenes featured an expressionistic ballet, up on the rooftops of London, in which Van Dyke hoofed it with a chorus of soot-covered chimney sweeps, and a charming setpiece called "Feed the Birds," beautifully designed to manipulate audience emotions into a bittersweet mood over an abandoned old woman. But children naturally preferred the nonsense number ("Super-cali-frag-ilistic-expi-alidocious") and sang it with the enthusiasm an earlier generation of tots had shown for "The Ballad of Davy Crockett." With *Mary Poppins,* the tradition of classic Disney children's films came, sadly, to an end. But, ah— what a way to go out!

David Tomlinson, Karen Dotrice, Matthew Garber, and Julie Andrews in *Mary Poppins.*

picture blended animated sequences with live actors, always a tricky business because the creation of a single tone for the piece is extraordinarily difficult to maintain. Also, they were again working from a classic book, which meant that many adults (if not necessarily children) had strong conceptions of how the stern *Mary Poppins* ought to look— more like Agnes Moorehead, some purists argued, than the sugary Julie Andrews. Finally, the Disney people insisted on making the movie a blockbuster—almost two and a half hours in length, an exceptional running time for a family picture considering that most of the finest Disney features, from *Snow White* to *Bambi,* averaged 75 minutes. Only the year before *Mary Poppins,* the Disney people had lavished much time, attention, and expense on an equally promising project—Victor Herbert's delightful operetta, *Babes in Toyland*— and produced a flat, foolish film that didn't even have the common sense to be short.

Wonderfully enough, with *Mary Poppins* the old magic worked, and the film emerged as a sort of *My Fair Lady* for children—with similar Edwardian costumes, a score of songs by Richard M. and Rob-

142

THE AMERICANIZATION OF EMILY

METRO-GOLDWYN-MAYER

Produced by Martin Ransohoff; screenplay by Paddy Chayefsky, based on a novel by William Bradford Huie; directed by Arthur Hiller.

CAST

Lt. Commander Charles Madison (James Garner); *Emily Barham* (Julie Andrews); *Admiral William Jessup* (Melvyn Douglas); *Lt. Commander "Bus" Cummings* (James Coburn); *Mrs. Barham* (Joyce Grenfell); *Admiral Healy* (Edward Binns); *Sheila* (Liz Fraser); *Old Sailor* (Keenan Wynn); *Captain Harry Spaulding* (William Windom); *Enright* (Alan Sues); *Pretty Girls* (Janine Gray, Judy Carne, Kathy Kersh)

In *Mary Poppins*, Julie Andrews proved she had the makings of a star; it only remained for her to prove she could also act. She found the right role in *The Americanization of Emily*, Paddy Chayefsky's significant screen adaptation of a novel by William Bradford Huie. Most of the scriptwriters who were well received in the Fifties found themselves unable to adapt to the concerns and questions posed by this new decade. Chayefsky, however, persevered by finding a theme he worked, and reworked, in various settings: the cynical individualist up against a blind system. In *The Hospital,* he pitted a singular, dedicated doctor (George C. Scott) against the bureaucracy of a major big city medical complex; in *Network,* he set a strong-willed newsman (William Holden) against the plastic people of the McLuhan age. But first, in *Emily,* he created an image of a self-confessed coward bucking the system of the armed service and, along with it, the insanity of war.

Emily is perhaps the most impressive example ever of an ardently pacifist film being produced by one of those notoriously patriotic major studios— and turning out to be commercially successful simply because it couched its doctrine in ingratiating romance, comedy, and melodrama. By succeeding, *Emily* paved the way for the strong anti-war ideology that would make itself felt in both the society, and the films, of the late Sixties. Lt. Charles Madison (James Garner) is a "dog robber"—that is, an aide to an American officer chosen for his ability to track down high quality booze, food, and women.

English innocence encounters American cynicism. Julie Andrews and James Garner in *The Americanization of Emily*.

James Garner, as an unpatriotic American officer, throws off-balance the unquestioning lifestyle of Julie Andrews and Joyce Grenfell in *The Americanization of Emily*.

James Coburn, as a cynic turned super-patriot, receives a lesson in the politics of survival from James Garner. *(The Americanization of Emily)*

He is a coward and a cynic, who hates war and beats the system by making it work for him. He considers patriotism an immoral attitude, insisting pacifism is the highest form of morality. "So long as valor is a virtue," he insists to the shocked English war widow, Emily Barham (Andrews), "we will have soldiers."

She has been assigned to Madison as a motor pool driver and, before long, they are involved in a love affair—another breakthrough for the film, seeing as the female star was, after all, Mary Poppins to millions of viewers. The affair was handled in a most casual manner—as something which could transpire just as easily in a Hollywood movie as in real life. The changing attitude toward sexuality received one of its first major illustrations in this romance which rejected the Doris Day problems of will-she-or-won't-she and substituted instead believable people attempting to satisfy their hungers for passion and companionship with other equally imperfect beings. The prim, proper, and very patriotic Emily resists her lover's attitudes at first, then gradually is "Americanized"—as she becomes aware of the luxury the officers enjoy in their London hotel suites. Complications arise when Madison and Annapolis man Lt. Commander "Bus" Cummings (James Coburn, in a strong supporting performance) receive a difficult assignment. Admiral Jessup (Melvyn Douglas) becomes convinced that the Navy's image must be improved by more impressive heroes, and assigns his two aides to make sure the first American who dies on the Omaha Beachhead during the great upcoming invasion is a Navy man. As the self-confessed coward sails toward Omaha, he realizes suddenly the trick fate has in store for him: he will more than likely be the first American to die on the beach; the propagandistic use that will be made of his death will contradict everything he stood for in life.

In the late Fifties, Garner had played a similar character in western setting—*Maverick*, TV's only cowardly cowboy. Now he carried that image to motion pictures and, in an era ripe for cynicism, emerged as a significant screen personality. Andrews was equally effective as a precursor of the smalltown girl turned anti-war activist of the late Sixties. If only Julie had been wise enough to balance her roles in lightweight, frothy musicals with meaty parts like this, she might have remained a major star for many years. Instead she buried herself in overly lavish musical extravaganzas (*Star!*, *Thoroughly Modern Millie*) and passed up the kinds of parts (*The Prime of Miss Jean Brodie*, for example) that would have kept her acting abilities on view. After one extravagant failure too many, she slipped out of the public's interest.

D-Day became a popular subject for Sixties filmmakers, ranging from the elaborate staging in *The Longest Day* to such other films as *36 Hours* and *Up from the Beach*, as well as this reenactment in *Emily*.

Anthony Quinn as Zorba.

ZORBA THE GREEK

INTERNATIONAL CLASSICS

Produced by Michael Cacoyannis; screenplay by Michael Cacoyannis, based on the novel by Nikos Kazantzakis; directed by Michael Cacoyannis.

CAST
Alexis Zorba (Anthony Quinn); *Basil* (Alan Bates); *The Widow* (Irene Papas); *Madame Hortense* (Lila Kedrova); *Mavrandoni* (George Foundas); *Lola* (Eleni Anousaki); *Mimithos* (Sotiris Moustakas); *Manolakas* (Takis Emmanuel); *Pavlo* (George Voyajis); *Soul* (Anna Kyriakou)

In the mid-Sixties, life in all its complexity, as it really is lived, suddenly replaced the dream factory images that had dominated American movies. Finally, the dictates of the Production Code were crumbling, as evidenced by the fact that a commercial/romantic film such as *The Americanization of Emily* could feature a heroine as clean cut as Julie Andrews—already considered by many moviegoers as England's answer to Doris Day—in a casually sexual but emotionally serious love affair outside of marriage with James Garner, who spouted pacifist attitudes that indirectly berated the government's current policies in Viet Nam. Another significant step toward a more mature cinema came when one of America's great older stars, Anthony Quinn, appeared as a symbol of the life force itself in a picture which—though tame enough by today's standards—still seriously altered the then-current image of what was fit material for an entertainment film.

Michael Cacoyannis—who wrote, directed, and produced the film—based his project on Nikos Kazantzakis' highly regarded novel, previously considered unfilmable—at least for any kind of major studio production: the material was not "commercial" enough, while important incidents in the story might prove too "controversial." But after its release, *Zorba* proved phenomenally successful, with its tale of an anglo-Greek named Basil (Alan Bates), a scholarly, over-serious Establishment-oriented young man who inherits an old lignite mine in the hills of Crete from his father, and journeys there with plans of putting it into operation. At the seaside town of Piraeus, Basil encounters an old itinerant named Alexis Zorba (Quinn) and is badgered by the man into taking him on as a traveling companion and assistant. On Crete, the two encounter a stark landscape: an uninvitingly rocky shoreline, barren villages, windswept hills. But they try to make their business venture work, and as they do, Zorba gradually teaches the younger man his secret of life—the dance he does, a celebration of spontaneity and enjoyment of the present moment. At times of cru-

145

Alan Bates and Irene Papas, in a moody and complex shot that effectively shows the visual style of *Zorba the Greek*.

The death of the widow: Irene Papas and Alan Bates in *Zorba the Greek*.

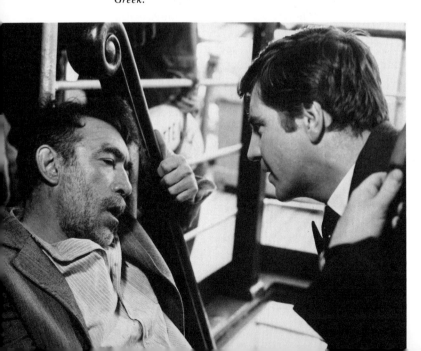

elty (which repel Zorba as much as Basil) the young man is often ready to run away from the hardened people of his village, and at first cannot understand Zorba's begrudging acceptance of them—their cruelty and ignorance being too much to bear. Gradually, though, Basil learns to understand Zorba's love of life itself, and life—sadly enough—encompasses cruelty and ignorance as well as joy and beauty. In the unforgettable final image, Basil joins Zorba on the beach, where the two dance together as the waves roll in: if Zorba is, in a sense, a natural "hippie," Basil become the first social dropout to join him.

Was *Zorba* an American commercial film or a European art film? On the one hand, it was the product of a major Hollywood studio, 20th Century–Fox, and featured a big name Hollywood star in the leading role. On the other, it represented the highly personal work of a European auteur, and featured the bawdy, brutal moments previously accepted only in pictures on the art-house circuit. In point of fact, with *Zorba*, the distinctions between art and entertainment, between Hollywood product and European creations, between mass audience and art-house audience began, at last, to blur—and, shortly thereafter, to disappear entirely. *Zorba* features terrifyingly pessimistic moments, as when the peasants kill the beautiful young widow (Irene Papas) Basil has made his mistress, or when a group of old women strip the possessions of an ancient courtesan (Lila Kedrova) from her bed before the deceased woman's body is even cold. *Zorba* featured mements of exuberant, exhilaratingly earthy lust (including Basil's passionate relationship with the widow and Zorba's with the courtesan) but also provided humor in the form of Zorba's irresponsible business trip undertaken for his young boss, when all their money is squandered in a brothel. When the humor is not sexual, then it is irreverent, as when Zorba must manipulate some naive monks into allowing him to cut down the trees on their hillside for mine timber; the dialogue all sounded amazingly racy in 1964. Today, *Zorba* may appear as nothing more than a charmingly robust celebration of life, but in its time, it represented a giant step forward in the maturation of the commercial cinema.

A precursor of the hippies and a spokesman for the Establishment: Anthony Quinn and Alan Bates in *Zorba the Greek*.

1965

THE SOUND OF MUSIC

20TH CENTURY-FOX

Produced by Robert Wise; screenplay by Ernest Lehman, from the musical play by Richard Rodgers and Oscar Hammerstein II; directed by Robert Wise.

CAST

Maria (Julie Andrews); *Captain Von Trapp* (Christopher Plummer); *The Baroness* (Eleanor Parker); *Max Detweiler* (Richard Haydn); *Mother Abbess* (Peggy Wood); *Liesl* (Charmian Carr); *Louisa* (Heather Menzies); *Friedrich* (Nicolas Hammond); *Kurt* (Duane Chase); *Brigitta* (Angela Cartwright); *Marta* (Debbie Turner); *Gretl* (Kym Karath); *Sister Sophia* (Marni Nixon)

Mary Poppins introduced Julie Andrews to the movies; *The Sound of Music* made her a star. Maria Von Trapp, as played by Julie, naturally turned into an extension of Ms. Andrews' screen personality—and metamorphosed into a Mary Poppins for adults, a supremely self-confident soul who can always defeat any foes that try to dim her perennial optimism.

Unlike Mary Poppins, though, Maria's story begins in a nunnery, where the postulant nun Maria continually finds herself in confrontation with the Mother Abbess (Peggy Wood). Eventually, Maria realizes she is far too free-spirited to ever successfully subscribe to the strict rules and steady discipline of so formalized a lifestyle, and must always sneak away to the neighboring hills where she can lose herself amid the beauty of nature. Leaving the retreat, Maria attempts to do a nun's work in the world at large, bringing the basic values she shares with the Mother Abbess with her, only applying them as a practical part of everyday life. Like Mary Poppins, she takes on a job as a governess—caring for seven children of an aristocratic widower, Captain Von Trapp (Christopher Plummer), a stern, cynical, embittered man. Maria realizes she must teach her young wards how to enjoy life, an enterprise she undertakes wholeheartedly. Eventually, they learn to see the Austrian Alps, and the quaint town of Salzburg, through Maria's sparkling eyes and, as they do, their own eyes begin to sparkle. Maria must help Captain Von Trapp resist the advances of a wealthy baroness (Eleanor Parker) and also ward off a wild-eyed impresario (Richard Haydn) who attempts to sign the singing Von

"The hills are alive . . .": Julie Andrews in the classic opening shot of *The Sound of Music*.

Trapps to a contract. But these problems are minor compared to the calamity they must finally deal with. When their storybook world is invaded by the Nazis, the Von Trapps flee their beloved city and make their way over the mountains to freedom.

Though this Richard Rodgers–Oscar Hammerstein II musical is, in fact, a modern operetta, director Robert Wise insisted on filming it against the actual locations, and brought his camera crew to Salzburg in order to shoot even the most stylized musical numbers—Julie and the children singing and dancing their way down a street—against backdrops that were unmistakably real, thereby giving his film the same sort of strange blend of the real and the expressionistic that had marked his earlier musical movie approach to another unforgettable Maria—in *West Side Story*. In fact, the opening scenes of the two films are almost identical: just as *West Side* began with a shot of the camera carrying us at first slowly, then at a dazzling pace, down from the sky to the tenement streets where the drama was to unfold, so too does *Sound of Music* begin with a camera moving in an identical motion—only this time, it is over the Alps, through the clouds and down to the hilltop where Maria, dancing amid the wild flowers and high grass, sings out the title song: "The hills are alive . . ."

Sound of Music is, like the stage show, pure saccharine—a combination of sentiment and corn, blended brilliantly and staged handsomely enough that the film quickly became the number one box-office champ of all time, providing a final bastion of optimistic escapism as an alternative to those new, more "realistic" films suddenly appearing. Despite its vast success, the picture was nonetheless the last of its breed and, arriving at mid-decade, served to close a chapter in the history of a brand of cinema that could take even a true story and make it appear like a fairytale. It's worth mentioning, though, that *Sound of Music* did in fact deal with the very themes that would be central to the radical counterculture, since Maria is a dropout nature lover intent on "finding herself"!

Julie was, of course, nominated for yet another Oscar for her role. But the upcoming change in cinematic styles was already in the wind, for the Academy awarded the 1965 statuette to yet another English lass (also named Julie) and, by so doing, legitimized the more intelligent, sophisticated, and modern breed of films that was about to dominate the commercial cinema.

Julie Andrews and Christopher Plummer with family in *The Sound of Music*.

The Sound of Music: Julie Andrews serenades the children on a hillside near Salzburg.

The first drop-out: Julie Andrews and Peggy Wood. *(The Sound of Music)*

Julie Christie as Darling.

DARLING

EMBASSY PICTURES

Produced by Joseph Janni; screenplay by Frederic Raphael; directed by John Schlesinger.

CAST

Diana Scott (Julie Christie); *Robert Gold* (Dirk Bogarde); *Miles Brand* (Laurence Harvey); *Malcolm* (Roland Curram); *Prince Cesare* (José-Luis de Villalonga); *Tony Bridges* (Trevor Bowen); *Sean Martin* (Alex Scott); *Estelle Gold* (Pauline Yates)

The great surprise of the Academy Award ceremonies came when a near unknown British "bird" named Julie Christie was named Best Actress of the Year—an honor that had once been the hard earned prize of long-time stars. Christie came, seemingly, out of nowhere, having been seen briefly in two memorable supporting roles: the swinging English girl who offers Tom Courtenay's modern day Walter Mitty a chance to live out his wildest fantasies in *Billy Liar,* and the lovely Irish lass who inspires Sean O'Casey (Rod Taylor) to write great poetry in *Young Cassidy.* The Oscar made it clear Ms. Christie would follow James Bond and the Beatles into the pop consciousness of Sixties America, already overcrowded with strong images from Britain. Many people doubted, though, that Christie could even act, for there was the lingering notion that in *Darling,* she had merely been employed by screenwriter Frederic Raphael and director John Schlesinger as an extension of her own self—a symbol of the amoral, live-for-the-present, media-hyped youth of modern London.

Bosley Crowther of the New York *Times* aptly and succinctly described *Darling* as the "tale of a London photographer's model who goes from bed to worse." Diana Scott (Christie) leaves an ill-advised marriage to make it on her own, and quickly comes in contact with Robert Gold (Dirk Bogarde), a cynical, caustic intellectual currently going completely commercial in his own eyes by working for the B.B.C. She falls into a quick affair with the man, but cannot commit herself to him any more than she could her first husband; has an abortion when she becomes pregnant; wanders into another relationship, this time with a slick, slimy advertising executive, Miles Brand (Laurence Harvey); ultimately becomes a pop celebrity after using them, and others, to get herself photographed for magazines and cast in television commercials; and finally ends up in a dazzling but sexless marriage with a bona fide Italian Prince, Cesare (José-Luis de Villalonga).

By cinematically travelling along Diana's road in life, the filmmakers were able to document a cross-section of modern English types and, by so doing, turn their picture into a work of social commentary without that aspect ever overshadowing our melodramatic interests in the central characters. As in Fellini's *La Dolce Vita,* we see the *paparazzi* of a major city—the celebrities, the hangers-on, but mostly the ambitious photographers and reporters who chronicle them for the media-hyped and media-hungry public. *Darling* is, more than anything, a movie about the superficiality of the Sixties, all dressed up to look chic and sophisticated, in which the surface of things is readily available from a deluge of media outlets but nothing is explored in depth. This is a movie about the world of the McLuhan prediction: the new order of the complicated media machine presenting only an empty message, the world of form over content, of style over substance. The element that stands out most clearly in *Darling* is the total lack of honest emotions on the part of anyone in the drama. Harvey's advertising man is too Machiavellian, Bogarde's TV interviewer too embittered and absorbed in self-defeat, and Christie's model too totally amoral to feel anything honest or meaningful for another person or, for that matter, to elicit a strong feeling from us. In 1965 *Darling* appeared cold and strange, impossible to reconcile with the conventional films in which we feel strongly about almost everyone—even the heavies. But *Darling* would set a pace for the films of the latter half of the decade: cool, clinical, clever, and committed to the theme of lack of commitment.

This, of course, had already been explored in the films of important, artistic filmmakers like Michelangelo Antonioni, whose pictures had impressed intellectual moviegoers with their abililty to capture the empty, amoral ambience of the Sixties. But these films appealed almost exclusively to intellectuals. With *Darling,* the commercial cinema suddenly appeared to be catching up. *Darling* contained explicit four letter words, graphic bed scenes, and most significant of all, a refusal to offer any simple moral conclusion about this ennui-ridden existence.

By closely studying and scrutinizing Julie Christie's character, Raphael and Schlesinger were able to focus on the person behind the perfect face we encounter every day on television, seducing us into buying products we neither want nor need; the moviemakers finally concluded that the character is as empty a vessel as the image itself. At one moment, as she is caught by a camera from precisely the right angle, Diana Scott displays an almost classic beauty; a second later, all sorts of sordid, superficial emotions cross over her face, making her appear cheap and sluttish.

At the beginning of *Darling,* a television documentary maker is seen interviewing people on the streets, his question being: "What's wrong with England today?" Without ever slipping into easy, obvious moralizing, *Darling* set out to answer that question by showing us precisely what the filmmakers considered worst about the evolving lifestyle.

Dirk Bogarde and Julie Christie in *Darling*.

Between two men: Laurence Harvey, Julie Christie, and Dirk Bogarde in *Darling*.

Peter Sellers and Peter O'Toole: two superstars who rode the crest of the wave of British popularity. (*What's New Pussycat?*)

WHAT'S NEW, PUSSYCAT?

UNITED ARTISTS

Produced by Charles K. Feldman; screenplay by Woody Allen; directed by Clive Donner.

CAST

Fritz Fassbender (Peter Sellers); *Michael James* (Peter O'Toole); *Carol Werner* (Romy Schneider); *Reńee Lefèbvre* (Capucine); *Liz* (Paula Prentiss); *Victor Shakapopulis* (Woody Allen); *Rita* (Ursula Andress); *Anna Fassbender* (Eddra Gale); *Jacqueline* (Katrin Schaake); *Tempest O'Brien* (Nicole Karen); *Man in Bar* (Richard Burton)

What's New, Pussycat? was *the* comedy of 1965, containing almost every element then popular with the moviegoing public. This was obvious even from the title sequence, which featured a tune by Burt Bacharach (just emerging as the composer who most completely captured the spirit of the times in song) sung by Tom Jones (who had, in the last year, established himself as the leading male pop-vocalist); meanwhile, the titles themselves appeared as a kind of Tiffany-type colored glass slide show, in the pop-art tradition that had recently caught hold of

the American imagination. The cast featured Peter Sellers who, thanks to *The Pink Panther*, had made the transition from art house celebrity to the comedy star of the decade, and Peter O'Toole, another highly popular import from England who had established himself as a new leading man thanks to *Lawrence of Arabia* and *Becket* (his equally popular co-star, Richard Burton, even popped up for a cameo in *Pussycat*). Ursula Andress, who had made big waves when she emerged from the ocean wearing a scanty bikini in *Dr. No.*, was also on hand, along with an eclectic trio of beauties—the kookie American Paula Prentiss, the sleek French sophisticate Capucine, and the kittenish Austrian Romy Schneider. Most significant of all, though, was that *Pussycat* boasted a screenplay by Woody Allen (as well as a supporting performance by him), thereby representing the first significant screen appearance by the man who would soon emerge as the modern Chaplin. Director Clive Donner's suitably "campy" style created a package that had audiences—if not the critics—rolling in the aisles.

The storyline is archetypal Allen. Michael James (O'Toole) works as the feature editor on a slick Paris fashion magazine. His job brings him into constant contact with some of the most beautiful women in the world, all of whom find him quite irresistible. That is a perfect situation for him, since he is obsessed with gorgeous girls: he coins the word "pussycat" to describe the sexually desirable and totally available women who cluster around him. Despite this, he suffers from anhedonia—an inability to enjoy even the most pleasant situations—because of one catch. Michael falls in love with Carol (Schneider), one of the loveliest of the lovelies, and wants to marry her, though he cannot get over his obsession with all beautiful women—which Carol will not tolerate. Michael then becomes obsessed with his obsession, and, in order to discover a release from it so he can be happy with the girl of his dreams, seeks help from a psychiatrist (Sellers) who, unfortunately, turns out to be a stark raving madman and, what's more, even more obsessed with beautiful women than Michael himself.

If the situation sounds vaguely like an old Marx Brothers routine, it should—Woody Allen has always admitted his great respect for their madcap style of frantic slapstick. But if Groucho, Harpo, and Chico predated Camp, Allen's film was consciously created in that pop-art style of the Sixties which, ever since the publication of an important essay by Susan Sontag, suggested that bad taste is in fact good, that excessiveness is preferable to art, that the lowbrow entertainments of youth which we uncritically enjoyed (Saturday matinee movies,

Backstage at the Crazy Horse Saloon, Woody Allen helps a chorus girl prepare for her act. (*What's New Pussycat?*)

Woody Allen demonstrates his romantic prowess in *What's New Pussycat?*

Ursula Andress (center) displays her talent for frolicking on a bed in *What's New Pussycat?*

comic books, and the like) are more significant to our culture than the high art we have to be taught to enjoy. In an era that saw the Campbell's soup can enshrined by Andy Warhol and the comic-strip panel aggrandized by Roy Lichtenstein, *Pussycat* revived Marxian madness but did so with a special sort of self-consciousness. Whether it was Paula Prentiss stripping at the decadently elegant Crazy Horse Saloon, Ursula Andress as a parachuting nymphomaniac, Peter Sellers prancing around in a Beatle wig or the surrealistic sets which loudly announced the movie's total removal from reality, *Pussycat* provided the perfect movie comedy for the society that had embraced the plasticity of pop art.

153

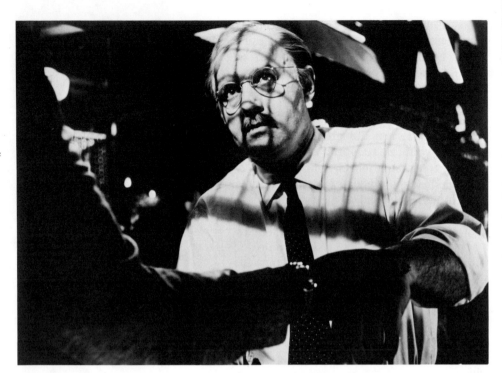

Rod Steiger as the pawnbroker.

THE PAWNBROKER

LANDAU-UNGER FILMS

Produced by Roger H. Lewis and Philip Langer for Executive Producer Worthington Miner; screenplay by David Friedkin and Morton Fine, based on the novel by Edward Lewis Wallant; directed by Sidney Lumet.

CAST

Sol Nazerman (Rod Steiger); *Marilyn Birchfield* (Geraldine Fitzgerald); *Rodriguez* (Brock Peters); *Jesus Ortiz* (Jaime Sanchez); *Ortiz' Girl* (Thelma Oliver); *Tessie* (Marketa Kimbrell); *Mendel* (Baruch Lumet); *Mr. Smith* (Juano Hernandez); *Ruth* (Linda Geiser); *Tangee* (Raymond St. Jacques)

The picture which spearheaded the innovative wave of American cinema at mid-decade was *The Pawnbroker,* the highly controversial film which gave Rod Steiger his first impressive shot at a character lead: Sol Nazerman, a middle-aged Jewish American who runs a dilapidated pawnshop in Harlem. Nazerman's background, as sketched in for us, is relatively unique: the man survived the concentration camps in Europe twenty years ear-

lier, after the rest of his family perished. But Nazerman's personality, in the present, is clearly an extension, and exaggeration, of a state that was beginning to infect the American public. Nazerman survives in the Sixties by eschewing all relationships, loyalties, and commitments, either to other people or to causes. The world around him is heightened in its ugliness—slums and suffering are everywhere—and Nazerman makes no attempt to do anything about it, since he has gradually convinced himself that things cannot be altered for the better. He exercises a passionless affair with the widow of his one-time best friend; he berates the spontaneous, flippant young Puerto Rican–Negro, Jesus (Jaime Sanchez), who works as his assistant; he spurns the attempts of a well-meaning welfare worker (Geraldine Fitzgerald) to strike up a friendship. Nazerman operates as an island unto himself, until a series of shocking accidents and outrages force him to extend himself back into the world at large.

Though Nazerman's story is a far cry from the experiences of most people, it still served as an allegory for current events. Non-involvement emerged as a major social wave of the Sixties, in response to the ever growing rate of crime, and became the subject of moviemakers who attacked this latest brand of amorality with a heated anger. *The Pawnbroker* was a case in point, though the film was immediately attacked from a number of corners. It was accused of being anti-Semetic, offering an image of a Jew who believes in nothing but money; of being anti-Negro, for presenting blacks in villainous roles; and of being pornographic, for featuring exposed breasts for the first time in a modern American commercial film.

These attacks were, of course, all ridiculous. Though Nazerman happens to be a Jew, he is in no way presented as representing Jewish characters in general, but rather an unpleasant modern trend toward alienation that cuts across all cultural barriers. For the character of the black Harlem gangster, the filmmakers hoped to cast any of a number of big name black stars. Brock Peters finally agreed to do the role, with a clear understanding that portraying nothing but clean-cut, highly intelligent, almost infallible black characters—as Sidney Poitier was doing in such films as *The Slender Thread, A Patch of Blue, Guess Who's Coming to Dinner* and *To Sir, With Love*—only offered an unrealistic image of the Negro in America, and thus was essentially counter-productive. And the exposed breasts—occurring in a scene in which a desperate young Negro hooker offers herself to Nazerman, reminding the man of his own wife—could not be considered pornographic, since the scene is anything but erotic or arousing. We are moved to feel anguish for the woman and for Nazerman, who is once again learning to feel pain, sorrow, and humiliaton.

There are some very legitimate complaints which can be levelled against the film but they are artistic, not moral, ones. The opening title sequence, in which Harlem is seen in a gritty, black and white, near documentary fashion, never quite jells with the scenes inside the pawnshop, which are played as a film version of a stage play. Even the writing in these scenes is as overly conscious as in a theatrical production: the gangs of blacks who wander in are clearly meant to be taken as a modern counterpart to the Greek chorus, while the wise old black man (Juano Hernandez) is too explicitly a symbol of the ancient figure of wisdom. Though in fact based on a novel, *The Pawnbroker* often looks like a dramatic work transferred to the screen without its theatrical origins ever being left completely behind. Even the flashbacks, a purely cinematic device, to Nazerman's youth in Europe are overly obvious, and set into the film in predictable, contrived ways. Despite this, the adult handling of such volatile and controversial subject matter qualifies *The Pawnbroker* as a significant movie milestone.

Juano Hernandez and Rod Steiger in *The Pawnbroker*.

Hoodlums (including Raymond St. Jacques, second from right) invade the world of the pawnbroker.

Rod Steiger in a flashback scene in *The Pawnbroker*.

Warren Beatty as Mickey One, in the spotlight . . .

. . . and out of it.

MICKEY ONE
COLUMBIA PICTURES

Produced by Arthur Penn; screenplay by A. M. Surgal; directed by Arthur Penn.

CAST

The Comic (Warren Beatty); *Jenny* (Alexandra Stewart); *Castle* (Hurd Hatfield); *Ruby* (Franchot Tone); *Berson* (Teddy Hart); *Fryer* (Jeff Corey); *The Artist* (Kamatari Fujiwara); *Beautiful Girl* (Donna Michelle)

Yet another major breakthrough for the American art film came when Arthur Penn's *Mickey One* arrived on neighborhood theater screens. Like *The Pawnbroker,* it offered a striking alternative to the commercial Hollywood product and, also like that film, it combined realistic scenes with stylized ones. The difference was that, in *The Pawnbroker,* such a combination seemed a major flaw: streetwise scenes clashed with studio shots, and the resultant picture lacked a definitive tone. In *Mickey One,* the antithetical style of certain shots—ranging from moments of extreme realism to a heightened expressionism—jolted viewers in a strange but satisfying manner. In many respects, *Mickey One* resembled one of those much discussed but little seen avant garde underground pictures. Yet it was made with a considerably larger budget (though still small, by Hollywood standards) and was the product of a major studio, featuring an important young star.

After incarnating the innocent teenager in *Splendor in the Grass,* Beatty had assayed some youthful heel-as-non-hero roles. He was truly a rebel without a cause—a reckless and casual symbol of Sixties youth, in strong comparison to Dean's highly intense young man in search of something worth commiting himself to. Now, though, the hero of his age was no longer a young man in search of truth but rather one who had abandoned the search and slipped willingly into the meaninglessness of the world around him. In *All Fall Down,* Beatty had calmly, coldly seduced, then abandoned Eva Marie Saint; in *Roman Spring,* he did the same to Vivien Leigh, and in each case, the symbolism of the casting was perfect: this representative of the new Hollywood was emotionally destroying those women who best represented the old order of picture making. In *All Fall Down,* Beatty even had Brandon de

Wilde to witness his action. The non-hero lives out the actions that the more introspective de Wilde can only fantasize about. De Wilde's ultimate rejection of both Beatty and Paul Newman at the ends of *All Fall Down* and *Hud* stood for a greater, more universal rejection of the new non-hero by the more traditional American. As our representative in the film, de Wilde made clear that total acceptance of the new amorality was not a necessity; that no matter how attractive it might appear at first glance, the final solution was to walk away from it.

In *Mickey One*, Beatty's screen persona at last congealed into its complete form: a young man of nervous energy, flippant humor, and gross insecurity always masked by a supremely confident manner. *Mickey One* is on the run—but from who is never made quite clear. Perhaps from the people who hired him as a nightclub comic, and on whom he has run out. Perhaps from the young woman (Alexandra Stewart) he discovered living as a derelict, and who asks him only for a normal, old-fashioned man-woman commitment, which he cannot abide by. Perhaps from the enigmatic stranger (Hurd Hatfield), who slithers around the city and

Alexandra Stewart and Warren Beatty in *Mickey One*.

appears to view Mickey from a homosexual obsession. Perhaps it is The Mob, that unspoken, unspeakable force of evil that apparently controls everything, everywhere, and from which there is no escape. Most likely, though, it is himself Mickey is running from.

Director Arthur Penn's previous picture was the touching *The Miracle Worker*, which he had also mounted on the Broadway stage. But Penn's background as a theater person was in no way evident with this experimental project, for *Mickey One* is pure cinema: a fascinating if occasionally confusing mixture of film techniques. Characters appear outside a high hotel window, bouncing up and down as in a dream; a late night chase through a nightmarish city spills over into total surrealism when a great machine on the city's edge explodes and endlessly regurgitates objects, parts, bubbles; finally, the hero stands before an unresponsive audience, his "act" and his reality becoming inseparable, as he frantically tries to make out the faces in front of him but is caught in the glare of lights. At moments, *Mickey One* resembles a Hitchcock thriller as it might have been done by Andy Warhol. For Mickey is the archetypal wrong man: hunted and pursued by forces he cannot understand, haunted and chased by his own private demons. *Mickey One* offered a surrealistic psychodrama for the emerging Sixties audiences: more youthful and more tolerant of artistic experimentation than the audiences of a decade before.

Warren Beatty and some low-life characters in one of the scenes that displayed filmmaker Arthur Penn's amazing ability to play realistic scenes for surrealistic effect. *(Mickey One)*

Omar Sharif as Dr. Zhivago.

DOCTOR ZHIVAGO
METRO-GOLDWYN-MAYER

Produced by Carlo Ponti; screenplay by Robert Bolt, from the novel by Boris Pasternak; directed by David Lean.

CAST

Tonya (Geraldine Chaplin); *Lara* (Julie Christie); *Pasha* (Tom Courtenay); *Yevgraf* (Alec Guinness); *Anna* (Siobhan McKenna); *Alexander* (Ralph Richardson); *Yuri* (Omar Sharif); *Komarovsky* (Rod Steiger); *The Girl* (Rita Tushingham); *Amelia* (Adrienne Corri); *Prof. Kurt* (Geoffrey Keen); *Petya* (Jack MacGowran); *Yuri at age 8* (Tarek Sharif)

The decision by M.G.M. executives to have screenwriter Robert Bolt and director David Lean (fresh from their success with *Lawrence of Arabia*) adapt Boris Pasternak's brilliant novel to the screen had little to do with interest in great literature. Twenty-five years had gone by since *Gone With the Wind* captured moviegoers with its personal love story set against an important epoch of the past. Numerous attempts to create another *Gone With the Wind* (including David O. Selznick's own *Duel in the Sun, GWTW* as a western) were less than successful. But here was the chance to provide audiences with a *Gone With the Wind* for the Sixties, and at the same time allow the filmmakers to sympathetically explain the socialist takeover of Russia—a move which, only ten years earlier, would have caused the moviemakers to become automatic targets of the House Committee on UnAmerican Activities.

Though the film was in many ways impressive, it was not, by any stretch of the imagination, another *GWTW*—even though it featured a haunting song, "Lara's Theme," which was the most memorable such number since "Tara's Theme." Part of the problem was that *Zhivago* seemed too synthetic. The filmmakers were clearly modeling their products on the format of an earlier success, whereas much of the peculiar chemistry of *GWTW* grew from the fact that numerous directors and writers were all stumbling in the dark, not knowing what they were after and then, by a miracle of good luck and a happy combination of talents, just happened to produce the greatest commercial film of all time. No great picture has ever been created by imitating a former triumph. Still, many *good* films may be

Dr. Zhivago (Omar Sharif) romances his wife (Geraldine Chaplin) . . .

turned out by such a process, *Zhivago* included. Also noteworthy is the fact that *GWTW* was based on a "junk novel"—Margaret Mitchell's tale of the vanished glories of the South was a superbly sentimental potboiler, a delightfully done work of superficial fiction. So the gloriously glossy screen treatment it received at the hands of Selznick and his people was perfectly in keeping with the book's style and, if anything, improved on it. But Pasternak had written a weighty, demanding work, so the approach taken toward his novel subverted his artistic intentions. Everything in the book that did not conform to a *GWTW* type treatment was cut out, and much that was cut had been responsible for the book's greatness.

Still, the film was not without merit. Bolt's screenplay was lean and literate; the performances by many cast members were striking; and best of all, David Lean's instinctive feel for the spectacle lent some of the major scenes a truly unforgettable quality: the execution of socialist protesters in a Moscow Square during the last days of the czar's reign; the battle between Communist troops and Communist deserters on a lonely Russian road; the transportation of exiles, by train, to the frozen outskirts of the country following the victory of the revolutionary forces. Less effective were the love scenes between Zhivago and Lara. Pasternak's characters were softspoken, submissive types, and

. . . and his mistress (Julie Christie).

159

therefore necessarily lacked the explosive passion of a Rhett and a Scarlett. Also, a basic part of the lot was Zhivago's transition from a bourgeois doctor to an inspired poet, and there is nothing less cinematic, or less dramatically effective, than watching someone writing. In one wordless scene, Lara and Zhivago—isolated together in a breathtaking ice-covered mansion—sit together as he writes of

One of the spectacular scenes of Russia in transition. *(Dr. Zhivago)*

his love for her, causing Lara to shed a tear. But nothing about Zhivago, as depicted in the film, led us to believe (as we had in the novel) that the character really did possess genius—that their love af-

Julie Christie as Lara. (*Dr. Zhivago*)

fair was an important, larger-than-life one. Instead, they seem sad victims, and our emotional response is more pathos than the full blown tragedy we witness in *GWTW*.

The essential problem, though, was the casting of Omar Sharif as Zhivago. What might have made the film work, would have been an actor/star of the Montgomery Clift/Marlon Brando magnitude, for such a person would have carried his own impressive presence with him to the part, and made us immediately sense Zhivago's intrinsic greatness. The film was also burdened by a choppy sense of narration, which made the experience of watching it rather like flipping through a copy of a great historical novel without being allowed enough time to read each page properly. For this reason, many of the characters—so believable and real in the book—were underdeveloped in the film.

Despite all this, there was a stunning visual beauty to the film. If it never metamorphosed into a milestone of the commercial cinema ("Not since *Gone With the Wind* has a motion picture . . ."), it did at least provide one of the last epic screen romances, in which a man and a woman desperately attempt to achieve happiness together despite revolutionary social forces. Very shortly, America—and Hollywood with it—would be rocked by just such forces, changing drastically the quality of life in America, and American films.

161

Overleaf: The revolutionary fervor engulfs Russia. (*Dr. Zhivago*)

1966

164

THE RUSSIANS ARE COMING
THE RUSSIANS ARE COMING

UNITED ARTISTS

Produced by Norman Jewison; screenplay by William Rose, based on the novel *The Off-Islanders* by Nathaniel Benchley; directed by Norman Jewison.

CAST

Walt Whittaker (Carl Reiner); *Elspeth Whittaker* (Eva Marie Saint); *Rozanov* (Alan Arkin); *Link Mattocks* (Brian Keith); *Norman Jonas* (Jonathan Winters); *The Captain* (Theodore Bikel); *Fendall Hawkins* (Paul Ford); *Alice Foss* (Tessie O'Shea); *Alexei Kolchin* (John Phillip Law); *Alison Palmer* (Andrea Dromm); *Luther Grilk* (Ben Blue); *Airport Worker* (Michael J. Pollard)

The most impressive element in *Doctor Zhivago* was not its updating of the *GWTW* formula in a different setting, but the particular setting the filmmakers casually chose: Russia, at the time of the revolution. And, on a less serious level, the second James Bond film, *From Russia With Love,* matched the super-patriotic secret agent with a beautiful Russian. Clearly, the atmosphere was changing, as we came to understand the Russians were no longer necessarily our natural enemies and that an understanding might, in the near future, be reached. Such sentiments were cleverly brought to the screen by Norman Jewison in his comedy *The Russians Are Coming the Russians Are Coming,* a box-office success not only owing to the charm it provided, but also the perfect timing of its message.

The story begins as a not-so-bright Russian Captain (Theodore Bikel) brings his submarine too close to Cape Cod, for no better reason than that he wants to get a good look at America through his periscope. When the sub accidentally becomes lodged in the sand of a small island, the Captain desperately trusts his second in command, Rozanov (Alan Arkin), to take a landing party and quickly pilfer some sort of power boat, in order that they can get their craft off American soil before any incident can take place. But all does not go well for Rozanov. For he ends up at the home of a vacationing Manhattan TV writer, Walt Whittaker (Carl Reiner), and his quiet suburbanite wife, Elizabeth (Eva Marie Saint). Whittaker is in a jumpy mood, for after a full summer on this isolated place, he can't wait to return to the rat race in the big city.

Theodore Bikel and Alan Arkin: In the sixties, Russians were suddenly portrayed in a less villainous light. *(The Russians Are Coming the Russians Are Coming)*

Brian Keith and Alan Arkin try to negotiate a peace in *The Russians Are Coming the Russians Are Coming)*

Townsmen form a militia to fight off a possible invasion in *The Russians Are Coming the Russians Are Coming*.

And when he comes face to face with the surly Russian, hysteria quickly sets in. The Russian and the American share mutual misunderstanding and unfounded fears of each other and, before long, a new Paul Revere (Ben Blue) is riding through the nearby town, shouting: "The Russians Are Coming! The Russians Are Coming!"

Young Norman Jewison directed William Rose's script as a TV-style situation comedy, though done with a sparkle and sophistication rarely found in that medium. A number of prominent TV personalities, like Reiner, Paul Ford, and Jonathan Winters, added to this effect. Some, like Brian Keith, received the chance to demonstrate an ability at comic delivery that had previously gone untapped, as when his garrulous sheriff tries handling the problem of the Russian invasion by serving them a ticket for illegally parking their submarine. The film's real find, though, was Alan Arkin, who here made his premiere in a major motion picture (though he had done some experimental, avant garde films, including a classic of the genre in which he portrayed an out-of-work Puerto Rican happily strumming a guitar in the park) and was quickly accepted as an important new comic and dramatic actor, making his mark in such pictures as *The Heart Is a Lonely Hunter* and *Wait Until Dark*. Arkin in many ways epitomized the new actor-star of the Sixties, with his ethnic looks and off-the-cuff,

down-to-earth acting style. He pioneered the way for such personalities as Dustin Hoffman, who would help redefine the term "movie star" by bringing the current New York acting approach to Hollywood, as Brando and Clift had done a decade earlier.

But the real impact of *Russians* was in its tacit suggestion that the problems between Americans and Russians were essentially based on stupid prejudices that for twenty years had made communication impossible. As the situation in the film escalates, the problems on this small island become clearly symbolic of the international problem. The only weak moment in the movie is the upbeat but unlikely ending, in which the distraught townspeople quickly calm themselves down in order to save an innocent Russian boy (John Phillip Law) who has fallen in love with a teenage American girl (Andrea Dromm); more likely, they would (in the scary tradition of *The Ox-Bow Incident* mob) have killed him on sight. But this overly optimistic ending, in which everyone makes friends and American-Russian relations are smoothed over, can be taken as a notable fantasy projection of America at mid-decade. Clearly, we perceived the world situation as shifting once again, and the transition was already being chronicled for public consumption by the movies.

BORN FREE

COLUMBIA

Produced by Sam Jaffe and Paul Radin as a Carl Foreman Production; screenplay by Gerald L. C. Copley, based on the book by Joy Adamson; directed by James Hill.

CAST

Joy Adamson (Virginia McKenna); *George Adamson* (Bill Travers); *Kendall* (Geoffrey Keen); *Nuru* (Peter Lukoye); *Makkede* (Omar Chambati); *Sam* (Bill Godden); *Baker* (Bryan Epsom); *Indian Doctor* (Sura Patet)

In the mid-sixties, an old word took on a new significance: ecology. As fear of instant atomic oblivion receded, only to be replaced by the growing realization that atomic fallout from routine testing, coupled with various industrial wastes from such long-accepted institutions as factories and businesses, were throwing off the world's natural balance, an ecology crusade began to take shape. At first, this was a small movement which, like the simultaneous peace and civil rights movements, began on college campuses, then spread to society at large. Before the decade's end, however, a concern for both the animal and vegetable kingdoms, and a desire to protect them from the ravages of pollution, had firmly taken hold of the American mentality. The film which first brought such a way of thinking to the screen, popularizing the guardians of the natural life as the new heroes for our age, was *Born Free*.

The film was based on a surprisingly non-sentimental book by Joy Adamson, the wife of a British game warden living in Africa, and related a number of her first-hand experiences while caring for nature's creatures on the dark continent. In the film—which is extremely true to the intent, tone, and the letter of the book—Joy (Virginia McKenna) and her husband George (Bill Travers) discover a nest of lion cubs whose mother has been destroyed. Unable to leave the animals to starve in the wilderness, they bring the creatures home and adopt them as pets. Their favorite is Elsa, a cub who quickly loses her cuteness and grows to enormous size, but still wanders around the house like an oversized puppy dog—obliviously destroying furniture. The love between the Adamsons and the animal is touching, as they walk through the wilds together, or enjoy a swim in a nearby river on a hot summer day. Even-

Bill Travers and Virginia McKenna, with Elsa in *Born Free*.

Virginia McKenna: the birth of an ecological impulse. (*Born Free*)

167

tually, though, Joy realizes Elsa must learn to live on her own, and sets about teaching the lion—born free, but raised among humans—how to feed and care for herself in the jungle.

Born Free was a family film, in the finest sense of that term. It was a delight for children, who were moved to laughter by the lovable antics of the little lion cubs, and swept up by the fierce battle sequences between Elsa and another lioness as she attempts to re-adjust to her life in the jungle. At the same time, adults could respond to the predicament of the Adamsons, for they were no mere cartoon level adults as might be discovered in a typical juvenile programmer. Since the people were played by a real life husband and wife team of performers, there was an understated but very strong tenderness constantly in evidence between Joy and George; and the actors, working from an intelligent script by Gerald L. C. Copley, were able to turn them into believable, multi-dimensional people, with moments of weakness and surges of strength and courage. Best of all, director James Hill drew as much humor and drama from Elsa as had been evident in such earlier animal-star epics as *Lassie* and *Flicka,* without ever turning her into Elsa, The Wonder Lion.

The documentary flavor of the picture, shot entirely on location in East Africa, also added to the sense of authenticity, as well as the powerful drama in the last scene (which might easily have slipped into maudlin melodramatics) in which the Adamsons bid farewell to a de-civilized Elsa, and watch as she disappears into the bush—only to return later, for a short visit, bringing her cubs with her. The sense that Elsa and the Adamsons have gone their separate ways, without breaking the beautiful tie between them, was communicated. There were, of course, a number of respectable but lesser sequels—*Living Free, The Lions Are Loose*—some featuring McKenna and Travers as the Adamsons, others starring different performers. Eventually, there was even a short-lived TV series in the mid-Seventies, at a time when the ecology movement had reached a peak. But it was the original *Born Free* which best conveyed Joy Adamson's dedication to the world of nature, and also effectively established the back-to-nature movement as a significant subject for Sixties filmmakers.

Virginia McKenna and friend care for the lions in *Born Free.*

"What's it all about, Alfie?" Michael Caine as the amoral swinger enjoys Millicent Martin's attentions.

ALFIE

PARAMOUNT

Produced by Lewis Gilbert; screenplay by Bill Naughton, based on his stage play; directed by Lewis Gilbert.

CAST

Alfie (Michael Caine); *Ruby* (Shelley Winters); *Lily* (Vivien Merchant); *Gilda* (Julia Foster); *Annie* (Jane Asher); *Harry* (Alfie Bass); *Siddie* (Millicent Martin); *Carla* (Shirley Ann Field); *Abortionist* (Denholm Elliott); *Lady Doctor* (Eleanor Bron)

"What's it all about, Alfie?
Is it just for the moment we live?"

The simple words to the title song perfectly expressed the moral question posed by the movie. This latest in a series of phenomenally successful films from London—suddenly the fashion, music, and cultural center of the Sixties—dealt with some of the major themes everyone confronted during the decade. Bill Naughton adapted his own popular London and Broadway hit play into a screen project, in which the protagonist (Michael Caine) constantly comments to the audience in asides—a dura-

ble device that hails back to Shakespeare's day but which was nonetheless somewhat revolutionary for commercial movies. But *Alfie* threw convention to the wind in shocking, serious ways. Though a colorful and, for the most part, breezily entertaining picture, it presented a case study of that creature of the Sixties, a man unable to commit himself to anything or anyone, presenting us with a moral motion picture about the phenomenon of amorality.

When we first meet Alfie—when he, in fact, introduces himself to us—we are as taken by his brash, casual manner as the many "birds" who drift in and out of his life. Almost immediately, though, we begin to sense the suggestion of something sinister beneath the surface cool. Despite his playboy stance, Alfie lives in a relatively seedy East End flat. And while his escapades with women at first appear not very different from those the hero might enjoy in a typical Tony Curtis vehicle (in which various available, attractive women are romanced and then cast aside), director Lewis Gilbert was aiming at something deeper. For one thing, he made it a point not to cast typically pluperfect goddesses, or fantasy women types, and instead used a string of talented actresses who did indeed look very much like the ordinary, everyday women a normal single man might well encounter. Then, Naughton and Gilbert explored the consequences of casual sexual

169

encounters—"the good life" of the Sixties Fellini had explored, and condemned, five years earlier—finding the ultimately aimless conquest a saddening, dehumanizing thing. *Alfie* studied the swinging lifestyle of the Sixties, but the point of view was noticeably square.

Alfie's inability to develop any sort of lasting relationship ultimately forms the basis for the audience's moral rejection of the character. Early in the film, he becomes involved with Gilda (Julia Foster), a quiet, nondescript, decent young woman who becomes pregnant after sleeping with Alfie. He does not, on the one hand, play the typical heel and desert her. In fact, he helps her through the pregnancy, and loves the child. But he cannot totally commit himself to the relationship and, after a while, Gilda realizes she must marry a less flamboyant young man who believes in the old-fashioned idea of family, and wants to build something permanent in life. Some of Alfie's birds, like Carla (Shirley Ann Field) are as casual about their hedonism as he; others, such as Annie (Jane Asher) are manipulated by Alfie for ego gratification and a momentary sense of power, as when he steals her away from a truck driver in order to prove his prowess, then drops the relationship. But even a taker like Alfie

Vivien Merchant and Michael Caine in a moment of *angst* over the ramifications of their ill-advised love affair in *Alfie*.

Michael Caine and Julia Foster enjoy the "good life." *(Alfie)*

can be taken, as when he becomes the temporary gigolo of Ruby (Shelley Winters), a rich American widow, only to find himself dropped by her in favor of a younger lover.

The film's most powerful, and controversial, scene involved Alfie with a particularly vulnerable housewife, Lily (Vivien Merchant). She is the wife of a close friend, and has never experienced a passionate romance. Alfie seduces her with calculated charm; when she becomes pregnant, he arranges for an abortion. The sequence proved a shocker in 1966, but no one could deny its power, honesty, and dramatic effect, as the abortionist (Denholm Elliott) hands Alfie the destroyed fetus—and we finally see the character's facade crumble, realizing that he can, and does, feel, even if his lifestyle is based on repressing or hiding such human qualities. At the end, we find Alfie no wiser for his experiences than he was at the beginning, and that is the saddest thing that can be said about any character. Without heavy-handed moralizing, the film's writer and director conspired to subtly make us reject Alfie's approach to life. When he fades away at the end, heading toward yet another casual encounter, the viewer feels entertained by the comedy and drama and at the same time moved, and troubled, by the story's implications.

A MAN FOR ALL SEASONS

COLUMBIA

Produced by Fred Zinnemann with William N. Graf; screenplay by Robert Bolt, based on his play; directed by Fred Zinnemann.

CAST

Sir Thomas More (Paul Scofield); *Alice More* (Wendy Hiller); *Thomas Cromwell* (Leo McKern); *King Henry VIII* (Robert Shaw); *Cardinal Wolsey* (Orson Welles); *Margaret More* (Susannah York); *Duke of Norfolk* (Nigel Davenport); *Rich* (John Hurt); *William Roper* (Corin Redgrave); *Anne Boleyn* (Vanessa Redgrave)

In *Alfie,* the trend toward an amoral existence was analyzed; in *A Man for All Seasons,* a very different current syndrome was depicted and, signifi-cantly, once again protrayed in an English setting. The film was based on Robert Bolt's memorable play about Sir Thomas More, the sixteenth century Archbishop of Canterbury who stood up to the boisterous King Henry VIII by opposing his majesty's planned marriage to Anne Boleyn. Paul Scofield had played the lead in the stage version of Bolt's drama and, remarkably enough, was allowed the honor or repeating his interpretation in the expensive film version. There were changes made in the dramatic fiber during its metamorphosis from stage to screen, yet this talky but never longwinded historical tale proved popular at the box office, and at the following year's Academy Award ceremonies as well. Mr. Scofield was named Best Actor of the Year—and the Oscar was presented by England's best known "swinging bird," Julie Christie (named Best Actress the previous year), who made the presentation to her countryman while wearing a mini-skirt.

Re-interpreting his own play for the screen, Bolt

The calm before the storm: King Henry VIII (Robert Shaw) visits Sir Thomas More's family (Susannah York, Paul Scofield, and Wendy Hiller) before the beginning of the conflict that separates the king from his most idealistic subject. *(A Man for All Seasons)*

totally eliminated what, for many theatergoers, had been the source of its considerable power, a framing device featuring a symbolic character called "The Common Man." A kind of second cousin to the gravedigger in *Hamlet,* The Common Man opened the play, and provided a running commentary on the trials and tribulations of More. On the stage, the entire production had been acted amidst symbolic lights and shadows, on a set design which gave only the barest suggestion of not-so-merry old England. Clearly, viewers were not so much in the presence of a story about the historical Sir Thomas More as an abstract analysis of the fate of an idealist, here embodied by More. Such a technique works well in the theater, where the principle of suggestion and the power of the spoken word are primary. Rarely, though, do motion pictures opt for such a style. Bolt wisely decided to eliminate the emphasis on the symbolic nature of his story, and let the tale unfold in a more naturalistic manner—usually the most ef-

fective approach for a film. So The Common Man was out, and the picture was shot, by director Fred Zinnemann, on very concrete, specific locations in England.

On a surface level, at least, the film offered more of a historial re-creation than the play. An all-star cast was recruited, and the roles which had been small supporting parts in the theater were transformed into "cameos" for the film: Wendy Hiller, quite wonderful as the simple, down to earth, highly practical Alice More, who cannot understand her husband's willingness to lose his happy life with her over something as seemingly unimportant as a minor moral issue; Susannah York, radiant as the soft-spoken but strong-willed daughter, Margaret, and Corin Redgrave, as More's foppish young son-in-law, William; Robert Shaw as the tempestuous king; Vanessa Redgrave, playing Anne Boleyn as an empty-headed simpleton instead of the tragic heroine of other films; and Orson Welles as Cardinal Wolsey and Leo McKern as Thomas Cromwell, the arch villains of the piece. As exquisite as most of the cast members proved (only Shaw occasionally weakened the impact by overplaying his part), Scofield's More remained the focus of our interest, the center of our attention, the magnet for all our thoughts and emotions.

Importantly, *A Man for All Seasons* had something very specific to say about the mood of the mid-Sixties. For all the amoral, uncommitted Alfies currently drifting about, there were also the groups of highly committed moral idealists. A subculture of society was emerging and, like Sir Thomas More, they would soon prove themselves unafraid of opposing a national leader if they considered his actions wrong. Even as *A Man for All Seasons* was arriving in the theaters, protests against the controversial war in Viet Nam and the President's motivations for involving America in the war had begun. Like Sir Thomas, the peace protesters would at first constitute only a small minority, a voice crying out in the wilderness. But, in time, they would also—like More—change the outlook of the majority. Though set in England over 600 years ago, *A Man for All Seasons'* hero reminded many of the peace protesters of Senator Eugene McCarthy (who actually bore a strong physical resemblance to Paul Scofield); like the character of More, he opposed his leader's actions out of strong religious convictions. In short, *A Man for All Seasons* provided a blueprint for an idealistic turning away from the government's policies that would mark the second half of the Sixties.

Ideals versus survival: Confident that he is truly in the right, Sir Thomas More (Paul Scofield) enjoys a hearty meal while his more practical wife (Wendy Hiller), who cares only for her husband's future, finds herself unable to eat. *(A Man for All Seasons)*

The romance that created a martyr: Vanessa Redgrave as Anne Boleyn and Robert Shaw as King Henry VIII in *A Man for All Seasons.*

In a more innocent era, they would have been the bad guys, but this was the Sixties, and they were the nearest thing to heroes we had: Burt Lancaster, Robert Ryan, Lee Marvin, and Woody Strode as The Professionals.

THE PROFESSIONALS

COLUMBIA

Produced by Richard Brooks; screenplay by Richard Brooks, based on the novel *A Mule for the Marquesa* by Frank O'Rourke; directed by Richard Brooks.

CAST

Bill Dolworth (Burt Lancaster); *Rico/Henry Fardan* (Lee Marvin); *Hans Ehrengard* (Robert Ryan); *Jesús Raza* (Jack Palance); *Maria Grant* (Claudia Cardinale); *Grant* (Ralph Bellamy); *Jack Sharp* (Woody Strode); *Ortega* (Joe DeSantis); *Chiquita* (Maria Gomez)

In the Sixties, there were the amoral Alfies and the committed, idealistic men for all seasons. But there was a third cultural prototype, too: the ultra-professional. From the beginning of the decade, the cool, calculated professional who goes about his job

Claudia Cardinale, as the abducted wife, begins to find captor Jack Palance interesting. *(The Professionals)*

173

without much concern as to its morality emerged as a non-hero for the times. In a western setting, this syndrome gave way to the first distinctive horse opera of the decade, *The Magnificent Seven*. In a more modern milieu, we were offered James Bond, the licensed-to-kill super-agent who dispenses with men and seduces women in the same uninvolved, uninterested but unmistakably professional manner. When Columbia Pictures released *The Professionals* late in 1966, the studio harbored no great hope that their picture would prove anything but a modestly successful action-adventure yarn. Instead, to the surprise of almost everyone, audiences lined up around the theater blocks to wait for a chance to see it.

Essentially, the film might be subtitled "The Magnificent Four": when a fiery, lush young wife (Claudia Cardinale) is kidnapped by a mad Mexican bandido, Jesús Raza (Jack Palance), her aged millionaire husband, Grant (Ralph Bellamy), hires a quartet of professional gunmen to journey into the badlands and rescue her. They include Dolworth (Burt Lancaster), a womanizing demolitions expert; Fardan (Lee Marvin), a superb shot with a rifle and the uncrowned leader of the group; Jack (Woody Strode), a silent giant who proves himself deadly with a long bow; and Ehrengard (Robert Ryan), the only weak link in the group owing to his single sensitive trait—an inability to see an animal suffer. The four men lock into combat with the outlaws in a number of striking settings, where they dynamite entire squadrons of the enemy and are involved in a devastating raid on a train.

The unique style of the Sixties' westerns was apparent in a number of aspects. First, there was the early twentieth-century setting, in which cars and even machine guns emerged as part of the landscape for western films. In earlier years, westerns were employed to communicate a sense of the integrity of our country during the days of the early pioneering spirit. In the Sixties, as a cynicism with American institutions began to set in, westerns turned more often toward a view of the fading frontier, and the replacement of the hardy pioneer lifestyle by modern machinery. Second, there was the strong Mexican influence, which had first made itself felt in *The Magnificent Seven*. Mexican music and culture had heretofore been relegated to a minor role in western films, but in the new western, it dominated—as Sam Peckinpah's *The Wild Bunch* and *Pat Garrett and Billy the Kid* demonstrate. In such films, Mexico came to symbolize the last land where machismo still ruled supreme, where an un-

spoiled culture still awaited the romantic, Hemingwayesque American male.

Third, and finally, there was the ever more intense depiction of sex and violence. The killings are graphic, and the heroes are no less merciless than the villains. Often, the two groups are very hard to tell apart, except perhaps that the heroes are more effective—more professional—than the bad guys. Maria is always in danger of being raped—either by bad guy Palance or good guy Lancaster. At one point, a handsome Mexican woman, Chiquita (Marie Gomez) actually bares her large breasts for a moment, to luxuriate in a makeshift, open air shower, and as she does, nudity enters the once sacrosanct world of the western. Essentially, the great difference between the new western genre and the old was the nature of the value system at work (white hats were quickly going out of fashion) and the personality of the hero himself. No longer the good knight of *Shane* or the fair-minded moralist of *High Noon*, he is the cynical professional such previous characters were matched against.

BLOW-UP

METRO-GOLDWYN-MAYER

Produced by Carlo Ponti; screenplay by Michelangelo Antonioni and Tonino Guerra; directed by Michelangelo Antonioni.

CAST

Thomas (David Hemmings); *Jane* (Vanessa Redgrave); *Patricia* (Sarah Miles); *Girl* (Jane Birkin); *Models* (Verushka, Jill Kennington, Peggy Moffitt, Rosaleen Murray, Ann Norman, Melanie Hampshire)

The new international trend in cinema, and the simultaneous bridging of the gap that previously existed between "art" and "entertainment" films, reached a milestone with *Blow-Up*—shot in swinging London by an Italian director, Michelangelo Antonioni, who had established his reputation as a significant artist of the Sixties by directing such classics of existential ennui as *La Notte*, *L'Eclisse*, and *L'Avventura*, studies of the rootless society and morally alienated characters. Antonioni transplanted his vision of the modern condition from his native land to the single city that captured the imagination of the world during this peculiar decade, and

Blow-up's moment of truth: Is Vanessa Redgrave killing the man or kissing him?

A new kind of nonhero: David Hemmings as Thomas in *Blow-up*.

The moral complexity of *Blow-up* was reflected in its visual scheme.

Sarah Miles and David Hemmings in *Blow-up*.

Blow-Up presented a parable that, in its view of human affairs, offered a symbolic vision of the fast, furious, and ultimately unfulfilling world in which the surface of life is so intensely experienced that the underlying substance often goes unnoticed.

Blow-Up begins as a typical Antonioni film, with that same deliberate buildup of events that caused this moviemaker to become known as the Chekhov of the cinema. Thomas (David Hemmings) is a hip young photographer, who has no strong commitment to any particular subject. He can shoot documents of flophouse derelicts or chic, sleek young models with equally disinterested craftsmanship. Then one day, an incident occurs which gives *Blow-Up* a Hitchcockian quality. While relaxing in a park, Thomas notices a couple necking on one of the benches, and shoots a roll of film. But as he leaves, the woman (Vanessa Redgrave) pursues him, demanding he turn over the film. When he refuses, she follows him to his studio and there offers herself sexually in trade for the film. Though Thomas takes advantage of her offer, he deceives the woman by giving her a different roll of film. Developing the

pictures that evening, he at first sees them only as conventional shots of a couple making love. Then, a dark spot in the nearby bushes catches his eye, and he begins to blow individual details of the photograph up into large, nearly wall-sized images, studying and scrutinizing what is before him. Calmly, he returns to the park and finds, near the bench, exactly what he expected: a body, since the pictures revealed the woman was killing, not kissing, the man. Returning to his studio to collect the pictures and perhaps take them to the police, he finds the place has been entered and ransacked, the pictures, gone. Returning again to the scene of the crime, he finds the body gone also. And eventually, without any sort of proof, he begins to doubt his own mind; if there is no tangible evidence that the event took place, can he continue to believe that it happened?

On the surface, then, *Blow-Up* is an old-fashioned thriller done in the new style of the Sixties. But there is more to it than that. This is, essentially, a parable about human perception. The young photographer cannot discern the truth with his eyes, but only with his camera. The initial conflict of the film—and the necessity for making the blow-ups in the first place—is the distinction between what his eyes see and what the camera sees; he assumes that he can perceive reality well enough, but his pictures, examined in detail, suggest there is a reality going on around us that our eyes cannot understand. All truth, finally, is subjective, as we cannot know what is "out there," only what we see of it, and this notion is made clear by the maddeningly symbolic ending. The distraught, alienated Thomas wanders onto a tennis court, where a troupe of mime-like hippies are pretending to play. At first, Thomas merely stares at their mute game, watching with a fixed stare as they go through the motions of an actual match. Then, the camera closes in on his face, as his eyes move back and forth—as if watching the ball in an actual game—and we begin to hear the sound of the ball being hit back and forth on the soundtrack. The moment Thomas believes the ball is there, it *is* there—for him.

A striking early scene, in which Thomas enjoys an Alfie-ish orgy with two young London birds, caused the film to be denied a Production Code Seal of Approval upon its American release. The brief touches of nudity and sex, in the context of what was obviously a film with major aesthetic pretensions and serious social commentary, caused an upheaval which would eventually cause the Code to lose its impact, paving the way for the new rating system which would take effect shortly.

WHO'S AFRAID OF VIRGINIA WOOLF?

WARNER BROTHERS

Produced by Ernest Lehman; screenplay by Ernest Lehman, from the play by Edward Albee; directed by Mike Nichols.

CAST

Martha (Elizabeth Taylor); *George* (Richard Burton); *Nick* (George Segal); *Honey* (Sandy Dennis)

"No one under the age of 18 will be admitted unless accompanied by a parent or guardian." That adage would become the obligatory accompaniment of any film receiving an "R," when the policy of rating motion pictures was established in the late Sixties. The first film to carry this commentary was *Who's Afraid of Virginia Woolf?*, which in its time marked not only the significant screen translation of an important play (the best drama of the decade, according to some) but also the latest of those important movie milestones which help redefine the notion of the Hollywood product. Here were two of our current superstars, Elizabeth Taylor and Richard Burton, fresh from their success in the ultimate,

Who's Afraid of Virginia Woolf?: Elizabeth Taylor as Martha.

Elizabeth Taylor, Richard Burton, George Segal, and Sandy Dennis in *Who's Afraid of Virginia Woolf?*

Elizabeth Taylor and Richard Burton in *Who's Afraid of Virginia Woolf?*

Richard Burton and Sandy Dennis in *Who's Afraid of Virginia Woolf?*

and last, of the old-fashioned Hollywood super-spectacles, *Cleopatra;* but here they were now speaking language that had never been heard in an American commercial movie before, as they forsook the glamor of their previous pictures. *Virginia Woolf* created a strong public outcry for more stringent censorship of films, simultaneously excited and upset various portions of the moviegoing public, and forever left behind the notion that American films could not deal with adult material.

In point of fact, Edward Albee had managed to shock even the legitimate theater when his play was first produced in 1962. In the early Sixties, Albee's symbolic shorter plays—including *The Sand Box, The Zoo Story,* and *The American Dream*—had been presented off-Broadway, where these searing studies of the sickness in American society had been perfectly in keeping with the avant garde attitudes of the audiences. Then, Albee's first full-length play was presented in the legitimate Broadway theater. Though his characters were no longer allegorical figures, but believable people caught up in a domestic situation of infidelity, self-deception, and an inability to discriminate reality—themes clearly in the tradition of the great twentieth century naturalistic theater since Ibsen and Strindberg first pioneered the form—*Virginia Woolf* still contained the acerbic implications and outlandish language of Albee's earlier works. By bringing them to Broadway, even in the guise of a domestic melodrama, Albee proved himself to be a creative force in the new, evolving generation of important playwrights. *Virginia Woolf* altered both the mentality and the conventions of legitimate drama and when, only four years later, the play was transferred to the screen, almost everyone assumed it would have to be hopelessly watered down—since movies were at the very least ten years behind Broadway in terms of maturity.

But Jack L. Warner, the old-fashioned studio head who personally stood behind the project, insisted it be done without the expected hedging. So producer/screenwriter Ernest Lehman was given the go ahead to keep almost all the film's language intact, making only minimal changes in locale (the single room setting was opened up slightly to include the entire house) and retaining words such as "bitch," "bastard," and the like. Anyone who feared the supersexy couple of the decade would glamorize the frustrated college professor, George, and his blowsy wife, Martha, quickly discovered Burton and Taylor were actors as well as movie stars. Burton successfully squelched his strong

Elizabeth Taylor. *(Who's Afraid of Virginia Woolf?)*

screen magnetism, making himself look every bit the meek, mousey fellow, while Taylor ranted and raved with enough conviction that she came off as a miserable college town matron rather than a long-time Hollywood celebrity. In order to assure the project would be handled properly, Warner decided to hand the directorial chores to a young man who had never before done a motion picture—but was clearly in tune with the current styles of the Sixties. Mike Nichols had worked as a popular satirist with Elaine May, then achieved notoriety with his handsome direction of several Broadway plays by Neil Simon. Sensing the material in *Virginia Woolf* marked so drastic a departure from the usual screen fare that his stock directors might be at a loss as to how the material should be handled, Warner rather took the risk of setting the untried Nichols free to mount the movie as he saw fit. The result was one of the most adult and satisfying films of the decade.

A MAN AND A WOMAN

ALLIED ARTISTS

Produced, written, and directed by Claude Lelouch.

CAST

Anne Gauthier (Anouk Aimée); *Jean-Louis Duroc* (Jean-Louis Trintignant); *Pierre Gauthier* (Pierre Barouh); *Valérie Duroc* (Valérie Lagrange); *Head Mistress* (Simone Paris); *Antoine Duroc* (Antoine Sire); *Françoise Gauthier* (Souad Amidou)

If the American cinema was just now coming of age, so too was the American audience. Which helps explain the immense popularity of *A Man and a Woman* not only on college campuses, where it quickly emerged as a cult favorite, but in other, less likely areas as well. In one small American city, the picture played for over a full year at a suburban movie house, to an adoring public made up of both young and older viewers. *A Man and a Woman* exuded a kind of magic, perhaps because it cleverly blended an old-fashioned, sentimental love story—complete with obligatory happy ending—with the new style of cinematic story telling that embodied the Sixties' notion of sophistication. As one writer for *Look* magazine put it: "*A Man and a Woman* allows us to feel sophisticated about our sentimentality."

The story is so simple it could be summarized on

A Man and a Woman: Anouk Aimee and Jean-Louis Trintignant as the two would-be lovers, separated by memories of the past that keep each from living a fulfilling life in the present.

Anouk Aimee and Pierre Barouh as husband and wife in the romantic fairy-tale vision of their marriage. *(A Man and a Woman)*

Anouk Aimee and Pierre Barouh enjoy the simple pleasures of life shortly before he is killed while working as a movie stunt man. *(A Man and a Woman)*

the back of the proverbial book of matches. Jean-Louis Duroc (Jean-Louis Trintignant) is an attractive young widower, who drives racing cars and, on weekends, visits his little boy Antoine (Antoine Sire) at the child's sleep-away school; Anne Gauthier (Anouk Aimée) is an attractive young widow who works as a movie script girl and, on weekends, visits her little girl Françoise (Souad Amidou) at her sleep-away school. The children happen to attend the same institution and, one rainy evening, Anne finds herself without a ride back to Paris. Jean-Louis obliges; before long, the two are dating, though their relationship is plagued by Anne's deep-seated inability to free herself from lingering thoughts of her deceased, but still much loved, husband. The final confrontation takes place in a bedroom, where Anne and Jean-Louis have gone to consummate their relationship. The honesty of their decision to carry their friendship to a hotel room, and the graphicness of their lovemaking (though there is in fact almost no actual nudity, since they are under the sheets, and the scene can, without much editing, be shown on late night TV today), made it at least mildly shocking, though always within the bounds of good taste.

The story was, simply, trite—but that word can hardly be used to describe writer/director/cinematographer Claude Lelouch's approach to the material. He totally fragmented his story and told it through rapid flashbacks and flash forwards, converging on the film's present tense, to make the characters' pasts and futures inseparable from what is happening at the moment. The photography was done through extreme telescopic lenses used when they were not absolutely necessary, producing extreme lack of normal visual perspective: characters run toward each other down a beach at sunrise without seeming to get any closer. Beautiful shots of sunsets were blended with the soft, lyrical, pseudo-poetic music of Francis Lai, and with voiceovers in which the characters speak (rather superficially, actually) about profound philosophical issues: commitment, art, love, and the like. Many of the shots were created with special colored filters and even sepia tones, though this was done without any real consistency of effect—making many critics complain it was only a clever, impressionistic-looking gimmick rather than a well-thought-out style for the film.

In fact, all of the film's various devices led cynics to complain Lelouch was a charlatan, who had given the audience what appeared to be a European New Wave "art film" but was actually nothing more than a facile, commercial bit of emotional exploitation which proved the absolute lack of sophistication among those who adored it. Certainly, there was at least a grain of truth in the complaint. One might have asked, like *Hamlet* addressing the players, for more matter with less art. Nevertheless, *A Man and a Woman* does—even upon repeated viewings—radiate an undeniable magic. Much of it is due to the radiant, unique charisma of Anouk Aimée, who had never been properly utilized by filmmakers before. *A Man and a Woman* won her an Academy Award nomination and some choice film roles during the next few years. But, following the commercial failure of such expensive pictures as *Justine* (from the Lawrence Durrell classic), she soon drifted back into relative obscurity. The loss was ours, for Ms. Aimée had the potential to be a latter day Garbo, with her enigmatic eyes and marvelously mysterious mien. Still, *A Man and a Woman* proved two things: first that, in terms of subject matter, American audiences yet loved the old formulas that had always been the primary staple of movies; and second that, in terms of style, they were now ready to have those stories presented in the nouvelle vaguish look of Europe's more sophisticated filmmakers.

THE WILD ANGELS
AMERICAN INTERNATIONAL PICTURES

Produced by Roger Corman; screenplay by Charles B. Griffith; directed by Roger Corman.

CAST

Heavenly Blues (Peter Fonda); *Mike* (Nancy Sinatra); *"Loser"/Joey Kerns* (Bruce Dern); *Gaysh* (Diane Ladd); *Joint* (Lou Procopio); *Bull Puckey* (Coby Denton); *Frankenstein* (Marc Cavell); *Dear John* (Buck Taylor); *Pigmy* (Michael J. Pollard); *Mama Monahan* (Joan Shawlee); *Suzie* (Gayle Hunnicutt); *Members of Hell's Angels of Venice, California* (Themselves)

In the mid-Fifties, Marlon Brando created an unforgettable archetype of the hell-raising motorcyclist in *The Wild One*. Surprisingly, despite the film's phenomenal appeal—and the mass acceptance of the cyclist as modern anti-hero—the wave of cycle flicks did not really begin until a full decade later. In 1966, Roger Corman and American International Pictures joined forces to create one of the most extravagantly successful exploitation films of all time. *The Wild Angels* was applauded by youthful American audiences at drive-ins and double bill houses, was loudly hissed by critics from coast to coast, and then turned up as the only American entry at the Venice Film Festival—by invitation, no less! The Europeans did not share the popular American prejudice against such sensationalized stories, and found the film—on the level of its madcap editing and wild imagery, rather than the banal dialogue—a cinematic work of art. At any rate, the film was quickly followed up by dozens of lesser imitations. After Peter Fonda emerged as a youth cult hero following his performance in *The Wild Angels,* his friends among Hollywood's counterculture tried their hands at similar projects, so Jack Nicholson was soon riding the highways in *Hell's Angels on Wheels,* while Dennis Hopper raced across the landscape in *The Glory Stompers.* Eventually, the three of them were united for *Easy Rider,* a film which would transcend the cycle genre completely, and temporarily redefine the American cinema.

There was practically no plot to *The Wild Angels.* A band of Hell's Angels type cyclists, led by Heavenly Blues (Fonda) and "Mike" (Nancy Sinatra), cruise the countryside, involving themselves with

Peter Fonda as Heavenly Blues in *Wild Angels.*

Hell's Angels on wheels: Can you pick out Peter Bogdanovich, Bruce Dern, and Michael J. Pollard in the group? *(Wild Angels)*

heavy drinking, pot smoking, gang fighting and various sorts of criminal activity, ranging from violent vandalism to heavy rape. One can clearly see the passing of the years by comparing *The Wild Angels* to *The Wild One*. In Stanley Kramer's film, considered shocking for its day, the character of Johnny (Brando) was, despite his moments of rebellion, a traditional American hero: a misunderstood romantic who falls for a pure smalltown girl, avoids violence whenever possible, and really means no harm to anyone. The heavy of the piece is Chino (Lee Marvin), a filthy, grotesque character without values or morals. Despite the charge that it "glamorized hoodlums," *The Wild One* looked like a conservative commentary when compared with *The Wild Angels*. For the Brando type character was now completely eliminated, while the Marvin character had been elevated to heroic proportions. In the morally confused, emotionally complex world of the Sixties, the maniac had supplanted the crusader as pop idol.

American International Pictures once again proved uncannily able to spot trends among the large youthful audience, oftentimes dealing with subjects the "major" studios would not (then, at least) deign to touch. In the Fifties, at the onset of the juvenile delinquency problem, A.I.P. marketed items like *High School Confidential* with Russ Tamblyn and Mamie Van Doren; they would soon find plenty of natural material for their exploitation flicks in such Sixties subjects as the campus radicals *(The Love Ins)*, the LSD experience *(The Trip)*, the spread of marijuana use *(Mary Jane)*, and the hippie movement *(Revolt of the Flower People)*. Corman, meanwhile, proved himself an unabashed exploitation-oriented entrepreneur, quick to spot young talents and use them for his own ends while providing them with their first necessary exposure and experience. Among the important stars of upcoming films featured in *The Wild Angels* were Bruce Dern and Michael J. Pollard, while Peter Bogdanovich not only played a part but also worked on the script and helped with the direction. *The Wild Angels* may not have been a class production, but it arrived at a time when many class productions were doing disappointing, even disastrous business at the box office; *The Wild Angels* was made by people clearly in touch with their audience, and hence offered sensationalism that spelled commercial success.

A bizarre marriage ceremony in *Wild Angels*.

Peter Fonda and Nancy Sinatra in *Wild Angels*.

1967

184

BAREFOOT IN THE PARK

PARAMOUNT

Produced by Hal Wallis; screenplay by Neil Simon, based on his play; directed by Gene Saks.

CAST

Paul Bratter (Robert Redford); *Corie Bratter* (Jane Fonda); *Victor Velasco* (Charles Boyer); *Ethel Banks* (Mildred Natwick); *Harry Pepper* (Herb Edelman); *Aunt Harriet* (Mabel Albertson); *Restaurant Owner* (Fritz Feld); *Delivery Man* (James Stone); *Bum in Park* (Paul E. Burns)

Every era has its perfect movie couple, providing the idealized image in which every young couple likes to believe it is reflected. In the Thirties, there was Clark Gable and Claudette Colbert in *It Happened One Night;* in the Forties, Robert Walker and Jennifer Jones in *Since You Went Away;* in the Fifties, Rock Hudson and Doris Day in *Pillow Talk.* In the Sixties, such a coupling was provided by Robert Redford and Jane Fonda, who looked better together than any other young stars, and clicked with a chemistry every time they appeared on screen. Earlier attempts to match young Redford with Natalie Wood *(Inside Daisy Clover, This Property Is Condemned)* proved disappointing, and then in their very first outing together, Fonda and Redford were trapped in a dismal mish-mash of soap opera and message melodrama, Arthur Penn's *The Chase,* starring Marlon Brando. But in *Barefoot in the Park,* they were charmingly united in a lovely light romantic farce by Neil Simon that had previously introduced Redford as a major star on Broadway.

The film begins in a suite at the Plaza Hotel, where Paul (Redford) and Corie (Fonda) Bratter are enjoying the last moments of their honeymoon. She cannot stop thinking about lovemaking; he can't keep his mind off problems in the office. So when he marches out to the elevator, she follows in the skimpiest of negligees and then, in full view of an elevator car full of strangers, plays the role of a classy call girl by smilingly saying: "Next time you're in town, Mr. Bratter, be sure to look me up." Shortly thereafter, they've moved into their first apartment, which Corie's mother (Mildred Natwick) finds depressing because of the five-flight walk up from the street—though she does admit to being begrudgingly atttracted to Victor Velasco

The mod couple: Jane Fonda and Robert Redford discover that her bohemianism may wreck their marriage before it is even off the ground. *(Barefoot in the Park)*

Jane Fonda, Mildred Natwick, and Robert Redford barely survive the terrors of a New York apartment building without a working elevator. *(Barefoot in the Park)*

(Charles Boyer), the European bohemian, bon vivant, self-confessed gourmet cook and lovable phony who inhabits the apartment upstairs. Not so pleasant, though, is the friction that begins to develop between Corie and Paul, as she finds his lifestyle as a straight-laced lawyer far too confining, and wants to express her no longer repressed kookiness by running barefoot through the park.

185

Robert Redford and Jane Fonda discover that despite serious differences, they can still salvage their relationship. *(Barefoot in the Park)*

In the time-honored tradition of romantic farce, this problem causes a respectable amount of marital discord, which is at least somewhat resolved in the ending: Corie tries acting a bit more reserved while her husband attempts to meet his wife halfway by becoming almost as bohemian as she. In point of fact, the situation represented between these two characters would become a very real problem for many young people, as the changing value system in American society began to split happily married couples apart. The escalation of the war in Viet Nam, the growing militancy within the civil rights movement, the rash of assassinations and the sudden extension of hippie-ish fashions into middle-class and even middle-aged lifestyles would leave many people, and many couples, reeling in a state of culture shock. Though written in the mid-Sixties and filmed before the Chicago Democratic Convention introduced radicalism to the mainstream of American society, *Barefoot in the Park* contains, beneath its surface of delightful entertainment, a hint of the great rifts to come. Though the Generation Gap would capture most of the headlines, an equally important conflict would grow between people who had coupled during the relative quiet of the early Sixties Kennedy-era idealism, only to find

themselves questioning the validity of their relationship as the world around them changed drastically. The Bratter marriage appeared as the first screen image of a young man with strong Establishment leanings married to a young woman with counter-culture inclinations. If, at the end of the movie, their divided loyalties are dismissed as unimportant, in real life such philosophic differences would prove far more permanently divisive. As a couple, then, Redford and Fonda provided the Hollywood image of a relatively young, comfortably affluent modern pair, facing the tidal wave of cultural change that was just then hitting the country.

IN THE HEAT OF THE NIGHT
UNITED ARTISTS

Produced by Walter Mirisch; screenplay by Stirling Silliphant, based on the novel by John Ball; directed by Norman Jewison.

CAST

Virgil Tibbs (Sidney Poitier); *Police Chief Bill Gillespie* (Rod Steiger); *Deputy Sam Wood* (Warren Oates); *Mrs. Leslie Colbert* (Lee Grant); *Purdy* (James Patterson); *Delores Purdy* (Quentin Dean); *Eric Endicott* (Larry Gates); *Webb Schubert* (William Schallert); *Mama Caleba* (Beah Richards); *Harvey Oberst* (Scott Wilson)

In 1957, producer-director Stanley Kramer offered his image of a solution to the racial problem in America by pitting Tony Curtis, as a white racist, and Sidney Poitier, as an embittered black, against one another in *The Defiant Ones;* the two men, escapees from a prison, were bound together by chains but slowly, eventually learned not only to respect but even to love one another as human beings. Ten years later, with the eruption of the ghetto riots and the beginning of black radicalism, such an attitude appeared quaintly out of date. In 1967, Norman Jewison—who had, the year before, turned the Cold War into the subject of a sophisticated sitcom with *The Russians Are Coming*—offered an updated image of our country's racial situation. *In the Heat of the Night* once again offered a mental duel between two men—one white, one black—but if this time around the outcome was something less than a loving handclasp between them, the film did still acknowledge the possibility of a growing respect, and admiration, despite prejudices on both sides.

The story, based on a forgettable potboiler by John Ball, is on the surface a conventional whodunit. Virgil Tibbs (Sidney Poitier), a black man waiting for a late night train at a deserted station in a small Mississippi town, is rudely arrested by a sneering deputy (Warren Oates) and dragged before Sheriff Bill Gillespie (Rod Steiger), an overweight, gum-chewing, fast-talking, no-nonesense law officer. The problem is, a white man—a northern industrialist with plans for building a new, integrated mill in the town—has just been murdered and, in his over-eagerness to find someone to arrest, the deputy assumed an unknown black man must be the guilty party. Not so; when asked for proper identification, Virgil reaches for his badge: he is himself a law officer. Before long, Virgil has formed an uneasy alliance with the redneck sheriff, using his own superior intelligence and insight to help the plodding policeman solve the crime.

Stirling Silliphant's script fleshes out the characters who pop in and out of the story. Though each could be branded a stereotype, there is an immediacy to them that makes these people transcend the cliché and come momentarily to life: a frustrated housewife (Lee Grant), a politically powerful white (William Schallert), an angry young punk (Scott Wilson), a sluttish teenage girl (Quentin Dean), a noble, long-suffering black woman (Beah Richards), and a not-so-bright cop (Peter Whitney) all strike exactly the right note. Jewison's flashy and striking visual scheme, augumented by an appropriately atmospheric soundtrack by Quincy Jones, cre-

"They call me *Mr. Tibbs!*" Sidney Poitier in action. *(In the Heat of the Night)*

Scott Wilson, Rod Steiger, and Sidney Poitier. *(In the Heat of the Night)*

ated the mood of believability and left audiences with the impression they were indeed momentarily dropped into the stiffling aura of a hot summer evening in the deep south. But always at the forefront of the film's focus was the ever growing, ever changing relationship between the two central characters. Even the final solution to the mystery was so played down that, a few days after seeing the picture, many viewers confessed to being unable to remember whodunit.

At the end, Poitier is once again standing at the station, waiting for his train, and now the feeling between the men is interestingly ambiguous. A kind of begrudging respect and perhaps undesired affection has crept into each man's conception of the other. Though there is no great moment of reconciliation—no cathartic scene reminiscent of those unforgettable clasped hands of precisely one decade earlier—the two men at least move away from one another with their prejudices having been, if not done away with, then at least challenged.

Sidney Poitier's performance presented something of a problem. As fine as he was in the role, Poitier was now clearly playing the same character over and over: a neatly tailored, refined acting, soft-spoken, intellectually superior and emotionally gracious man. Poitier first introduced this persona in the charming *Lilies of the Field,* for which he won an Oscar. But he made the mistake of repeating the role in a succession of lesser films, first in *The Slender Thread* with Anne Bancroft, then in *A Patch of Blue* with Shelley Winters, finally in *Guess Who's Coming to Dinner* with Spencer Tracy and Katharine Hepburn. Once hailed as the black Brando, he began to seem more like a Negro Rock Hudson, as

The final moment: Sidney Poitier and Rod Steiger. *(In the Heat of the Night)*

the repetitiousness, conventionality, and predictability of his character became less ingratiating with each picture. Steiger, however, created one of his most notable characterizations as the southern cop—a man of limited intelligence, and a unique human being who grabbed the audience's interest in a way Poitier's stereotype of perfection could not. For his performance, Steiger received the Academy Award many people felt he had been unfairly denied the year before, when the Oscar had gone to Lee Marvin for his comic burlesque role in *Cat Ballou.*

189

Opposite page: The plot thickens: Sidney Poitier and Rod Steiger. *(In the Heat of the Night)*

Katharine Ross and Dustin Hoffman: new archetypes for a new youth. *(The Graduate)*

THE GRADUATE

EMBASSY PICTURES

Produced by Lawrence Turman; screenplay by Calder Willingham and Buck Henry, based on the novel by Charles Webb; directed by Mike Nichols.

CAST

Mrs. Robinson (Anne Bancroft); *Ben Braddock* (Dustin Hoffman); *Elaine Robinson* (Katharine Ross); *Mr. Braddock* (William Daniels); *Mr. Robinson* (Murray Hamilton); *Mrs. Braddock* (Elizabeth Wilson); *Carl Smith* (Brian Avery); *Mr. Maguire* (Walter Brooke); *Mr. McCleery* (Norman Fell); *Second Lady* (Elizabeth Fraser); *Mrs. Singleman* (Alice Ghostley); *Room Clerk* (Buck Henry); *Miss De Witt* (Marion Lorne)

Once in the course of every decade, thanks to an impossible-to-predict combination of timing, talent, and luck, a film appears which captures the spirit of the times, and allows America's youth to perceive in the action onscreen an image of themselves which they can both identify with and emulate. In the Fifties, it was *Rebel Without a Cause*; though originally shot as a youth-oriented exploitation film it metamorphosed into the central cultural experience of an entire generation. In the Sixties, the key film turned out to be *The Graduate*, taken from a clever but minor novel by Charles Webb.

The story, as adapted by Buck Henry and Calder Willingham, follows the basic premise of Webb's novel: Benjamin Braddock (Dustin Hoffman), a Holden Caulfield-ish college graduate, returns home to Southern California and finds he's unable to commit himself to anything. Adoring friends and family wait to see what he's going to do with his expensive education, but Ben only hangs around his affluent parents' swimming pool, sensing a general repugnance for, and superiority to, the pretentious upper-middle-class lifestyle that surrounds him— though he lacks the ambition and courage to break away from it. Then, Ben is propositioned by Mrs. Robinson (Anne Bancroft), the frustrated wife of his father's law partner, and after first nervously rejecting her, the boy calls the older woman for a rendezvous. Their long-term affair, which Ben eventually finds decadent, causes complications when Ben is railroaded into a blind date with the Robinsons' college-senior daughter, Elaine (Katharine Ross), and finds himself falling in love with the girl, despite the hysterical objections of the distraught Mrs. Robinson.

Director Mike Nichols was, as a result of *Who's Afraid of Virginia Woolf?*, already established as one of the most promising young directors of the "New Hollywood." But *The Graduate* made him (for a while, at least) the most powerful and influential of those people who were reshaping the American motion picture product. First, Nichols decided to make a major motion picture with no name stars, and in so doing, introduced Dustin Hoffman, who would quickly become, ironically enough, the new name to be reckoned with. Second, Nichols employed a series of camera techniques that had been extensively used in television commercials and avant garde pictures, but were new to the Hollywood product. The camera seemed suddenly free from the old limitations—a shot of Ben driving across the Golden Gate Bridge suddenly sweeps us far into the air; the camera cuts at a rapid rate to

convey a sense of Ben's subjectivity. Cinematographer Robert Surtees was given a chance to experiment with "arty" techniques like those used by his European counterparts, and created moments that were both original and effective; the best remembered example comes when Ben, rushing madly to stop Elaine's marriage to a fraternity row type, is seen running toward a camera that photographs him in extreme depth through a telescopic lens; though Ben runs at a phenomenal speed, the technique makes him appear to be running in place, never getting anywhere. Thus, the film's essential theme is wordlessly conveyed. Third, there was the equally important decision to change the notion of the musical score, and instead of just featuring music composed expressly for the picture, Nichols included currently popular songs by folksingers Simon and Garfunkel ("The Sound of Silence"; "Scarborough Fair") without necessarily correlating them directly to a scene.

The film, which might easily at any moment have degenerated into an enjoyable but forgettable bedroom farce, is continually turned into a deft work of social satire, establishing Nichols as a cultural humorist in the tradition of Preston Sturges and Billy Wilder. Numerous bits of Americana are effectively integrated into the story: when Ben visits Mrs. Robinson at her home, *The Dating Game* is blaring from the television set, adding a comic undercurrent to

"And here's to you, Mrs. Robinson!" Dustin Hoffman averts his glance as Anne Bancroft strips in *The Graduate*.

One angle on Ben's tragedy: removed from reality by a pane of glass. *(The Graduate)*

Another angle on Ben's tragedy: the modern crucifixion. *(The Graduate)*

their relationship; when Ben tries to stop Elaine's forced marriage, he finds it taking place in one of those modern churches that look more like an experimental art museum than a place of worship. There are numerous scenes that have become classics, including Ben's nervous routine when checking into a hotel with Mrs. Robinson for the first time, encountering an unperturbed desk clerk (Buck Henry), and Ben's early attempt to escape the banal small talk of his parents by submerging in their swimming pool with diving equipment, where he stares, in exasperation, directly into the camera.

But the most striking image of all was the last, in which Ben and Elaine rush away from her marriage ceremony and escape on a busload of old people, heading—they know not where. After their moment of exhilaration, they look down at Elaine's hand, and stare at her wedding ring. Mike Nichols would later cynically comment, "I think Benjamin and Elaine will end up exactly like their parents; that's what I was trying to say in that last scene." But audiences (especially youthful, affluent audiences) did not perceive it that way. What Elaine and Ben accomplish in *The Graduate* appeared to them as a significant act of outright rebellion against the confining lifestyle of their parents. Understandably, Dustin Hoffman emerged as the most significant youth cult star since James Dean. With a deadpan expression and an uncertain voice, he offered an entirely new concept of how a star should act and look, just as the artistic techniques employed in *The Graduate* presented audiences with an alternative to the earlier ideas of how a Hollywood movie ought to be made.

YOU'RE A BIG BOY NOW
WARNER BROTHERS—SEVEN ARTS

Produced by Phil Feldman; screenplay by Francis Ford Coppola, based on a novel by David Benedictus; directed by Francis Ford Coppola.

CAST

Bernard (Peter Kastner); *Barbara Darling* (Elizabeth Hartman); *Margery Chanticleer* (Geraldine Page); *I. H. Chanticleer* (Rip Torn); *Miss Thing* (Julie Harris); *Amy* (Karen Black); *Raef* (Tony Bill); *Policeman Graf* (Dolph Sweet); *Richard Mudd* (Michael Dunn); *Kurt Doughty* (Michael O' Sullivan)

At the same time Mike Nichols was analyzing modern alienated youth in *The Graduate*, Francis Ford Coppola turned his camera on a youthful theme with *You're a Big Boy Now*. Like *The Graduate*, the film studied the current syndromes facing young people and set their lifestyles to the beat of the latest pop music. Nichols had elected to include Simon and Garfunkel on the soundtrack; Coppola used several numbers by the Lovin' Spoonful. But the differences in style were just as noteworthy as the similarities. While both directors liberated their cameras and gave their films a sensation of visual freedom that borrowed from to TV commercials for the Pepsi Generation, they treated their subjects differently. *The Graduate* presented us with what was, essentially, a tragic situation with comic implications, while *Big Boy* combined Keystone Kops antics with more serious moments, following wild camera movements in flashy colors with dramatic confrontations between characters. The movie that emerged was a cartoon come to life, played out against the background of modern New York.

You're a Big Boy Now: Peter Kastner roller skates his way through the New York Public Library.

Elizabeth Hartman (in archetypal Sixties swinger costume, complete with miniskirt and plastic boots) seduces Peter Kastner. (*You're a Big Boy Now*)

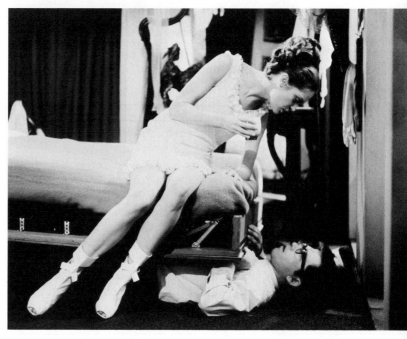

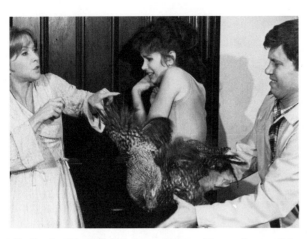

Julie Harris, Elizabeth Hartman, and Peter Kastner in one of the frenetic comedy sketches that often reminded audiences of work by improvisation groups. (*You're a Big Boy Now*)

Tony Bill, Elizabeth Hartman, and Peter Kastner—young people searching for an alternative lifestyle. (*You're a Big Boy Now*)

The story of how the film came to be made has long since become a legend. Coppola, a twenty-seven-year-old student at U.C.L.A., had to complete a movie as part of his Master's Degree fulfillment in that university's Cinema Studies Program. Coppola wrote the script for this film (based on a novel by David Benedictus), then set about persuading a number of his favorite movie actors and actresses to contribute their time and talents for his project. Before long, a number of major stars had been conned/charmed into doing roles, including: Geraldine Page and Rip Torn, a real life husband-and-wife team who were talked into playing the parents of a troubled teenager in the film; Julie Harris, who offered a wild, atypical characterization as the teenager's landlady; Michael Dunn, the dwarf star, as the companion in crime to a capricious go-go dancer out to steal a wooden leg; Karen Black, just

then emerging as an important young actress, as the nice girl who works at the New York Public Library; Tony Bill, as the hero's best friend; Elizabeth Hartman, fresh from her success as the sensitive blind girl in *A Patch of Blue,* changing her image by incarnating a gyrating queen of a discotheque; and Peter Kastner, who created a strong impression in the Canadian-made film about teenage problems, *Nobody Waved Goodbye,* as Bernard, the central character.

You're a Big Boy Now is more interesting, though less successful, than *The Graduate.* It takes more risks, and some of them don't pay off. At times, Coppola attempts a sincere, serious vision of misunderstood teenagers, in the tradition of J. D. Salinger's *The Catcher in the Rye;* at other moments, he goes in for Terry Southern-style satire, with bizarre, exaggerated characters who menace the innocent hero, and absurdist situations that strap poor Bernard in the straitjacket of life. If the desire was to throw convention to the wind, and make a movie free from Hollywood's conceptions about consistency of tone, then Coppola succeeded. But he also succeeded (if that is the correct word) in creating a film which has no real tone of its own. *Big Boy* jumps hysterically from one style to another as though a desperate, still immature artist were trying on a variety of possible styles in hopes that one would work. To a degree, this technique is consistent with the film's hero, who jumps from one possible lifestyle to the next; the prime justification for the picture's eclectic style may be that it suits its subject matter.

Interestingly enough, Coppola appeared at this time as one of the new wave of young American directors willing to experiment with odd camera angles and strange mixtures of comedy and drama. Ironically, though, he would next try his hand at a big, old-fashioned musical (*Finian's Rainbow*) that would turn out heavyhanded and lightweight instead of charming and airy. Next, Coppola attempted a downbeat social drama (*The Rain People*) about a young woman's search for personal freedom—a film which predated the popularity of the Women's Movement by five years. But it would not be until 1972, with *The Godfather,* that Coppola would live up to his promise as a major young talent. And, in that film, he would enshrine most of the old qualities of careful, intelligent, articulate moviemaking that has been developed by the American studios during the golden age of Hollywood—and which Coppola had appeared to be acting in open defiance of while shooting *You're a Big Boy Now.*

COOL HAND LUKE
WARNER BROTHERS

Produced by Gordon Carroll; screenplay by Donn Pearce and Frank R. Pierson, based on the novel by Donn Pearce; directed by Stuart Rosenberg.

CAST

Luke (Paul Newman); *Dragline* (George Kennedy); *Society Red* (J. D. Cannon); *Koko* (Lou Antonio); *Loudmouth Steve* (Robert Drivas); *The Captain* (Strother Martin); *Arletta* (Jo Van Fleet); *Carr* (Clifton James); *Boss Godfrey* (Morgan Woodward); *Girl Washing Car* (Joy Harmon); *Babalugats* (Dennis Hopper); *Gambler* (Wayne Rogers); *Alibi* (Ralph Waite)

Paul Newman as Cool Hand Luke.

Bucking the Establishment: that was to emerge as a key phrase in the last years of this turbulent decade, as a protest against the powers that be—and the parallel enshrinement as hero of anyone who stood up against the forces of absolute authority—became de rigueur. *Cool Hand Luke* was set in the deep South and dealt with a chain gang prisoner; but unlike the classic Thirties film, *I Am a Fugitive From a Chain Gang, Cool Hand Luke* was something other than a realistic case study of the inhumanity of such a form of punishment or a specific social treatise directed against one portion of the country. This time around, the chain gang existed as a metaphor for the American system, and the main character, Luke, emerged as an archetype of the individualist who makes his stand against the system—and ultimately pays the price for such an action.

Like McMurphy, the non-hero of Ken Kesey's then-popular novel *One Flew Over the Cuckoo's Nest,* Luke finds himself in the power of people who cannot understand his personal values, and are in fact antithetical to everything he stands for. Luke (Paul Newman) is arrested not for any major, dangerous crime, but only for an act of social defiance: knocking the tops off parking meters, those omnipresent representations of the governmental, bureaucratic regulation of our lives. Soon after, he is on a chain gang ruled by the Captain (Strother Martin), a small, sweet-voiced man, who rules the camp with an iron hand. At first, though, Luke's major conflict is with one of his fellow prisoners, Dragline (George Kennedy), who perceives Luke as a no-account con-man, out to rob the others of their paltry belongings through his charming manner and skill at

195

The chain gang: Wayne Rogers, Paul Newman, and Robert Drivas in *Cool Hand Luke*.

Paul Newman and George Kennedy in *Cool Hand Luke*.

cards. But when the muscular Dragline battles it out with Luke in an epic boxing match, he is amazed to discover the man's indomitability. Dragline can kill Luke, if he chooses to do so, but he can't beat him into submission. This realization makes close friends of the men, and a kind of hero out of Luke. The other prisoners congregate around him, and begin to live off his reflected glory. Ultimately, Luke senses the danger in this: like a power source used to revive batteries, he eventually finds himself spent. Hoping for self-survival, Luke pulls away from the others and tries to live by himself, for himself. Finding that he cannot exist in this way, he returns to the men, continuing his commitment to them by standing against the vast machine of the Captain—and, in so doing, seals his fate.

Stuart Rosenberg's striking direction lent the film the feeling of a folk ballad, and provided a number of unforgettable sequences. Chief among them: the boxing match between Dragline and Luke, a dynamic confrontation of strong wills, as well as powerful bodies; the egg eating contest, in which Luke brags he can down fifty hard-boiled eggs in one hour, and turns the event into a cause for exuberant gambling among the men; Luke and the other prisoners being taunted by a well-endowed teenage temptress (Joy Harmon), who hoses down her car, and herself, in clear view of the sun-scorched, frustrated men; the visit from Arletta (Jo Van Fleet), the sick old mother of Luke, who visits him one

"I don't care if it rains or freezes": George Kennedy and Paul Newman in *Cool Hand Luke*.

Sunday, propped up in the backseat of a truck, coughing terribly and just barely able to reminisce about their past together; and the "Plastic Jesus" song, in which Luke strums a guitar and sings a raunchy, irreverent pop song, "I don't care if it rains or freezes/ long as I got my plastic Jesus/ sitting on the dashboard of my car . . ." But no one scene quite so fully symbolizes the film's anti-Establishment attitude as a single line of diaglogue, spoken by the disciplinarian Captain as he confronts the unflinchingly idealistic Luke: "What we have here . . . is a failure . . . to c'mmunicate!" A breakdown in communication between the older and younger generations, between the government and the ever more embittered young people, between the haves and the have-nots became a fact of life in the late Sixties.

For Paul Newman, the role of Luke represented the symbolic characterization of loner/loser he adapted as his own special style of performance during the decade. It also provided him with his third Oscar nomination, and his third failure to receive the award. He had made many enemies in Hollywood, mainly because Newman proved to be as independent-minded and individualistic as the characters he played. He has not been nominated since, but each of the three strong performances in his classic films of the Sixties—*The Hustler, Hud,* and *Cool Hand Luke*—certainly merited the statuette.

Paul Newman and Lou Antonio in *Cool Hand Luke*.

197

The Trip: Peter Fonda emerged as the screen embodiment of the late-Sixties hero, symbolizing the era's loners just as his father had done for an earlier audience in *The Grapes of Wrath*.

THE TRIP
AMERICAN INTERNATIONAL PICTURES

Produced by Roger Corman; screenplay by Jack Nicholson; directed by Roger Corman.

CAST

Paul (Peter Fonda); *Sally* (Susan Strasberg); *John* (Bruce Dern); *Max* (Dennis Hopper); *Glenn* (Salli Sachse)

"Tune in—turn on—drop out."

The phrase, originally emanating from one Dr. Timothy Leary, haunted the college campus scene throughout 1967, as more and more students began to retreat from the growing complexity of the world situation into the alternative world of hallucinogenic drugs. The craze of "tripping" began in California, where it spread through the hippie community, then travelled from the original flower-power denizens of Haight-Ashbury to more middle-class campuses across the country. In less than one year, the early-Sixties Ivy League/Peace Corps conception of college life changed drastically into a haven for "hippiedom" and, as always, American International Pictures hurriedly rushed into production an

Images borrowed from voodoo and Bergman: Salli Sachse and hooded horsemen appear to Peter Fonda during his "trip." *(The Trip)*

198

exploitation picture designed to capitalize on this new youth craze. In the summer of 1967, *The Trip* played to saturation booking at drive-ins across the country. And while more sophisticated students who knew something of LSD laughed at the conventional images provided, more naive youngsters accepted the film's synthetically bizarre vision of "freaking out" as the real thing.

The story concerns a young director of TV commercials (Peter Fonda) who cannot stand the L.A. lifestyle any longer, and allows a close friend (Bruce Dern) to coax him into a psychedelic parlor of pleasure. At the Freakout, the proprietor (Dennis Hopper) slips him some acid, and before long Fonda is experiencing visions of his wife (Susan Strasberg) with whom he has just split. He also sees such sights as: two dark caped men on horseback, pursuing him down a deserted stretch of beach; his friend and the proprietor popping into his psychedelic visions to explain the nature of what he's experiencing; a beautiful blonde hippie (Salli Sachse), who shows up in flashy costumes that have little to do with what's going on, but at least allow her the opportunity to engage in a freaked-out fashion show; and all kinds of bizarre colors, coming together in a kaleidoscopic manner. The effects were often derivative of such artistic filmmakers as Federico Fellini, but that made perfect sense since the director was none other than Roger Corman, the uncrowned king of exploitation pictures, whose entire career was based on the notion of lifting whatever he wanted from the styles of more serious artists, and casually throwing them into his highly effective (and incredibly lucrative) little ventures.

The roles of hero and heroine were originally intended as a recoupling for Fonda and Nancy Sinatra, those second generation Hollywood youths who previously co-starred in Corman's successful, sensational item *The Wild Angels*. But Ms. Sinatra chose to drop out of the exploitation picture market, thanks to her sudden success as a recording artist with such songs as "These Boots Were Made for Walkin'." She was the only major cast member of the previous picture who did not make an appearance here. Fonda, Dern, and Hopper could not, at that time, find work in more important pictures, but along with *The Trip's* screenwriter, Jack Nicholson, they were already forming the basis of Hollywood's soon to emerge counterculture. In fact, American International provided a haven for the misfits of the movie business who, in the changing cultural patterns of the late Sixties, would soon appear as the non-heroes for this confused era. Shortly, with such films as *Easy Rider,* they would move out of the obscurity of sensationalized A.I.P. pictures (where they were already "underground superstars" with a built in audience of drive-in addicts), and take their act to a broader, more all-encompassing constituency.

"In Psychedelic Color," read the ads. The phrase was new, but the essential appeal was traditionally sensuous. *(The Trip)*

The Good Life gone sour: Sharon Tate, Martin Milner, Patty Duke in *Valley of the Dolls*.

Barbara Parkins becomes hooked on "dolls." (*Valley of the Dolls*)

VALLEY OF THE DOLLS

20TH CENTURY–FOX

Produced by David Weisbart; screenplay by Helen Deutsch and Dorothy Kingsley, based on the novel by Jacqueline Susann; directed by Mark Robson.

CAST

Helen Lawson (Susan Hayward); *Neely O'Hara* (Patty Duke); *Anne Welles* (Barbara Parkins); *Jennifer North* (Sharon Tate); *Lyon Burke* (Paul Burke); *Tony Polar* (Tony Scotti); *Mel Anderson* (Martin Milner); *Kevin Gillmore* (Charles Drake); *Miriam* (Lee Grant); *Reporter* (Jacqueline Susann)

Valley of the Dolls was to the late Sixties what *The Carpetbaggers* had been to the first half of the decade: the trash masterpiece which everyone went to see, even though they knew better; the irresistibly sleazy, great-bad movie which provided garrishly gaudy scenery, unbelievably exaggerated dialogue, a lusciously lurid plot, silly stabs at a serious message, and cartoon characterizations by a cast of ordinarily competent actors. All of this was wrapped up into a work of garbage which in no way qualified as high class entertainment, much less art, in any sense of the word, yet still sucked everyone in with the promise of a chance to go cinematically slumming in a marvelous bit of movieland madness. Like *The Carpetbaggers,* the film featured a combination of "bright" young stars and "reliable" old veterans, all of whom looked equally amateurish when confronting such masterfully maudlin material. And, as in the case of the earlier film, *Valley of the Dolls* provided a glimpse of the Hollywood Babylon—a sensationalized scandal sheet peep show view of life among show biz celebrities and their very chic, ultra rich, fantastically decadent friends. There was only one major distinction between *The Carpetbaggers* and *Valley of the Dolls:* the earlier picture centered around a male hero, while this was an updating of the classic women's tearjerker.

The Carpetbaggers, written by Harold Robbins, a master of junk novels, was told from a strong masculine point of view; *Valley of the Dolls* was derived from a best-seller by Jacqueline Susann, who turned out tawdry, true-confessional-type potboilers for female readers desiring to experience the ups and downs of an exciting, career girl existence vicariously—that is, without taking any of the risks. Essentially *Valley of the Dolls* is a turgid updating of the kind of films Joan Crawford, Bette Davis, and Lana Turner turned out a generation earlier, except it lacked the class of those old studio productions—and also the magic those then-young actresses brought to the roles. In *Dolls,* Barbara Parkins assumed the focal characterization of Anne Welles, a bright, brash young New England college grad who leaves her Peyton Place-ish small town and heads for Broadway, where she hope to find an exciting job and sophisticated men. Before long, however, her life is a total void. She's involved with a married man, and finds herself hooked on pills—"dolls," as the girls call them—which keep her energy level high from one day to the next. During her misadventures in Manhattan and, later, Hollywood, she shares experiences with two other young hopefuls: Jennifer North (Sharon Tate), a statuesque, Monroe-ish actress who wants to be accepted as a human being, but is regarded as a sex object by all the men she meets, and Neely O'Hara (Patty Duke), a superb young actress who uses devious means to reach the top, pulling an *All About Eve*-type deception on a great older star (Susan Hayward) in order to steal a good role away from her.

It was a mark of the film's strange sensibility that a brilliant young actress like Patty Duke (who had won an Academy Award only a few years earlier for her sensitive, in-depth performance in *The Miracle Worker*) actually came off worse in this context than non-actresses Parkins and Tate. Perhaps that was due to the demands made by such a script: actually attempting to act, to create any kind of a real character, caused the dumbness of the dialogue to show through more clearly. Like most potboilers, *Valley of the Dolls* pretended to look through liberated eyes at its material, while in fact assuming a reactionary view. Jennifer develops breast cancer, and kills herself upon realizing that her only asset—her beautiful body—will be scarred by an operation; Neely turns into a hysterical shrew, hooked on booze and pills, after having clawed her way to the top only to find it unfulfilling; and Anne finally returns to her small hometown where she weds the naive local boy still waiting there for her, amid the virginal snow and the fresh, clean evergreens. But even this note of morality struck false: while pretending to put down the fast life in big cities, *Valley of the Dolls* excited thousands of young female moviegoers with the prospect of living such splendidly sordid adventures themselves.

Susan Hayward, playing a fading star in *Valley of the Dolls.*

"We rob banks!" Warren Beatty and Faye Dunaway as Bonnie and Clyde.

BONNIE AND CLYDE

WARNER BROTHERS–SEVEN ARTS

Produced by Warren Beatty; screenplay by David Newman and Robert Benton; directed by Arthur Penn.

CAST

Clyde Barrow (Warren Beatty); *Bonnie Parker* (Faye Dunaway); *C. W. Moss* (Michael J. Pollard); *Buck Barrow* (Gene Hackman); *Blanche Barrow* (Estelle Parsons); *Malcolm Moss* (Dub Taylor); *Captain Frank Homer* (Denver Pyle); *Velma Davis* (Evans Evans); *Eugene Grizzard* (Gene Wilder); *Grocery Store Owner* (James Stiver)

Initially, *Bonnie and Clyde* was dismissed by serious critics as nothing more than another moronic gangster programmer: *Time* Magazine lambasted the film in a curt, cruel review, then did a complete turnabout the following week in which their critic retracted his statements and, in an elaborate cover story, announced that *Bonnie and Clyde* was one of the most significant motion pictures of the decade. Eventually, the picture that was in some areas marketed as nothing more than an exploitation flick was chosen to kick off the Montreal International Film Festival!

Screenwriters David Newman and Robert Benton based their story on the life and legends of Bonnie Parker and Clyde Barrow, real life Depression-era rural gangsters who terrorized portions of the southwest as they travelled about in stolen automobiles, accompanied by Clyde's strong, silent brother Buck (Gene Hackman), Buck's flighty female companion Blanche (Estelle Parsons), and a zany, impish rube named C. W. Moss (Michael J. Pollard). However, the writers also incorporated certain incidents which, historically, happened to members of the Dillinger gang, and in so doing made their tale a composite image of the early twentieth-century cult of the outlaw. Arthur Penn, meanwhile, incorporated various artistic techniques, recently developed by the French New Wave filmmakers of the early Sixties—Jean-Luc Godard, François Truffaut, Claude Chabrol—into his own directorial approach. Penn helped to further the developing sense of an international cinema by cross pollinating the techniques of the French filmmakers, bringing the devices they had initially discovered in American action films back to America.

Instead of the deadly serious approach of other recent rural gangster flicks, Penn purposefully speeded up the action in many key scenes, making his movie look amazingly like an old Keystone Kops slapstick comedy. The effect was disconcerting, and disorienting, because he featured such techniques at moments of extreme violence—bank holdups, shootouts, and the like—making the most upsetting scenes look silly. By shooting these sequences in a style diametrically opposed to what audiences expected, Penn created a unique viewing experience out of what could easily have been con-

Faye Dunaway taunts lawman Denver Pyle, while Warren Beatty looks on, in *Bonnie and Clyde*.

Fate closes in: Faye Dunaway, Michael J. Pollard, and Warren Beatty in *Bonnie and Clyde*.

203

ventional scenes. He also explored the relationship of sex and violence in society by concentrating on the shifting relationships between the characters. At first, Bonnie and Clyde are mindless, cold-blooded killers. Significantly, Clyde is impotent at the time, resisting all of Bonnie's sexual advances in favor of a close attachment to his gun. As he and Bonnie grow in stature as human beings, they become more interested in a meaningful relationship, less concerned about robbing banks. After Bonnie has actually learned to express herself in words, writing of their love in a crude but touching poem, they communicate their love physically. From that point in the film, they kill no one else. Critics noted that Lee Harvey Oswald, accused assassin of President Kennedy, was supposedly impotent, and the makers of *Bonnie and Clyde* reflected just such a concept. Sex and violence are seen as the positive and negative aspects of a single force: when one is repressed, the other is released in devastating proportions.

Bonnie and Clyde was preceded by an effective advertising campaign ("We rob banks!") and the film's popularity promptly launched a wave of nostalgia for the clothing styles and fashions of the thirties. But the most significant question raised by the movie was the technical manner in which Penn treated his big finale, depicting the ambush of Bonnie and Clyde by police officers: it was filmed as a montage sequence, alternating slow motion shots with normal depictions of time, repeating certain images from various camera angles and thereby extending what might have been a ten- or twelve-second sequence (if realistically portrayed) into a two-minute "ballet of blood." In the original script, the deaths take place offscreen, and Penn defended his instinctual decision to add the controversial ending by insisting he sensed, while making the movie, that Bonnie and Clyde were emerging as larger than life characters, and his treatment of the last scene was necessary in order to visually portray the deaths of legends rather than people. At once, though, the quality and quantity of screen violence emerged as the most controversial and heatedly debated issue in films.

A family portrait: Gene Hackman, Estelle Parsons, Warren Beatty, Faye Dunaway, and Michael J. Pollard. *(Bonnie and Clyde)*

John Forsythe (far left) and law officers take Robert Blake and Scott Wilson into custody. *(In Cold Blood)*

In Cold Blood: Scott Wilson is confronted with evidence of his guilt.

IN COLD BLOOD

COLUMBIA

Produced by Richard Brooks; screenplay by Richard Brooks, based on the novel by Truman Capote; directed by Richard Brooks.

CAST

Perry Smith (Robert Blake); *Dick Hickock* (Scott Wilson); *Alvin Dewey* (John Forsythe); *Reporter* (Paul Stewart); *Harold Nye* (Gerald S. O'Loughlin); *Mr. Hickock* (Jeff Corey); *Roy Church* (John Gallaudet); *Clarence Duntz* (James Flavin); *Mr. Smith* (Charles McGraw); *Officer Rohleder* (James Lantz); *Prosecutor* (Will Geer); *Herbert Clutter* (John McLiam); *Bonnie Clutter* (Ruth Storey); *Nancy Clutter* (Brenda C. Currin); *Kenyon Clutter* (Paul Hough)

Bonnie and Clyde offered an image of two real-life killers brought to a violent end; so too did *In Cold Blood*. But the style, treatment, and intentions of Arthur Penn's film were drastically different from Richard Brooks'. *Bonnie and Clyde* was shot in color, with European artistic flourishes; *In Cold Blood* was one of the last significant pictures to be flmed in black and white, in order that it might convey the quality of a 1950s documentary—altogether fitting, since it portrayed an incident that took place in 1959. Straightforward and simple in terms of its visual imagery, it did nonetheless feature a complex storytelling technique—with numerous flashbacks and disorienting jumps in time—in order to restructure the events it depicted: the killing of the entire Clutter family by two distraught young men, Perry Smith and Dick Hickock. Once again, it brought to motion picture screens a work based on the principle of social violence, to convey the growing concern with, and escalation of, violence in our time.

Truman Capote, previously regarded as the likable author of such charming tales as *Breakfast at Tiffany's,* undertook the elaborate job of interviewing Smith and Hickock in their jail cells, collecting his impressions of their lives in a book that changed the shape of modern writing. A "non-fiction novel," the critics called it, as *In Cold Blood* offered readers a chilling study of the mindless, merciless, meaningless murders, making the public aware of the way in which insane violence could creep into the lives of the most domestic, unassuming small-town middle Americans. But the basis of the book's power was in its exploration of the minds of the two men who entered an average, ordinary home assuming, for some unknown reason, that vast amounts of money were to be had, then—without any conscious plan—gradually realized their real reason for being there was to kill the innocent family. Following the Kennedy assassinations, it became ever more obvious that violence in our country was escalating and the central question everyone asked was: Why? By analyzing the actions and self-images of these two social misfits—the very kind of people who could easily be responsible for the casual killings either of an unknown man like Herbert Clutter or a world leader such as President Kennedy—Capote educated his audience as to the mentality and emotional forces responsible for such acts.

Richard Brooks, in both his writing and directing of the film version, chose to assault the sensibility of his viewers in a peculiar but effective style. He began his movie with an image of Smith (Robert Blake) and Hickock (Scott Wilson) stealthily approaching the Clutter house, then cut away to a shot of a cleaning lady arriving the following morning and discovering the bodies—which we were not allowed to see. The picture then followed the attempts to track down the killers by a relentless investigator, Alvin Dewey (John Forsythe), despite the lack of clues or motivation; the temporary es-

Scott Wilson and Robert Blake break into the victims' home. *(In Cold Blood)*

Robert Blake sketches in prison. *(In Cold Blood)*

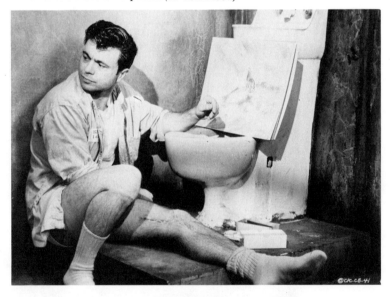

cape of Smith and Hickock to Mexico; their almost accidental arrest in Las Vegas some time later; the handling of the court case by a powerful prosecuting attorney (Will Geer); and finally, the execution of Smith and Hickock by hanging. All this time, the audience assumes it has been spared the grim experience of actually witnessing the murders. But, near the end, Smith describes the incident to a reporter (Paul Stewart) and we are forced to finally watch what we sensed was unavoidably coming all along. The enactment of the murders turns out to be a cathartic experience, at once terrifying and purging,

since the viewer senses an incredible feeling of relief that would not be possible without at last coming to grips with the act in all its ugly detail.

Like the book upon which it was based, *In Cold Blood* offers no easy moralizing or simple solutions. It merely recounts one of the most extreme cases of random, purposeless violence that had begun to plague us during the Sixties. And by studying the formative years of both Smith and Hickock, their flashbacks to incidents recounting their lack of strong relationships with their fathers, the picture suggested the sort of syndromes that spur people to become the emotional freaks of our society. With horrifying accuracy, *In Cold Blood* brought home the fact that our culture was fast becoming an extraordinarily—perhaps uncontrollably—violent one, and that motion pictures—in order to accurately reflect life as it was now lived—would necessarily become more violent.

THE DIRTY DOZEN

METRO-GOLDWYN-MAYER

Produced by Kenneth Hyman; screenplay by Nunnally Johnson and Lukas Heller, based on the novel by E. M. Nathanson; directed by Robert Aldrich.

CAST

Major Reisman (Lee Marvin); *General Worden* (Ernest Borgnine); *Joseph Wladislaw* (Charles Bronson); *Robert Jefferson* (Jim Brown); *Victor Franko* (John Cassavetes); *Sergeant Bowren* (Richard Jaeckel); *Major Max Armbruster* (George Kennedy); *Pedro Jiminez* (Trini Lopez); *Captain Stuart Kinder* (Ralph Meeker); *Colonel Everett Dasher-Breed* (Robert Ryan); *Archer Maggott* (Telly Savalas); *Samson Posey* (Clint Walker); *General Denton* (Robert Webber); *Vernon Pinkley* (Donald Sutherland); *German Girl* (Dora Reisser); *Additional Squad Members*: (Tom Busby, Ben Carruthers, Stuart Cooper, Robert Phillips, Colin Maitland, Al Mancini, George Roubicek)

The Dirty Dozen was to the late Sixties what *The Great Escape* was to the first half of the decade: a slick World War II entertainment yarn about a group of guys who take on an impossible mission; while most perish at the hands of the Nazis, a few manage to survive in order to give the movie a sense of optimism. What proved disconcerting about *The Dirty Dozen* were the underlying differ-

Lee Marvin leads the Dirty Dozen into action.

209

Telly Savalas in *The Dirty Dozen*'s most violent moment.

Jim Brown (far left) and fellow squad members arm for action in *The Dirty Dozen*.

ences in tone between this film and the earlier one. There, the characters were all heroic G.I.s, likable English and American soldiers whose mission is admirable; now, the fellows are murderers, rapists, and other assorted criminals, while their objective—killing not only defenseless German officers, but their women as well—is questionable for the basis of a heroic epic. This is no *Guns of Navarone*–style adventure, in which well-defended enemy cannons must be knocked out of commission by a few brave souls, but rather an unpleasant project in which non-combatants are to be murdered without mercy by frightening, despicable brutes whose personal escapades are presented as a new form of escapist entertainment. The change in the country's emotional climate between 1963 and 1967 was clearly reflected in the difference in attitude between these two films calculated to appeal to the vast moviegoing public.

Though Lee Marvin proved a strong choice for Major Reisman, the no-nonsense old-time warhorse, and Richard Jaeckel provided a fine performance as his young M.P. assistant, Sergeant Bowren, the film's focus remained on "the dozen" and the audience's interest on those actors who played them. Charles Bronson (soon to emerge as a superstar in Europe, where he was known as El Brute) made a career of such "group" projects, following his roles in *The Magnificent Seven* and *The Great Escape* with the only sympathetic character among the dirty dozen; movie director as well as actor John Cassavetes received a Best Supporting Actor nomination for his role as a manipulative, psychotic hustler; football hero Jim Brown suggested a strong screen presence with his performance as a militantly anti-white Negro, and singing star Trini Lopez properly fit the bill as Brown's Puerto Rican sidekick; intellectual English actor Donald Sutherland did a nice turn as a retarded southerner, while Telly Savalas (later to suck lollipops as TV's supercop *Kojack*) delivered a chilling performance as a sadistic killer who needlessly murders a beautiful German prostitute they capture—an act which disgusts even his fellows. That scene proved one of the most controversial in the film, since it was treated as an audience turn on: the filmmakers made this the most memorable scene in the picture, violent and erotic at the same time, as the man's knife entering the girl appears to be a demented substitute for the sex act.

Many critics wondered if perhaps the film wasn't irresponsible in its unabashed assumption that sex and violence were now the staple of popular enter-

Lee Marvin, George Kennedy, and Ernest Borgnine as the army officers who gamble that a dozen criminals can pull off a serious military operation. *(The Dirty Dozen)*

Telly Savalas as Maggot. *(The Dirty Dozen)*

tainment. But underlying this element was the movie's strong moral sensibility, added by action director Aldrich in his effectively exciting style. If the film's appeal is decidedly unsubtle, its anti-war message is constantly kept just under the surface. The officers (Ernest Borgnine, Robert Ryan, and Robert Webber) who assign Marvin to his mission appear partially corrupt, partially stupid, and partially insane, which helps explain their willingness to hand over this major job to such a deranged group of men; in the end, we like the men not so much for their own qualities but in comparison to the generals and colonels we meet along the way. Likewise, a significant sequence of the picture features an extended war game, in which the misfits prove their resourceful abilities as professional soldiers after being recruited and trained by Marvin; in this scene, Aldrich's notion of war (and, for that matter, life itself) as a great "game" is clearly communicated.

And, in the end, the raid is so ugly that any notions of war as a glorious endeavor are thoroughly dashed. With its cynical view of battle, its bevy of non-heroes and strong suggestions of where the "professional" men of violence really come from, coupled with a modern cinematic approach to violence in film, *The Dirty Dozen* proved not only one of the most popular audience pleasers of 1967, but also one of the most perceptive film studies of the emerging consciousness of that period.

1968

212

THE GOOD, THE BAD, AND THE UGLY

UNITED ARTISTS

Produced by Alberto Grimaldi; screenplay by Luciano Vincenzoni and Sergio Leone, based on a story by Age Scarpelli; directed by Sergio Leone.

CAST

Joe/"Blondie" (Clint Eastwood); *Tuco* (Eli Wallach); *Setenza/Colonel Matherson* (Lee Van Cleef)

For years, Italian and Spanish movie companies turned out their own versions of Hollywood westerns, usually starring American actors who had struck out in Hollywood. Many European moviegoers who had never heard of Marlon Brando knew and loved Charles Bronson as "El Brute." Then, a young Italian director name Sergio Leone fashioned the film *For a Fistful of Dollars,* which boasted enough crude brillance to make United Artists feel it might just have an American marketability, creating a craze for arty, existential, Europeanized westerns.

Though Leone's long, moody stretches containing virtually no dialogue may have been due to the practical consideration that he was working with an international cast—many of the performers being unable to communicate with one another—he nonetheless turned this defect into a virtue by directing for optimum visual potential. In the role of "The Man with No Name," Clint Eastwood sported a grisly beard, a beat-up sombrero, a long serape covering two huge guns, and rode a mule. Instead of the perennial fair-minded hero, this protagonist appears more like a villain.

The American idea of the gunfighter was filtered through an oriental-samurai consciousness, interpreted by an Italian artist who shot his films in Spain, but embodied once more by an American actor. In *For a Fistful of Dollars* Eastwood stood at the film's focus; in the sequel, *For a Few Dollars More,* he was given a friendly-enemy antagonist (Lee Van Cleef). Finally, for the third, largest, most expensive entry in the trilogy, another character—a cruel version of the robust peasant clown—was added with Tuco (Eli Wallach), a hysterical, greedy, lecherous bandit. Leone made a film that was unfathomably violent yet strikingly funny; the cinematography is as sweeping as in a John Ford epic, while the music (by Ennio Morricone) added a Eu-

ropean sensation of irony not unlike that in a film by Bergman or Buñuel. The film proved equally popular with college intellectuals and drive-in movie crowds.

The story concerned the epic search by each of the three professional gunmen for a man named Bill Carson, who presumably hid a fortune in some unmarked grave; our non-heroes struggle, sometimes alone, sometimes as a tenuous group, after the loot, and Leone's story turns into a *Treasure of Sierra Madre*–type fable. Leone focuses on scenes of violence—beatings, shootings, and the like—that might easily have become gratuitous or sensationalized, but are handled in such a way that they come off as a terrible kind of poetry. Such moments are also, importantly, part of the film's morality. For as these three characters struggle and maim their way to the gold, they continuously step in and out of the American Civil War going on around them. As the armies of gray and blue hurl themselves at one another, the three stand aside, awe-struck at what they see—their own violence, terrible as it may be, dwarfed by the socially "legitimate" violence of the war.

Clint Eastwood as the Man With No Name in *The Good, the Bad and the Ugly.*

Eli Wallach finds himself in an unpleasant situation in *The Good, the Bad and the Ugly.*

Eli Wallach and Clint Eastwood in *The Good, the Bad and the Ugly.*

The classic three-way shootout: Lee Van Cleef, Clint Eastwood (in serape), and Eli Wallach. *(The Good, the Bad and the Ugly)*

The parallel between the American Civil War and the then-current Viet Nam conflict was implicit. Eastwood's scene with a dying soldier is more touching than one might expect from such a film, while his comments about war—"Never have so many good men been wasted so terribly!"—hit home with equal impact. Meanwhile, other scenes shocked audiences into uneasy laughter by reversing the clichés and stock situations of past westerns. Eli Wallach rides across the prairie in a stereotypical manner, except for one detail—he carries a pink parasol; at another point, he luxuriates in a huge bubble bath, then shoots a passerby with a gun concealed under the suds. The final three-way shootout is filmed as a burlesque of the classic western showdown, yet is as suspenseful as it is over-stylized. Throughout, the film's effectiveness comes from Leone's uncanny ability to at once satirize conventions of the western films he cut his teeth on, while simultaneously reconstructing them as dark comedies. The success of the spaghetti westerns—especially the mammoth third entry in the series—introduced American audiences to a kind of import very different from the Fellini flicks, allowing us to share what the Italian moviegoing public actually spent their lire to see.

PLANET OF THE APES

20TH CENTURY–FOX

Produced by Arthur P. Jacobs; screenplay by Rod Serling and Michael Wilson, based on the novel by Pierre Boulle; directed by Franklin J. Schaffner.

CAST

Taylor (Charlton Heston); *Zaius* (Maurice Evans); *Zira* (Kim Hunter); *Cornelius* (Roddy McDowall); *President of Assembly* (James Whitmore); *Honorious* (James Daly); *Nova* (Linda Harrison); *Landon* (Robert Gunner); *Dodge* (Jeff Burton)

As talk of a "new consciousness" continued in the late Sixties, movies underwent drastic changes in attitude and style. While film producers were not yet ready to risk criticizing the government's official policies directly, they could nonetheless express their attitudes by masking them in the guise of a different time period. This was what Sergio Leone did in his spaghetti westerns set in the past, and what a number of other filmmakers did with the future—as in *Planet of the Apes,* one of the most expensive, and admirable, sci-fi films in years. The genre had fallen upon sad times in the late Fifties, when countless schlock monster movies gave it a bad name. *Apes* was the first Sixties sci-fi film to star a major Hollywood name, Charlton Heston, and also the first to use painstaking special effects which drew critical praise. In all respects, it was a class production: well liked and widely respected. But beneath the veneer of futuristic fantasy, there was a chilling commentary on America in the Sixties.

Apes began with that highly anticipated moment, the first manned space flight. Taylor (Heston) and three companions crash land on some apparently distant planet, where the oxygen, vegetation, and even animal life are not very different from Earth's. One by one, the members of Taylor's company die off until, alone, he encounters a tribe of human beings living in a primitive state. For the time being, he is content to remain with them, living off wild berries in the woods and making plans to try and contact Earth. Then, suddenly, he and the other people are surrounded by mounted riders with guns and nets, who capture them all and carry the helpless lot off to a large city. What astonishes Taylor is that his captors are apes; on this planet, the evolutionary trend has been reversed.

Charlton Heston and Linda Harrison in *Planet of the Apes*.

Three "apes" travel overland by wagon. *(Planet of the Apes)*

By playing off this premise, the filmmakers were able to make several points. First, the human beings Taylor encounters look amazingly like the love/peace flower children of the late Sixties, who flaunted a self-styled naivete as a form of moral superiority. The vulnerability of such a group is set against the more militaristic apes, whose brutish attack on the community of flower people could not help but remind audiences of the current clashes between anti-war demonstrators and National Guardsmen then taking place on college campuses. There is also, via a comic portrayal of the apes' political system—with its beleaguered President (James Whitmore) and outspoken senator of the Ape Establishment (James Daly)—an inherent criticism of our own congress. There are militantly military apes, who correlate to the hawks believing in the necessity of our keeping peace in the world through might, and "liberal" apes—the young couple Cornelius (Roddy McDowall) and Zira (Kim Hunter) as well as the ancient Dr. Zaius (Maurice Evans)—who oppose their government's activities with peaceful demonstrations. Interestingly, the

Kim Hunter, Charlton Heston, and Linda Harrison in *Planet of the Apes.*

216

film was based on a book by Pierre Boulle, who had written the novel *Bridge Over the River Kwai,* and directed by Franklin J. Schaffner, who would later make *Patton.* Their anti-war sentiments, so clear in their other works, are present in *Apes,* which cleverly avoids any possiblity of censorship by disguising such attitudes as enjoyable sci-fi.

Still, it was first and foremost through its quality as entertainment that *Apes* succeeded. Instead of ape masks, the distinguished cast went through the rigors of makeup sessions, lasting several hours, before each successive day of shooting. So instead of two-dimensional effects, the actors all maintained their complete ranges of facial gestures and their own unique personalities. Roddy McDowall, for instance, is totally recognizable as Roddy McDowall; it's as though he has been turned into an ape while still retaining his most characteristic facial qualities. The only major drawback to the film is screenwriter Rod Serling's tendency to camp up the proceedings with lines like "I never met an ape I didn't like," or having three of the ape/actors assuming the See No Evil/Hear No Evil/Speak No Evil stance. There are some ponderous, pretentious lines ("He goes to find his fate!") that are best overlooked. But such moments are forgettable considering the impact of the ending: in the picture's startling final moment, Taylor and his beautiful companion Nova (Linda Harrison) ride out onto a deserted stretch of beach and discover a half destroyed Statue of Liberty in ruins. At this point, Taylor realizes he has been travelling through time rather than space, as the forceful final image says more than dialogue ever could.

2001: A SPACE ODYSSEY

METRO-GOLDWYN-MAYER

Produced by Stanley Kubrick; screenplay by Stanley Kubrick and Arthur C. Clarke, from Mr. Clarke's short story, "The Sentinel"; directed by Stanley Kubrick.

CAST

Bowman (Keir Dullea); *Poole* (Gary Lockwood); *Dr. Heywood Floyd* (William Sylvester); *Moonwatcher* (Dan Richter); *HAL 9000* (Douglas Rain); *Smyslov* (Leonard Rossiter); *Elena* (Margaret Tyzack); *Halvorsen* (Robert Beatty); *Michaels* (Sean Sullivan); *Mission Controller* (Frank Miller)

Keir Dullea as an astronaut in *2001: A Space Odyssey.*

2001 begins with a sequence in which Neanderthal monkey men roam a prehistoric forest. But unlike *Planet of the Apes*—with its obvious entertainment values and willingness to make all its points clear by means of heavyhanded dialogue—*2001* remained obscure and artistic, a difficult, demanding film. Perhaps the psychedelic light show, which takes up almost a half-hour near the end of this nearly three-hour film, appealed to the youthful "turned on" moviegoers. Whatever the reasons for its success, *2001* quickly became a conversation piece among filmgoers and the cornerstone of the New American cinema: intellectually stimulating, aesthetically experimental, thematically ambiguous.

In terms of style and meaning, *2001* is best considered as part of a trilogy, along with two other of Kubrick's modern classics, *Dr. Strangelove* and *A Clockwork Orange.* All the films are, to a degree, futuristic, taking place during a time in the relatively immediate future. All make use of classical music as an ironic foil for what we see: images of

exploding atomic bombs, violent delinquency, or the emptiness of space are perceived more clearly when set against the order, intelligence, and emotional discipline of a Strauss waltz or one of Beethoven's symphonies. And, finally, all the films deal with the notion of human beings as set against machines of some sort—the Bomb and related war machinery in *Strangelove,* the computer H.A.L. in *2001*, the brainwashing by technological devices in *Clockwork.*

For the key roles of the astronauts in *2001,* for instance, Kubrick picked two actors not for their talent, but their blandness. When Bowman (Keir Dullea) and Poole (Gary Lockwood) realize, en route to Jupiter, that their computer companion H.A.L. has decided they are unfit to accomplish their mission, would do better to proceed without them, and must eliminate both men as stumbling blocks, the movie's moral complexity derives from the fact they are considerably less interesting than H.A.L. He (it?) possesses considerable charm and wit, while the two men are a pair of Ivy League,

217

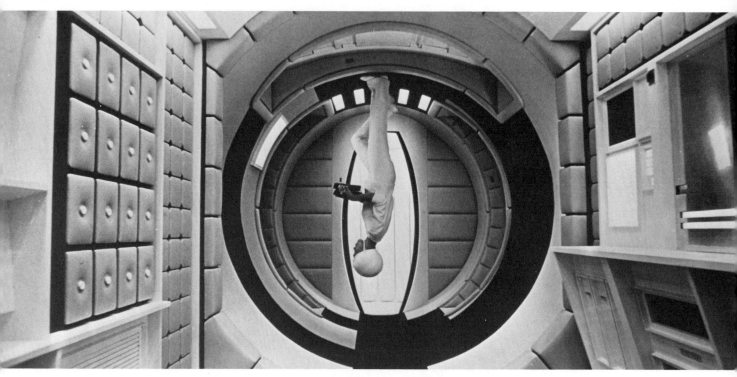

Stanley Kubrick's stunning widescreen vistas lent a surrealistic quality to the interior scenes of *2001*.

Opposite page: One of the dazzling images that made *2001* a "trip" in more ways than one.

clean-cut zombies, more machine-like than the machine. After Poole's death, as Bowman devises an effective means of destroying the electronic brain and goes about disconnecting H.A.L.'s thinking apparatus, the viewer experiences an extreme case of identity crisis: why do we keep sympathizing with H.A.L.?

Kubrick and sci-fi writer Arthur C. Clarke based their original screenplay on Clarke's short story, "The Sentinel," fleshing out an epic motion picture from one detail Clarke created: the idea of a strange slab, broadcasting information of high intelligence, which reappears throughout man's history of civilization. In the opening sequence, it is depicted as communicating on a visceral level with a number of frightened primitives, who regard the slab as some kind of god. Kubrick effectively creates a transition over several thousand years—from our animal past to our near future—by having one of the ape men throw a bone weapon into the air; in the split second that it rests suspended before beginning its descent

to earth, the object turns, before our eyes, into a modern spacecraft. The plot proper begins when two astronauts are ordered by their superiors to journey toward Jupiter in order to determine just what the slab (now broadcasting from Earth's moon) is communicating with. But for the surviving astronaut, the physical journey becomes a spiritual odyssey; the outer trip toward a distant planet metamorphoses into an inner search for himself—and, in essence, for man. As Bowman (his name draws memories of another great wanderer, Odysseus) nears Jupiter, the sense of space degenerates into a surrealistic image of the mind; the astronaut finds himself wandering down the corridors and into a bedroom from a period-piece movie. Finally, the concept of relativity and the idea of the cycle dominate; for when he moves as far from Earth as possible, he has in fact returned. What he discovers is what he already knew; as he suddenly ages, his last vision is of a fetus. By moving to the ultimate limit in space, man has returned to his origins.

218

Free floating: Keir Dullea experiences freedom from gravity. *(2001)*

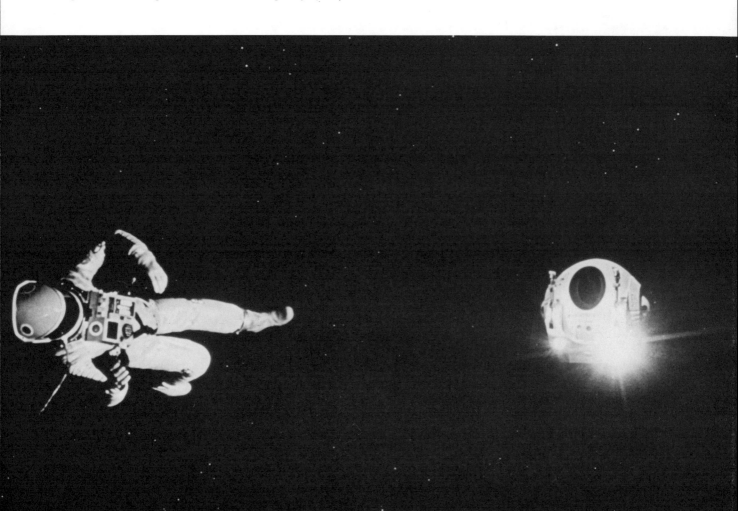

The ultimate in high camp: Jame Fonda and John Philip Law in *Barbarella*.

BARBARELLA

PARAMOUNT

Produced by Dino De Laurentiis; screenplay by Terry Southern, Brian Degas, Claude Brule, Jean-Claude Forest, Roger Vadim, Clement Wood, Tudor Gates and Vittorio Bonicelli, based on the comic strip by Jean-Claude Forest; directed by Roger Vadim

CAST

Barbarella (Jane Fonda); *Pygar* (John Philip Law); *The Black Queen* (Anita Pallenberg); *The Concierge* (Milo O'Shea); *Dildano* (David Hemmings); *Professor Ping* (Marcel Marceau); *Mark Hand* (Ugo Tognazzi); *President of Earth* (Claude Dauphin)

Barbarella offers the perfect example of how thoroughly a film designed for the most crass of commercial purposes can, in retrospect, be seen to mirror nearly all the significant social forces that were, at the time of the film's creation, at work in our society.

First, there is the very conception of the project, based on a risqué French comic strip for adults. In print form, *Barbarella* constituted a combination of Brigitte Bardot and Cinderella, a blending of adult sophistication and childlike innocence. Jean-Claude Forest, the strip's author, realized many modern, mature adults longed for the *Flash Gordon* serials of their youth, and so decided to combine those naive fantasies with a mildly pornographic story. Such a concept could never have been turned into a multi-million dollar motion picture by a major company like Paramount at any other time than in the late Sixties, when the pop art craze had already led to TV shows such as *Batman*. Adults were embracing the junk culture of the past and enshrining it now as respectable art; *Barbarella* was an extension of that syndrome.

But in addition to pop art, *Barbarella* also reveals the effects of high camp. The screenplay, as written by, among others, Terry Southern—whose novel *Candy* had set the tone for an era of intellectually acceptable satiric pornography—"camped up" *Barbarella,* giving it the same formula for success that had established the Bond films as the decade's most popular movie series: serious, kinky, even deadly scenes were played for laughs, in a Grand Guignol style of arch seriousness that finally spilled over into conscious comedy. Even the cast was "campy" in its eclectic assemblage of then-popular people: Jane Fonda, the all-American princess who

221

Milo O'Shea and Jane Fonda, enjoying an experiment in induced orgasms in *Barbarella*.

had run off and married a naughty European director, as Barbarella; David Hemmings, the hero of *Blow-Up,* as a revolutionary; John Philip Law, the young star of *The Russians Are Coming,* as the angel; Anita Pallenberg, then-current girlfriend of Mick Jagger, as the wicked queen; Milo O'Shea, scene-stealer from *Romeo and Juliet* and star of *James Joyce's Ulysses,* as an evil monarch; even Marcel Marceau, the great mime, as an outer space weirdo. The inappropriateness of them all being bundled together in a motion picture only added to the sensation of decadent fun.

The sexual revolution played an integral part in the picture's chemistry. Early in the story, *Barbarella* is depicted as an innocent if alluring creature, but as the tale progresses, she is subjected to a series of highly varied sexual experiences, including rape/seductions by an animalistic male, a computer programmed to induce orgasm, even a lesbian tryst with the queen of outer space. Fonda approached each of these love matches with a little girlish combination of playful naughtiness and nervous hesitation; her character emerged from each encounter a little more satisfied and sophisticated than before.

Coupled with the sexual revolution was, necessarily, the new freedom of the screen, without which the picture would have been quite impossible to film—at least for consumption by the American

Freudian symbolism dominates the set design, as Jane Fonda sets about rescuing the Angel in *Barbarella*.

Barbarella: Science Fiction meets the new freedom of the screen.

mass audience. The opening sequence featured a futuristic striptease as Fonda divests herself of a clumsy space suit and emerges nude onscreen. Nudity had become fashionable, as had mildly graphic love sequences: Fonda's orgasmic pleasure at each interlude was photographed with an erotic sensuousness that may have been controversial at that time, but would look tame enough when compared to the next wave of sex films.

It was during the Sixties that European art films and American commercial pictures, so long considered the polar opposites of one another, would become indistinguishable. *Barbarella* offers one of the best examples of that trend, since it starred an American actress and was directed by her European husband. Even the revolutionary fervor then seizing the emotions of so many Americans was present in the form of the character played by David Hemmings. He is seen as an absentminded revolutionary, plotting against fascistic forces at

work in the galaxy, and his presence in the film is a direct effect of the revolutionary chic then at work in the country. Finally, the fact that such a major motion picture is, essentially, a work of sci-fi is itself significant. Though *Planet of the Apes, 2001,* and *Barbarella* are as different from each other as possible, they do form a trilogy of blockbuster sci-fi fantasies that reflect man's preoccupation with the fact that, very shortly, he would indeed begin the conquest of space.

Only one concept of the Sixties seems more an intrusion than a legitimate part of the film's total effect. A very bad rock music score marred the softness and eroticism, and appeared to have been included for no better reason than that ever since *The Graduate,* the new rock had replaced traditional scores in all films designed to appeal to the new hip audience. Here, though, it only detracts from the overall impact of this sensuous, campy comic book on celluloid.

WILD IN THE STREETS

AMERICAN INTERNATIONAL PICTURES

Produced by James H. Nicholson and Samuel Z. Arkoff, with Burt Topper as executive producer; screenplay by Robert Thom, based on his original story; directed by Barry Shear.

CAST

Max Frost (Christopher Jones); *Sally Leroy* (Diane Varsi); *Mrs. Flatow* (Shelley Winters); *Senator Fergus* (Hal Holbrook); *Mary Fergus* (Millie Perkins); *Senator Albright* (Ed Begley); *Stanley X* (Richard Pryor); *Max Jacob, Sr.* (Bert Freed); *Billy* (Kevin Coughlin); *Abraham* (Larry Bishop)

"Don't trust anyone over 30!"

That catchphrase became the primary slogan of the youth movement in the latter half of the Sixties, following the disastrous Democratic National Convention in Chicago: the entire world watched on their television sets as thousands of youthful anti-war supporters of Senator Eugene McCarthy and the late Robert Kennedy were suppressed by police in the city's streets. For almost a year previous to that tumultuous event, students had been urged to express their ever growing resentment over the war in Viet Nam in legal ways —"through the system." But the rejection by the Establishment that young people felt after their year of idealistic work seemed an intentional slap in the face: they were ignored by their elders who had promised them a voice. Cynicism concerning the system skyrocketed, and a simultaneous reactionary feeling against the young set into motion a polarization of America—a Generation Gap, as it would be called. Anti-youth sentiments were especially strong among those who expressed concern that young people—who had recently been loudly campaigning for a lowering of the voting age—would soon make up the majority of the population and control the power to carry an election. The film which caught the then-current paranoia perfectly was the latest exploitation vehicle from A.I.P., *Wild in the Streets*.

Cheaply made and quickly produced pictures always bring new themes to motion picture screens fastest, but not necessarily with any subtlety or art. This was an exception. Robert Thom based the screenplay on his own original story and, instead of the overdone histrionics usually associated with the exploitation flick genre, turned this into a combination of dark farce and social satire: the effect was as if Terry Southern had written a youth-comedy in the style of Evelyn Waugh. The story begins by introducing us to a most unappealing boy, Max Frost (Christopher Jones), who shows his mother (Shelley Winters) his dissatisfaction with her middle-class lifestyle by poisoning the family dog and blowing up the car. On his own in the world, Max quickly becomes the most popular rock singer in the country, and his thousands of hippie fans devotedly follow him everywhere. An entourage consists of a fifteen-year-old graduate from Harvard Law School, a militant black drummer, and a wild-eyed hippie chick (Diane Varsi). When Senator Fergus (Hal Holbrook), a cool California liberal and manipulative power broker, asks them to lend their public appeal in support of his candidacy, they agree—if he will promise to lower the voting age to fifteen. The election is won, and the deal is kept. Only then do the young people begin to appreciate their new-found power. Youth groups riot in the streets, and pour LSD into the water furnished to Congressmen so that, in a freaked-out state, they can be tricked into lowering the Presidential eligibility age.

Before very long, the obnoxious punk has been elected President. One of his first acts is the incarceration of all citizens over the age of thirty in concentration camps. But all does not go well for Max Frost: for these radicals are eventually viewed as reactionaries by a group of three-year-olds, who make plans to overthrow the new Establishment. The absurdity of the plot was purely intentional— and the film's bizarre, arty, semi-surrealistic style made clear this was a satire on youth exploitation flicks in general, as well as the current emotional climate of the country. In the long run, though, *Wild in the Streets* proved unduly paranoid about its subject. For one thing, many of the country's young people turned out to be as conservative as their parents. For another, the prospect of a population made up largely of people under the age of twenty-five actually reversed itself in the early Seventies, when family sizes, and the birth rate, shrank drastically, owing to economic difficulties and the awareness of overcrowding on our globe. If anything, the possibility was of a population made up largely of geriatrics. But if the great fear of the late Sixties proved a cry of wolf, the film *Wild in the Streets* still stands as a vision—written in the lightning language of the cinema, and created in an uproarious style of grotesque comedy—of the future, not as it was actually to be, but rather as many people then feared it might turn out.

Chris Jones, as the first hippie president, is interviewed by a teenage reporter while peacenik-fascist bodyguards look on. *(Wild in the Streets)*

Richard Pryor, Chris Jones, Diane Varsi, and fellow hippies in *Wild in the Streets*.

"Don't trust anyone over thirty!" Richard Pryor looks on as Chris Jones berates his mother, Shelley Winters, and Bert Freed in *Wild in the Streets*.

Julie Christie and George C. Scott: the amoral swinger and the committed professional. *(Petulia)*

PETULIA

WARNER BROTHERS–SEVEN ARTS

Produced by Raymond Wagner; screenplay by Lawrence B. Marcus, based on the novel *Me and the Arch Kook Petulia* by John Haase; directed by Richard Lester.

CAST

Petulia (Julie Christie); *Archie* (George C. Scott); *David* (Richard Chamberlain); *Barney* (Arthur Hill); *Polo* (Shirley Knight); *May* (Pippa Scott); *Wilma* (Kathleen Widdoes); *Mr. Danner* (Joseph Cotten)

It was a nice style, Pauline Kael wrote of Richard Lester's moviemaking, but what could you do with it? *Petulia* was the film that answered that question.

Unfortunately, it arrived at a time when critics were realizing they had overpraised Lester's "modern" approach in such pictures as *A Funny Thing Happened on the Way to the Forum* and *The Knack*. In the mid-Sixties, Lester's TV commercial style of cutting and his frenetic pacing of a picture had seemed a breath of fresh air, especially when compared to the stiff, stodgy style of the conventional Hollywood product. Now, people were wondering if perhaps his technique weren't all gimmick and show, as empty as those very same commercials he borrowed so freely from; was he unable to artistically approach a serious subject? Could he do nothing but free-floating burlesque? With *Petulia*, Lester employed his singular style to tell a stunning story about an important subject; unfortunately, the tide had already turned against him, and his best movie was buried by the reviewers and ignored by the public. It remains, all the same, one of the most impressive motion pictures of the Sixties, a work which expresses the subtleties of the decade's paranoia with insight, artfulness, and a compelling mixture of humor and drama.

Based on the novel *Me and the Arch Kook Petulia*, the film introduces us to the Holly Golightly of the late Sixties. Petulia (Julie Christie) is a seemingly carefree and unpredictable member of California's social set, who calmly informs a hard-boiled surgeon, Archie (George C. Scott), that she plans on becoming his lover. A strange flirtation follows, during which her superficially charming husband, David (Richard Chamberlain), beats his beautiful wife savagely, causing Archie to realize he is viewing a world very different from his own. This is the land of the super-rich and, like Scott Fitzgerald, Archie comes to see that they are very different from you and me: The elite crowd is headed by Petulia's father-in-law, Mr. Danner (Joseph Cotten), an elegant acting but ultimately corrupt character. At first, Archie seeks revenge for the young woman's treatment, then realizes Petulia—despite her declarations of a desire to marry him—is incapable of leaving their gilt-edged existence of mansions, sleek cars, and luxurious yachts. But he himself is trapped in a lifestyle he would prefer dropping out of: saddled with a decent but uninspiring mistress (Pippa Scott), a clutching ex-wife (Shirley Knight), and a pair of meddling, well-meaning friends (Arthur Hill and Kathleen Widdoes) who

In a bizarre sequence in *Petulia*, Julie Christie descends to George C. Scott.

The new lifestyle: Julie Christie and George C. Scott. *(Petulia)*

227

push him toward a reconciliation, even though their own life together is hell. Ultimately, we learn Petulia is attracted to Archie because of his professionalism as a surgeon, his ability to ease pain and suffering, his dedication to the form of work that he believes in, and his kindness at a moment in the past. He is capable of honest emotion, and expresses everything her plastic existence lacks. But even though she drifts out of Archie's life and back into the world of the elegant living dead, she brings something of Archie with her—and leaves something of herself with him. Our last image of Petulia is a shot of her being "put under," at a hospital, where she is about to have her baby—Archie's baby. And while it is her husband who stands beside her, the woman's last conscious word is: "Archie?"

Nicolas Roeg's striking cinematography would soon earn him the chance to direct his own features, and his reputation would be established with such offbeat properties as *Walkabout* and (with Julie Christie) *Don't Look Now*. In *Petulia*, he carefully aimed his camera at every modern subject from underground parking lots to high-rise apartments, perfectly capturing the pop art landscape of Southern California and the myriad of lifestyles that co-exist there. Lester, meanwhile, paced the film in such a way that it vibrates with the rhythms of the era, emphasizing this effect with music by The Grateful Dead and Big Brother and the Holding Company. Richard Chamberlain, formerly one of TV's blandest leading men as *Young Doctor Kildare,* earned a reputation as a talented performer with his fruitcake performance as the sexually confused husband; George C. Scott, moving out of the character-actor category, headed directly for full stardom; and Julie Christie, in her most significant role since *Darling,* again proved she was clearly the primary symbol of the late Sixties female—replacing Audrey Hepburn, who had assumed that responsibility at the decade's beginning.

George C. Scott makes a time-honored escape from an angry husband in *Petulia.*

Mia Farrow as Rosemary. *(Rosemary's Baby)*

ROSEMARY'S BABY

PARAMOUNT PICTURES

Produced by William Castle; screenplay by Roman Polanski, based on the novel by Ira Levin; directed by Roman Polanski.

CAST

Rosemary Woodhouse (Mia Farrow); *Guy Woodhouse* (John Cassavetes); *Minnie Castevet* (Ruth Gordon); *Roman Castevet* (Sidney Blackmer); *Hutch* (Maurice Evans); *Dr. Sapirstein* (Ralph Bellamy); *Terry* (Angela Dorian); *Young Man* (Charles Grodin)

Roman Polanski's vision of evil—as portrayed in such films as *Repulsion, Knife in the Water,* and *Chinatown*—is an artistic commentary that cannot be separated from his personal life. Less than a year after his first major commercial success in America, *Rosemary's Baby,* portrayed devil worshippers invading the privacy of a young couple with designs on the pregnant wife, Polanski's own pregnant wife—the beautiful actress, Sharon Tate—was murdered by a cult of similar characters in the actor's home. There is, in Polanski's view, an obsession with the possible terrors of the world, which causes some of his movies to bog down in excessive florid violence (his *Macbeth,* for instance) and others to effectively reflect the violent climate of the times (most notably, *Chinatown*). Polanski's single blockbuster hit of the Sixties, *Rosemary's Baby,* offered the filmmaker's analysis of an ordinary couple confronting the evil at large around us, and the film's popularity eventually led to an entire cycle of such stories that reached its apex several years later with *The Exorcist.*

Polanski's picture was based on a clever, if routine, potboiler by Ira Levin. The movie version—like film treatments of other novels, from *Birth of a*

229

Mia Farrow and John Cassavetes. (*Rosemary's Baby*)

Nation to *The Godfather*—employed the basic elements of the plot as a source for a work of art far more impressive than anything the book had to offer. Rosemary Woodhouse (Mia Farrow) and her husband Guy (John Cassavetes) are a socially ambitious young couple of the Sixties, who move into an elegant old apartment. He is frustrated by an inability to make his mark as an actor, while she is just a bit terrified by the Castevets (Ruth Gordon and Sid-

ney Blackmer), the old couple who continually intrude on their lives. But they make do and, about the same time Rosemary becomes pregnant, her husband starts landing the good parts that have thus far escaped him. Gradually though, Rosemary begins to suspect Guy has made a pact with a cult of devil worshippers, that he was possessed by, and acting as an agent for, the devil at the time of her conception—and that the baby she is about to bring into the world is actually the anti-Christ. When she expresses her fears to doctors, they call it normal pregnancy hysteria; when she presses the issue, she is treated like a madwoman and very soon finds herself wondering if there is a vast conspiracy formed against her. Whether the plotting going on around her is real or imagined becomes difficult for even the heroine to discriminate; Rosemary only knows she is alone with the thing inside her womb.

Polanski directed with enough panache to make the film perfectly acceptable as an effective modern horror story. Simultaneously, though, he elevated the picture to a higher level of importance, making it a modern fable about life in the degenerate Sixties, where in the concrete jungle of New York such frightening old instincts can still rise to the surface. The role of Rosemary established Mia Farrow as a film star; she had already emerged as one of the decade's more singular young women, first through her role as Allison MacKenzie on TV's popular prime time soap opera, *Peyton Place,* and later through her short-lived marriage to Frank Sinatra. With her Beatle-style haircut and Twiggy-ish shape, Ms. Farrow incarnated a most fetching Sixties type. Still, she was a less than perfect choice for Rosemary. The role called for a substantial, strong-willed woman who gradually degenerates into a shadow of her former self. With Farrow in the role, the effect is distorted: when someone comments that Rosemary is looking terribly thin, she strikes us as looking no more undernourished than she did at the beginning. The role might better have been played by Jane Fonda (who was, in fact, the first choice) since she would have appeared more appropriately healthy at the beginning and then could have suggested Rosemary's gradual deterioration. By the same token, John Cassavetes played the role of the husband as though his mind were elsewhere (most likely, on the next film he would direct) and if Robert Redford had been re-teamed with Fonda, the primary couple of the mid-Sixties cinema might have made *Rosemary's Baby* the perfect picture it had the potential to be, instead of a film which just misses the mark of a true classic.

THE PRODUCERS

EMBASSY PICTURES

Produced by Sidney Glazier for Joseph E. Levine; screenplay by Mel Brooks; directed by Mel Brooks.

CAST

Max Bialystock (Zero Mostel); *Leo Bloom* (Gene Wilder); *LSD* (Dick Shawn); *Franz Liebkind* (Kenneth Mars); *Ulla* (Lee Meredith); *"Hold Me, Touch Me" Old Lady* (Estelle Winwood); *Eva Braun* (Renee Taylor); *Roger De Bris* (Christopher Hewett); *Carmen Giya* (Andreas Voutsinas)

All Mel Brooks movies are about movies, and what they mean to us. That recurring theme actually began before Brooks shot his first feature length film; in his Academy Award Winning animated short, "The Critic," we see a series of experimental, arty images onscreen, as they might appear in an expressionistic short subject—then hear (presumably from the audience) the voice of a garrulous viewer and self-styled critic (Brooks himself) as he deflates the pretensions of the pictures. Later, in *Blazing Saddles,* Brooks would burlesque the western; in *Young Frankenstein,* he would make light of monster movies; in *Silent Movie,* the director would provide a modern silent movie about the difficulty in trying to make a modern silent movie; in *High Anxiety,* he would create a homage to his favorite filmmaker, Alfred Hitchcock. But Brooks' breakthrough feature, *The Producers,* might at first seem an exception to the rule, as the story concerns itself with an odd couple of Broadway entrepreneurs. Even here, though, his heart is closer to the movies—and in this film, he redefined what movie comedy would become, in terms of taste and style.

The "producers" of the title are a sad, seamy pair. Max Bialystock (Zero Mostel) survives in show business by conning poor old women out of their lives' savings, giving them "one last thrill on the way to the cemetery." In the shocking opening sequence, a senile geriatric (Estelle Winwood) is, at length, pawed and caressed by Bialystock, even as he fleeces her out of her funds. "Hold me, touch me," she coos on and on and, in 1968, more than a few viewers rose and left the theater at once, unable to deal, at this point in time, with Brooksian humor. But the best (or worst!) was yet to come. Max is assaulted by one Leo Bloom (Gene Wilder), a nervous bookkeeper who gives Max an idea for the ultimate golden fleecing. Why not locate the world's

Gene Wilder and Zero Mostel consider the talents of Lee Meredith in *The Producers.*

"Springtime for Hitler." *(The Producers)*

worst play, one bound to be a flop, then oversubscribe backers? When the show closes on opening night, the two producers can run away with all the extra money they have solicited, and no one will be the wiser—since all the subscribers will assume their investment has been lost. "I want . . . I want . . ." Leo gasps as the two make plans by the Lincoln Center fountain at night, "everything I've ever seen . . . in the *movies!*"

That statement is Brooks' philosophy in a nutshell: even beneath Bloom's simple exterior, there beats a frustrated heart that longs for an escape from his quiet desperation into that wonderful fantasy world we experience—seemingly real—in the movies. The only possible downfall to their plan is, of course, the problem of the show being a hit—in which case they would have to pay off all those extra backers, and be ruined. To avoid this, they choose the most terribly tasteless play in the world: *Springtime for Hitler,* a musical written by a rabid fascist (he still wears a Nazi helmet) living in Yorkville, and a transvesite director who has never brought a play beyond rehearsal stage. For their star, they choose a hippie named LSD (Dick Shawn) whose mind is gone from drug use. Wonder of wonders, on opening night—as the pair gleefully await the angry audience they assume will come

storming out at any moment—they are instead faced by a hysterically happy crowd that takes all this as the new rage: Camp. According to the modern sensibility of the Sixties, the worse the taste, the better the play; Bialystock and Bloom are destroyed by the insane world of current culture, in which garbage can be enshrined as art.

Some viewers complained that Brooks' taste in *The Producers* was almost as lurid as the taste found in *Springtime for Hitler,* but the strong sense of vulgarity is only part of his total picture. Brooks scoffed at a world in which refined tastes are in a state of hibernation, and built his structure on our collective inability to judge by some standards of sanity. Everyone did agree that young Gene Wilder was one of the important new comic stars: Renata Adler of the *Times* described him as "Dustin Hoffman by way of Danny Kaye." As for Brooks' New York–based style of humor, it would be some time before the mass audience would catch up with him—and, in '68, *The Producers* flopped. But in 1974, when Warner Brothers released a gaudy Lucille Ball vehicle as their fiftieth anniversary package, and just barely threw Brooks' latest into release, they were astounded to find *Mame* showing to empty houses, while *Blazing Saddles* played to packed ones.

Mel Brooks coaches Zero Mostel in how to hold Estelle Winwood for the ''Hold me! Touch me!'' sequence in *The Producers*.

Zero Mostel with other inmates in *The Producers*.

Walter Matthau and Jack Lemmon in *The Odd Couple*.

THE ODD COUPLE

PARAMOUNT PICTURES

Produced by Howard W. Koch; screenplay by Neil Simon, based on his stage play; directed by Gene Saks.

CAST

Felix Unger (Jack Lemmon); *Oscar Madison* (Walter Matthau); *Vinnie* (John Fiedler); *Murray* (Herb Edelman); *Roy* (David Sheiner); *Speed* (Larry Haines); *Cecily* (Monica Evans); *Gwendolyn* (Carole Shelley)

Not all of the year's brilliant comedies were as offbeat as *The Producers*. Neil Simon proved he could provide his own odd couple—first on the Broadway stage, then in the context of a film adaptation. Simon has, unfortunately, been underrated as a competent gag man, a clever, commercial, high-level hack who churns out audience pleasers that ultimately add up to nothing more than a collection of lovely one-liners. On the surface his plays are, indeed, excellent as escapist entertainment. But Simon is, actually, the master of the sitcom form, and a writer who developed that genre to a very specific purpose. His plays contain, in the most unpretentious form possible, a strong social commentary: they all concern some aspect of the modern lifestyle, and what it does to people. They are also most deceivingly constructed because, despite the pleasant premises, plot always takes a backseat to characterization; the people are as thoroughly understood by the author as the ones in the most perceptive farces from Molière's to Ben Jonson's. Simon's characters are downright existential in their anguish, and the miracle is that they can be made to provide so much goodhearted laughter. None are richer in their humor and humanity than Oscar and Felix, the heroes of *The Odd Couple*.

As always, Simon bases his premise on a popular—indeed, almost stereotypical—situation of the times. In this case, two men (old poker pals, in fact) are both estranged from their wives, and attempt to join the single-swingers scene by rooming together. But the arrangement proves disastrous. Oscar Madison (Walter Matthau) is a garrulous sportswriter and a dedicated slob; Felix Unger (Jack Lemmon) is a hypochondriac, fussbudget, and gourmet cook. As the story progresses, each man's tolerance level for the other falters. Felix's constant mutterings about his wife cause Oscar to lose the chance of a swinger's lifetime with the ultimate English birds, the Pigeon Sisters (Monica Evans and Carole Shelley) by destroying the party mood and putting everyone into a thorough depression.

Jack Lemmon turned Felix into a variation of the character he played successfully in *Some Like It Hot, The Apartment,* and several other of his best pictures: a hypertense human being lost amid the unfeeling forces of modern society. And while some critics complained this was not the character as written by Simon (and played by Art Carney on Broadway), it was nonetheless a totally acceptable film actor's interpretation, as well as one of the most memorable performances in Lemmon's career. Matthau repeated the role he created on the stage and, with the success of *The Odd Couple,* finally moved from the character roles he'd been stuck in to full blown superstardom. Director Gene Saks virtually carved a career out of translating Neil Simon vehicles to the screen (he had served a similar function with the equally successful *Barefoot in the Park*) and with his effective, if unexceptional work, the picture came to life onscreen as a perfectly satisfying vehicle that offered two fine actors the roles of a lifetime, while continuing to assert Simon's status as the master of modern urban comedy.

Oscar meets the Pigeon Sisters. Carol Shelley, Walter Matthau, and Monica Evans. *(The Odd Couple)*

FUNNY GIRL
COLUMBIA PICTURES-RASTAR PRODUCTIONS

Produced by Ray Stark; screenplay by Isobel Lennart, based on her play and book; directed by William Wyler.

CAST

Fanny Brice (Barbra Streisand); *Nick Arnstein* (Omar Sharif); *Rose Brice* (Kay Medford); *Georgia James* (Anne Francis); *Florenz Ziegfeld* (Walter Pidgeon); *Eddie Ryan* (Lee Allan); *Mrs. Strakosh* (Mae Questel); *Branca* (Gerald Mohr); *Keeney* (Frank Faylen); *Mrs. Meeker* (Penny Santon)

Omar Sharif and Barbra Streisand in *Funny Girl*.

Barbra Streisand was the most unlikely star since Fannie Brice. Thus, it made perfect sense that Barbra reached stardom by playing Fanny in *Funny Girl:* the funny girl of the Sixties established herself by re-creating the funny girl of the Twenties. Streisand had already made her mark as an exciting new show business personality, thanks to a series of recordings which demonstrated the most perfectly pitched voice since the early Sinatra recordings in the Forties; a co-starring, scene-stealing role in *I Can Get It for You Wholesale,* a clever Broadway play which caught the eye of New York theatergoers; a number of club dates in Greenwich Village; and some spots on New York–based talk shows, in which she appeared as the worst-dressed woman in memory, an inveterate chain-talker, and a personality to be reckoned with. Her dream come true was star billing in a Broadway version of *Funny Girl.* But the final question was whether or not Streisand could make the jump to Hollywood, and rival Julie Andrews as the reigning queen of lavish musicals. Would the public that had just embraced a delicate, softspoken English lady also accept an overweight, slang spitting Jewish princess? As it turned out, Ms. Andrews' latest vehicles—*Star!* and *Thoroughly Modern Millie*—were bombing at the box office, as the public had already tired of her perky style. Streisand arrived at precisely the right moment: the changing scene of the late Sixties created a vacuum for new, offbeat stars—Jack Nicholson, Elliott Gould, Donald Sutherland, Steve McQueen, and Dustin Hoffman were even then beginning to make a strong impression in films—and Streisand provided the perfect female counterpart to them.

As a movie, *Funny Girl* left much to be desired. Though the sets were lavish and the songs (including the classic "People") lovely, the picture—as di-

236

Opposite page: A new kind of movie star: Barbra Streisand as Fanny Brice. *(Funny Girl)*

Last of the ''backstage musicals'': Barbra Streisand in rehearsal. *(Funny Girl)*

Drama as well as comedy: Barbra Streisand displays her dramatic intensity with Lee Allen in *Funny Girl*.

rected by old Hollywood hand William Wyler—suffered from many of the qualities of stage-bound stodginess that were causing such other expensively packaged musicals as *Finian's Rainbow* and *Camelot* to misfire in this era of new movie styles. But *Funny Girl* didn't end up a disaster like those other films, thanks mainly to its star. Some stage personalities cannot transplant their chemistry to the wide screen; Streisand conquered the new medium with ease, becoming the most important musical movie star since Judy Garland—and, a decade later, would go on to star in a modern remake of Garland's most famous vehicle, *A Star Is Born*. Pauline Kael put it better than anyone else when, in her *New Yorker* review, she declared: ''the 'message' of Barbra Streisand in *Funny Girl* is that talent is beauty . . . Barbra Streisand is much more beautiful than 'pretty' people.'' She was, of course, quite right. Essentially, the appeal of Streisand is the appeal of Bogart: the charisma of the ugly-beautiful person, whose conventionally unattractive fea-

238

tures are transformed by the magnetism of their personalities into a new definition of attractiveness. Part of the problem with the film is that her co-star, Omar Sharif, projected none of that quality; he failed to provide a man of equal interest to Streisand's heroine. *Funny Girl* might have been more successful if an idiomatic American tough guy actor—like Tony Curtis or Marlon Brando, both of whom turned down the role—had played Arnstein.

But Curtis and Brando were no fools: they knew instinctively that this was a one-woman show and, no matter how "right" they might have been for the part, they would be overshadowed by Streisand. Streisand also established a pattern that would most perfectly suit her, as the chutzpah-ish Jewish girl of great talent and·depth of personality who must, sadly, keep a constant vigil so that her more conventionally attractive mate does not leave her for a superficially attractive woman. It was a role Streisand would repeat often, most effectively in *The Way We Were,* with Robert Redford. Unfortunately, as she grew older in real life, the age of her screen characters decreased; as her face was taking on ever more character, she was seized by a desire to play one of those superficially pretty girls who had served as her foils in earlier pictures. A decade after *Funny Girl*—in *A Star Is Born*—Streisand made an embarrassment of herself by trying to portray a teenaged sex symbol. But she will, hopefully, be remembered for the *Funny Girl–Way We Were* roles which best express the star quality audiences responded to.

PRETTY POISON
20TH CENTURY–FOX

Produced by Marshal Backlar and Noel Black, with Lawrence Turman as executive producer; screenplay by Lorenzo Semple, Jr., based on the novel *She Let Him Continue* by Stephen Geller; directed by Noel Black.

CAST

Dennis (Anthony Perkins); *Sue Ann* (Tuesday Weld); *Mrs. Stepanek* (Beverly Garland); *Azenauer* (John Randolph); *Bud Munsch* (Dick O'Neill); *Mrs. Bronson* (Clarice Blackburn); *Pete* (Joseph Bova)

One of the strangest aspects of Hollywood casting is that very often, an actor is picked for a significant role because he seems so interestingly wrong for it, and then finds himself emerging from the film

as the new living symbol of that quality. James Cagney received the lead in *The Public Enemy* (1931) because, as a brash song 'n' dance man, he would make a more offbeat film gangster than the macho male types, but after that picture's release, he was shocked to find himself forever branded as the archetypal tough guy; James Stewart was chosen for the part of a cowboy in *Destry Rides Again* (1939) since it was generally agreed he (who had never done a western before) was the least likely leading man in Hollywood to portray a plainsman, though at once he became every bit as associated with the genre as John Wayne. Likewise, when Alfred Hitchcock cast Anthony Perkins as Norman Bates in *Psycho,* he did so out of the belief that Perkins—who had always played sensitive, clean-cut all-American boys—appeared the antithesis of a psychotic killer, thereby increasing the suspense in that audiences would never suspect him. But Perkins proved so perfect in the part that he at once found himself typed. Only once did he find a project in which the quality was as high as his first venture into neuroticism—a cult classic called *Pretty Poison.*

Anthony Perkins, in his best psycho role since *Psycho. (Pretty Poison)*

Anthony Perkins and Tuesday Weld in *Pretty Poison*.

Beverly Garland, Tuesday Weld, and Anthony Perkins in *Pretty Poison*.

The plot is a nightmare-come-true that captured the ambience of the Sixties. Dennis (Perkins), a paranoid with a strong penchant for extended, imaginative fantasies, wanders into a small New England town, where he grows obsessed with a pretty young cheerleader, Sue Ann Stepanek (Tuesday Weld), whom he befriends. Dennis quickly convinces Sue Ann that he is a C.I.A. spy and that a Communist ring is about to take over her village. Eagerly, Sue Ann joins him in a counterespionage movement—although it is never spelled out whether she actually believes him or just enjoys indulging in the fantasy. The great irony of the film is that her hometown is so mundane, so deadeningly quiet, in contrast to the amazing adventure they project on everything, and everyone, around them. The point is, Sue Ann has been so conditioned by spy movies—the James Bond, Matt Helm, Harry Palmer, and Our Man Flint series—along with their television counterpart, *The Man From U.N.C.L.E.*—that she is a helpless victim of the mass media, which have thoroughly programmed every young woman in every small town in America to half expect a double agent to enter her life and reveal that her neighbors are in fact enemy agents. *Pretty Poison* suggested that in the Sixties, even the most average person was in fact a potential paranoid, waiting for someone to pull the pin that would unleash the forces inside them. In the picture's most chilling sequence, the pretty little cheerleader calmly, calculatingly guns down her own mother

(Beverly Garland)—moving her tongue across her upper lip, *Lolita* style, as she does—so completely has she allowed herself to be drawn into the spy fantasy.

With *Pretty Poison,* Tuesday Weld found the role that established her as the unchallenged cult queen of the Sixties. Even as an overdeveloped twelve-year-old girl dancing wildly in the chorus line of exploitation flicks like *Rock, Rock, Rock,* she generated a special kind of chemistry. In the Sixties, Weld proved she could play a good girl (*The Cincinnati Kid,* with Steve McQueen) or a bad one (*Wild in the Country,* with Elvis Presley) with equal effectiveness. And yet it was her rejection of important roles that might have turned her into a great star—her conscious self-destructiveness, as it were—that made her an irresistible figure to movie buffs. She turned down the leads in varied films, from Stanley Kubrick's *Lolita* to Roman Polanski's *Macbeth,* and instead chose to do trash like *Return to Peyton Place* and *I'll Take Sweden.* A mark of her versatility as an actress can be seen by comparing two roles she turned down in 1969—the pre-teenage Mattie in *True Grit* and the bored, sophisticated middle-aged suburbanite in *Bob and Carol and Ted and Alice.* Those roles were played by Kim Darby and Dyan Cannon, respectively; the point is, neither of those actresses could even have been considered for the part in the other picture. Weld would have been as believable as the child as she would have as the woman, yet she cautiously avoided all pictures which smelled of success and instead concentrated on offbeat projects she felt assured would bomb at the box office. Of those, *Pretty Poison* stands as her most perfect vehicle.

THE GREEN BERETS

WARNER BROTHERS–SEVEN ARTS

Produced by Michael Wayne; screenplay by James Lee Barrett, based on the novel by Robin Moore; directed by John Wayne and Ray Kellogg.

CAST

Col. Mike Kirby (John Wayne); *George Beckworth* (David Janssen); *Sergeant Petersen* (Jim Hutton); *Sergeant Muldoon* (Aldo Ray); *Doc McGee* (Raymond St. Jacques); *Colonel Morgan* (Bruce Cabot); *Colonel Cai* (Jack Soo); *Captain Nim* (George Takei); *Jamison* (Patrick Wayne); *Sergeant Provo* (Luke Askew); *Lin* (Irene Tsu)

At first, there were only the newspaper reports, hinting at battles in the night and American casualties. But no one paid them much attention; they were, after all, bothersome—none of us wanted to believe we were involved in yet another operation as tedious and hopeless as the Korean conflict. Then, there were the first of the protests—isolated flag burnings by apparent crazies, heated diatribes against our government's "illegal" involvement in another country's civil war—all of which perplexed and disturbed the public at large. But then, how did one explain the ever escalating number of young men being called up for the draft? Or the reports of combat that were now making front page headlines and turning up as the lead stories on the six o'clock news? Or the contention that somehow, we had once again slipped into what amounted to an all-out war—only this time, without a formal announcement or national consensus, or even understanding as to who we were fighting and why. Americans sharply divided over the issue, so understandably Hollywood did not choose to mass produce propaganda films for the war cause, as it had during World War II. In fact, only one major film was then made about Viet Nam and, since it was to be the single example of super-patriotic cinema produced during the decade, director/star John Wayne amassed almost every cliché that had ever been used in a pro-war film of the past, assembling them all together into one anguished argument in favor of American involvement. Based loosely on Robin Moore's best-selling book *The Green Berets,* Wayne's picture was of course viewed as a stunning tribute to our fighting men by many, and as a fascist document by just as many others.

The film is presented as a Socratic argument between old-line soldier Mike Kirby (Wayne) and a weak-kneed liberal journalist, George Beckworth (David Janssen). He arrives in Viet Nam to cover the war with a wise guy chip on his shoulder, and immediately starts grumbling about American tactics. Through experience, he learns to see things differently. Colonel Kirby guides the naif through a long series of atrocities, showing the man firsthand how young American soldiers are tending orphaned children, as well as the old and homeless. American atrocities to the enemy (including the use of Punji sticks for torturous deaths) are adamantly defended, and opposition to any such tactics is scoffed at as mere bleeding heart meddling with the work of real men.

The sets for the film were incredibly unauthentic, so much so that the battlegrounds of Asia often

John Wayne: the Last Warrior. *(The Green Berets)*

John Wayne leads the Green Berets into action.

looked like a suburban backyard. There were ridiculous *Terry and the Pirates*–type adventure sequences, one of which featured a seductive woman who offers herself to an enemy guerrilla leader so that the Green Berets can capture the man and sport him off to headquarters at the end of a helicopter line. Like the decadent, insidious German officers in World War II films, the guerrilla leader is depicted as living in a mansion, enjoying a chauffeur-driven Citröen, feasting on caviar and champagne—and, naturally, breaking down into cowardly hysterics at the moment of the Americans' arrival. What had legitimized such cartooning of the enemy a quarter decade earlier was the feeling of unison among American audiences; we may have known, deep down, the Nazis and Japanese were not really like this, but it made us all feel good to go on believing they were. But in the schizophrenic state of the late Sixties, the effect was rendered embarrassing. The people who proved to be most of-

David Janssen rescues a wounded child in *The Green Berets*.

fended by the film were, ironically, those men who
had actually served in Viet Nam, and understood
the disservice such a patently phony picture was
doing by turning the very real world of jungle warfare into just another grand scale escapist fantasy
adventure, in which any American boy can easily
lick ten of the enemy.

At the film's end, the journalist admits his initial
ignorance, having had his "eyes opened" about
"what's *really* going on out there," promising to return to America and spread the word so that everyone might get behind the effort. That proved to be
wishful thinking on Wayne's part. In fact, most of
the liberal journalists who visited Viet Nam returned with, if anything, a stronger conviction that
we were engaged in a desperate, disillusioning
struggle, and the reports they filed in their papers
continued to stir more and more people to question
the validity of our current conflict.

244

Catherine Deneuve experiences decadence in *Belle de Jour*.

BELLE DE JOUR

ALLIED ARTISTS

Produced by Robert and Raymond Hakim; screenplay by Luis Buñuel and Jean-Claude Carrière, adapted from a novel by Joseph Kessel; directed by Luis Buñuel.

CAST

Séverine Sérizy (Catherine Deneuve); *Pierre Sérizy* (Jean Sorel); *Mme. Anais* (Genèvieve Page); *Henry Husson* (Michel Piccoli); *Renée* (Macha Mérill); *Hyppolite* (Francisco Rabal); *Marcel* (Pierre Clementi)

Luis Buñuel's *Viridiana* (1961) presented viewers with a novice nun who believes she has been raped by her uncle (she has not) and abandons the church in order to carry on religious principles in a secular society. But just as surely as her self-conception as a fallen woman has nothing to do with the reality of her situation, so are her attempts at humanistic endeavor (raising the level of the peasants) doomed to failure. Ultimately she is nearly raped by the very people she has dedicated her life to healing, and finally enters into a casual sexual relationship with her own cousin—while rock 'n' roll music replaces the Mass as the music which defines her life rhythms. *Viridiana's* journey from the church to "la dolce vita" stands as a symbolic representation of the popular odyssey of the 1960s. Buñuel's vision of the hopelessness of the human condition dated back to his early silent works, including *Un Chien Andalou*; but in the Sixties, he ceased to seem a perverse avant garde artist, and emerged as a spokesman for the times; in short, the world at large had caught up with Buñuel's vision.

Understandably then, in 1968 *Belle de Jour* won both popular and critical acclaim, since Buñuel's once controversial vision was now perfectly in tune with a public enraged over Viet Nam, exasperated over the new explicitness in films, and seized by a

The Lesbian influence: Catherine Deneuve and Genevieve Page in *Belle de Jour*.

Catherine Deneuve's latest lover inspects a photograph of her husband. *(Belle de Jour)*

A peephole on the world: Catherine Deneuve, in a shot that symbolizes the philosophy of *Belle de Jour*.

sudden popularity in anti-Establishment radicalism. First, it was erotic enough to lure viewers interested in the sudden sexual revolution in movies, as the new "X-rating" allowed for graphic nudity and even lovemaking sequences; though relatively tame by today's standards—with only mild nudity and a suggestion of the sex act rather than depictions of the act itself—*Belle de Jour* was nonetheless, in 1968, accepted by some audiences as elegant pornography. Second, it attracted the highbrow and college audiences who had come to regard Buñuel as a major film poet. Third, the film offered yet another example of the new international trend in cinema, wherein certain types of European movies which would have formerly been regarded as fit only for art house audiences were now being seen, and enjoyed, by a surprisingly large and broad public. *Blow-Up* had introduced Antonioni to viewers outside of the art house circuit, and *Belle de Jour* did the same for Buñuel.

Like *Blow-Up*, the film was based on the notion that all reality is subjective—perhaps the single most significant theme of the latter half of the decade—and the notion that all reality finally exists solely in the mind. At the film's beginning, we meet young Séverine (Catherine Deneuve), a beautiful and bored upper-middle-class housewife living in France. Henry (Michel Piccoli), an acquaintance, mentions the existence of a sophisticated but decadent bordello, to which Séverine immediately jour-

neys. There, she talks the prim and proper Madame (Geneviève Page) into giving her an afternoon job and, from that point on, the presumably frigid young woman spends all her days entering into the most unmentionable of acts with a strange assortment of men. Buñuel insists that reality is determined only by context; whether Séverine is frigid or a nymphomaniac can never be stated in any objective sense, but only by virtue of her current situation. She responds to people and places as a chameleon might, changing psychological colors to fit her environment—decadent in the whorehouse, cold in the home. At the same time, we are never (very) certain whether Séverine's journeys to the brothel are actual, or only fantasies. The point is, of course, that it doesn't matter. If all reality exists in the mind, and she mentally makes these journeys, then they are "real" for her. Thus, viewers who attempted to sort out Séverine's fantasies from her reality missed the point of the picture.

Buñuel makes the brothel itself a symbol, by having it appear to us as a cross between a respectable, upper-middle-class household and efficiently run business. Ultimately, the brothel becomes Buñuel's central symbol for the bourgeois lifestyle, a place where someone like Séverine is trapped part way between fantasy and reality. In a sense then, *Belle de Jour* is not so much a case study of one woman's own sexual odyssey as it is a parable for modern man's state of existence.

248

RACHEL, RACHEL

WARNER BROTHERS–SEVEN ARTS

Produced by Paul Newman; screenplay by Stewart Stern, based on the novel *A Jest of God* by Margaret Laurence; directed by Paul Newman.

CAST

Rachel Cameron (Joanne Woodward); *Nick Kazlik* (James Olson); *Mrs. Cameron* (Kate Harrington); *Calla Mackie* (Estelle Parsons); *Niall Cameron* (Donald Moffat); *Preacher* (Terry Kiser); *Hector Jonas* (Frank Corsaro); *Leighton Siddley* (Bernard Barrow); *Reverend Wood* (Geraldine Fitzgerald)

Rachel, Rachel represented an offbeat choice for Paul Newman's directorial debut. At a time when the hip young filmmakers were dealing with the powerful wave of cultural changes and necessarily experimenting with bizarre, surrealistic styles in order to suggest the paraphernalia of psychedelia onscreen, Newman instead chose to scrutinize middle America, looking closely at the people who were least affected by—and least aware of—the revolutionary forces electrifying the country. The setting was Small Town, USA, the emphasis on a thirty-five-year-old virgin (Woodward) who, at the halfway point in her life, takes her first lover (James Olson), finally comes to understand the latent lesbian attractions of her closest friend (Estelle Parsons), and at last escapes from the clutches of her domineering mother (Kate Harrington). Rachel is one of those middle-Americans the sexual revolution has bypassed, and her only "trip" comes in the form of a flight from her home, her job, and her life as a schoolteacher when, in the movie's closing sequence, she boards a bus headed for Oregon where she will attempt to make a new life for herself.

For Ms. Woodward, the role indicated a break with the kinds of parts she had played during the

Joanne Woodward as Rachel, leading her students through a flight of fantasy. *(Rachel Rachel)*

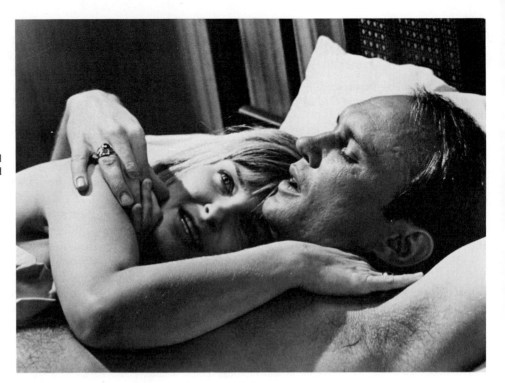

Sexual awakening without a sexual revolution: Joanne Woodward and James Olson in *Rachel Rachel*.

The old-fashioned way: Geraldine Fitzgerald in *Rachel Rachel*.

earlier portion of her career. In the Fifties she was forced into the glamor girl mold, as movie studios alternately tried to turn the obviously gifted actress into either another sophisticated blonde like Grace Kelly or else a slut goddess like Kim Novak. But despite such sex symbol roles, Woodward always seemed uncomfortable in the confines of Hollywood, a misplaced Broadway-based "serious" actress who clicked only once, in her memorable, Oscar-winning *The Three Faces of Eve*. *Rachel* opened up a whole new career for her, and at exactly that point when most Hollywood actresses begin their decline, Woodward's star started to rise. During the next decade, she would play a succession of troubled heroines, in films such as *Man in the Moon Marigolds* and *Summer Wishes, Winter Dreams*, becoming movieland's resident neurotic.

Rachel was not, by any means, a perfect film. For one thing, Newman displayed great difficulty in dealing with the fantasy sequences, which portray Rachel's inner life. Early in the film, all her fears are visualized: falling down in public, fainting in front of friends. Likewise, we see a vision of herself as she believes she ought to be—standing up to her school principal in defense of a misunderstood student, instead of letting the man torment the child. But these images were presented, then dropped, far too quickly: audiences were left wondering why they were introduced at all. Also, a final fantasy image, at the very end, was unnecessary: it was enough to offer us a portrait of Rachel boarding the bus and leaving the ennui of her small town, yet Newman went a step further by including a sugary, sentimental tableau of Rachel walking along a beach with children, as a possible "new life" for the character. Far more effective was the dramatic storytelling device which lent the film its offbeat title: Woodward's grown-up Rachel is, throughout the film, constantly replaced on screen by an image of "Rachel" as a child: in essence, there are two Rachels cohabiting: the mature Rachel who has not yet come into being and the adolescent Rachel who has not yet been left behind.

Understandably, then, when Rachel the woman boards the bus and leaves town, we see her waving goodbye to Rachel the child (played by Woodward and Newman's own daughter); Rachel is at last leaving behind the child she has remained for thirty-five years and moving out into the world in search of herself. Interestingly enough, in *Rachel, Rachel*, Paul Newman—hailed as the most macho of all film stars by many people—guided his wife through a softspoken, understated story of a woman's dilemma, thereby providing a film which presaged the Women's Movement in motion pictures.

I LOVE YOU, ALICE B. TOKLAS!

WARNER BROTHERS—SEVEN ARTS

Produced by Charles Maguire, with Paul Mazursky and Larry Tucker as executive producers; written by Paul Mazursky and Larry Tucker; directed by Hy Averback.

CAST

Harold (Peter Sellers); *Nancy* (Leigh Taylor-Young); *Mother* (Jo Van Fleet); *Joyce* (Joyce Van Patten); *Herbie* (David Arkin); *Murray* (Herb Edelman)

"I love you, Alice B. Toklas!" Peter Sellers exclaims after devouring a plateful of hashish brownies made from a recipe by the famous bohemian lady of letters; the line lent the film its improbable title, although in Europe, where a literal translation of the meaning was impossible, the picture was popularly known as *Kiss My Butterfly*, referring to a sensuous sequence in which Sellers enjoys the fruits of free love with his hippie girlfriend. The significant point is that these sequences would have been impossible to include in an American commer-

"Kiss my butterfly!" Leigh Taylor-Young and Peter Sellers in *I Love You, Alice B. Toklas.*

cial movie only a year or two earlier, and were suddenly a part of a major Hollywood project. Since *Blow-Up*, the Production Code had been disintegrating, and once controversial sequences—including "illicit" love scenes and illegal behavior—could be presented without eyebrows even being raised. In that same vein, *Alice* featured a significant breakthrough in terms of its treatment of hippiedom. Earlier epics had either been gentle, naive pleas for flower power, like *You Are What You Eat*, or drive-in quickies (*Psyche Out*) which exploited the emerging subculture by allowing viewers to vicariously enjoy love-ins and pot parties, then put such behavior down in a heavy moralistic ending. *Alice* scrupulously avoided either extreme, which helps explain why even today it stands as one of the few films of that era made about hippiedom that comes off as neither condescending nor propagan-

The straight life: Peter Sellers and Joyce Van Patten. (*I Love You, Alice B. Toklas*)

The hip life: Leigh Taylor-Young and Peter Sellers. (*I Love You, Alice B. Toklas*)

Queen of the hippies: Leigh Taylor-Young in *I Love You, Alice B. Toklas*.

distic—but is a clever, critical analysis of both the pleasures and the problems caused by the counterculture.

In the opening sequence, a neat, well-tailored, early-middle-aged Jewish lawyer (Sellers) is about to make his mother (Jo Van Fleet) extremely happy by marrying the nice girl (Joyce Van Patten) the family has picked for him. She is sincere, sweet, and—boring! At the altar, he finally realizes he cannot go through with the ceremony and live his life according to the pattern that has been set for him; suddenly, he turns and runs from this Establishment-oriented ceremony into the streets, where the flower people enjoy a freedom of personal and sexual experience that has been denied him thus far in his life. Before long, he can be seen sporting long hair, wearing love beads, and hawking copies of the Los Angeles *Free Press* on street corners. He also finds a beautiful hippie girl (Leigh Tayler-Young) to share his "pad." They smoke pot, make love, and live from sweet moment to moment. But this ecstasy ultimately proves to have its limitations. Flower power friends invade their apartment without warning and, in total freedom, we discover a surprising lack of freedom. His girlfriend's inability to commit herself to him in any way ultimately becomes unpleasant. "I like him—I like you too!" she says as a casual explanation for her sleeping with another man. "Isn't there *anybody* you don't like?" he complains. Finally, his basic middle-class values resurface; he wants his own apartment, not one that is a virtual commune; he wants things to be clean, not gloriously dirty; he wants occasional peace and quiet, not endless Grateful Dead records blaring on the stereo system; he wants a woman who loves him for himself, not just promiscuous free sex.

Understandably enough, the disillusioned dropout eventually drops out of the counterculture and returns to square, normal life. In the last sequence, we see him about to go through with the marriage ceremony after all. But that is where the film offers its surprise ending. Instead of the heavy-handed morality play—in which the protagonist can get away with indulgence in forbidden pleasures, as long as he returns repentant to the fold at the finale—he once again senses the constraints of the straight life that are closing in on him and, once again, bolts and runs. This time, however, he will not return to the counterculture, which he found equally unsatisfying; for it is no better or worse, in the final analysis, than what it presents an alternative to. Sellers is seen disappearing into the lonely crowd, laughing hysterically as he shouts: "I don't know where I'm going!" He has rejected all simple, easy solutions and pat, readymade answers; more important, so has the film itself.

253

BULLITT
WARNER BROTHERS–SEVEN ARTS

Produced by Philip D'Antoni; screenplay by Alan R. Trustman and Harry Kleiner, based on the novel *Mute Witness* by Robert L. Pike; directed by Peter Yates.

CAST

Bullitt (Steve McQueen); *Chalmers* (Robert Vaughn); *Cathy* (Jacqueline Bisset); *Delgetti* (Don Gordon); *Weissberg* (Robert Duvall); *Capt. Bennett* (Simon Oakland); *Baker* (Norman Fell)

Steve McQueen as the honest cop and Robert Vaughn as the politician who hampers his effectiveness in *Bullitt*.

Steve McQueen was born to be a star: the only problem was in discovering his "personality" onscreen. McQueen came very close to finding it early on in *The Magnificent Seven*, in which he played a young gunman with darting eyes that suggested an innate intelligence and a strong moral constitution. In *The Great Escape*, he proved he could do comedy, but too often McQueen found himself lost in pictures that negated, rather than expanded, his star potential. The ponderous anti-war picture *The War Lover* allowed him to be laconic without purpose; the moody *Baby, the Rain Must Fall* never allowed his chemistry to click; the misguided *Soldier in the Rain* had him mugging mercilessly and outacted by Tuesday Weld at every turn. But McQueen persevered, and the Hollywood studios stuck by him despite a string of duds. Then, even as Paul Newman's shining star began to dim, McQueen assumed a Newmanish stance and gave a striking performance in *The Sand Pebbles* as the kind of doomed loner Newman had been doing so well since the beginning of the decade. In *The Thomas Crown Affair*, he was matched with *Bonnie and Clyde*'s Faye Dunaway in a sophisticated crime caper that came off rather like a Sixties' version of *The Thin Man*. But by far, the film which most clearly established McQueen as the new box-office champ was a police thriller called *Bullitt*.

Even the title had its significance: for while the James Bond spy sagas were still doing well at the box office, there was a growing sentiment against the cold-blooded, ruthless types who never lost their cool, who sauntered with superficial grace through comic book situations, who dispensed with men as calmly as they seduced an endless line of beautiful women. The emotionless man had been presented as the new hero of our age, and if he was widely accepted as just that, there were still plenty of people who wistfully recalled the old Bogart hero

Jacqueline Bisset and Steve McQueen made a perfect romantic pairing for the late Sixties, as a swinging English bird and a nonconformist American man in *Bullitt*.

255

Opposite page: Steve McQueen as Bullitt.

of the Forties *film noir* classics—the detectives, policemen and even gangsters who walked down mean streets with a sense of duty and an aura of dignity, who could not kill without moral compunction or make love without some strong sense of commitment. In 1965, Paul Newman took Ross Mac-Donald's "Lew Archer" novel *The Moving Target* and turned it into an exquisite private eye picture, *Harper*, in which a vulnerable, fallible man found himself enmeshed in a sleazy situation instead of the Bondian tableaux of beautiful scenery and pluperfect sex objects. Just as McQueen had followed Newman's *The Hustler* with his own similar project, *The Cincinnati Kid*, so did he do his own turn on the single-named title character. In Bullitt's complex relationship with his girlfriend (Jacqueline Bisset), his deep commitment to his partner (Don Gordon), his friendly-enemy dealings with his own police captain (Simon Oakland) or his antipathy toward a corrupt bigwig (Robert Vaughn), McQueen projected an ardent stoicism that clearly hid an inner anguish; like Newman, he emerged as a kind of existential hero, suffering without complaining and following the dictates of his conscience despite endless obstacles.

While the plot of the picture was a conventional cops-and-robbers outing, the approach taken by the filmmakers gave it an immediate distinction. Director Peter Yates employed the most modern camera techniques to lend his film an elevated sense of action, projecting the audience into the San Francisco scene on a level that had not been possible before the new technical achievements that changed the form of filmmaking in the mid-Sixties. This was most obvious in the car chase sequence, up and down the Frisco hills, which was filmed with such an incredible sense of immediacy and edited so brilliantly that everywhere the picture played, some viewers found themselves sick to their stomachs in a way they had not been since the original *Cinerama* roller coaster ride. The sequence made such an

impact on viewers that it quickly became a conventionalized part of every police flick that followed, including producer Phil D'Antoni's followup, *The French Connection*, as well as dozens of lesser pictures. But if *The French Connection* featured the best of the car chase sequences, *Bullitt* delivered the first and therefore most memorable one. It also established McQueen as a star of the first order, a man who would make his mark on Hollywood pictures.

Steve McQueen in action. *(Bullitt)*

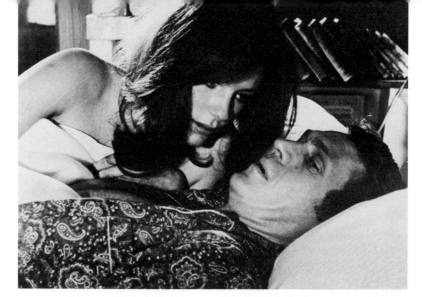
Jacqueline Bisset and Steve McQueen in
Bullitt.

ROMEO AND JULIET

PARAMOUNT PICTURES

Produced by Anthony Havelock-Allan and John Brabourne for Dino De Laurentiis; screenplay by Franco Brusati, Masolino D'Amico and Franco Zeffirelli, based on Shakespeare's play; directed by Franco Zeffirelli

CAST

Romeo (Leonard Whiting); *Juliet* (Olivia Hussey); *Friar Laurence* (Milo O'Shea); *Tybalt* (Michael York); *Mercutio* (John McEnery); *Nurse* (Pat Heywood); *Lady Capulet* (Natasha Perry); *Prince of Verona* (Robert Stephens)

The major problem in translating drama to the screen has always been destroying the heavy-handed act divisions and singleness of locale which dominates most theatrical work. Shakespeare, by all means, should be the easiest dramatist to film successfully: he used the scene, not the act, as his basic unit for plot development and, considering the abrupt changes of locale and wide diversity of action, his plays bear far more resemblance to a film scenario than they do to a modern work of the theater. Ironically enough, the successful Shakespearean films are few and far between. But in 1968, Italian filmmaker Franco Zeffirelli offered a new version of *Romeo and Juliet* which sparkled as brightly as any Shakespeare ever done on the screen.

After the prologue was solemnly recited while travelogue shots set the scene, audiences were whisked into the marketplace, where the ancient feud is first seen on the level of pranks between the servants, leading up the social chain until the heads of both households are involved. Shakespeare could not have asked for a more perfect visual metaphor for his perpetual theme as, in a matter of seconds, jokes turn into serious insults, and a prank undergoes an unintentional metamorphosis into pure chaos in the public streets.

Zeffirelli's cast was magnificent to behold. Pat Heywood, as the nurse, provided low comedy at its highest range of intelligence. Milo O'Shea, who already had tried his hand both at protagonist (Leopold Bloom in *Ulysses*) and antagonist (Jane Fonda's near-nemesis in *Barbarella*) found himself more at home as a character actor. Teenagers Leonard Whiting and Olivia Hussey didn't so much play Romeo and Juliet as they lived out the parts. Although each proved perfect in his role, Hussey

Leonard Whiting and Olivia Hussey: In Zeffirelli's production of the Shakespearean classic *Romeo and Juliet,* the two teenagers suggested the flower children of the Sixties, trying to find free love in spite of the Establishment and being destroyed by the Generation Gap.

Milo O'Shea and Olivia Hussey in
Romeo and Juliet.

Despite the modern implications of the story, Zeffirelli insisted on an authentic and dazzling costume design for *Romeo and Juliet*.

The duels in the street in *Romeo and Juliet* were filmed in a strikingly modern cinematic style, which helped lure young audiences into the theaters and let them realize that Shakespeare is not boring, when done properly.

was the standout of the two only because she looked to be precisely the right *person* for Juliet, while he was exactly the right *type* for Romeo. Whiting was natural, honest, and never ruined the show by trying to "act"; probably dozens of other young men could have fared as well. Hussey, however, seemed irreplaceable; in the balcony scene, her face changes in a matter of seconds from the innocent smile of a child to the mature stare of a woman. But rather than waste a great actor in the role of Romeo (the part doesn't demand one), Zeffirelli wisely saved his young talent for the part of Tybalt: Michael York brought the "prince of cats" to life, as his eyes burned with a brooding feline intensity and his ears actually seemed to be as pointed as Mr. Spock's.

Zeffirelli's most masterful touch came in his use of montage. Unlike so many modern moviemakers, who employed it promiscuously and continually in fear that their films might look either static or old-fashioned, Zeffirelli reserved it for the proper moments. At the Capulets' dance, the camera carries the viewer into the action with a pace which would have made even Richard Lester dizzy and the double duels occupy a central place in the pacing of this picture not unlike the chase sequence in *Bullitt*.

But the film's appeal went beyond aesthetic quality. During the opening days of the decade, Robert Wise, Leonard Bernstein, and Arthur Laurents had re-interpreted Shakespeare for the early Sixties by transplanting the star-crossed lovers to New York tenements in *West Side Story*; now, as the decade neared its end, Zeffirelli showed that *Romeo and Juliet* could prove equally relevant to the Free Love generation. Despite the exquisite period costumes, this 350-year-old tale appeared amazingly in tune with the current situation. Romeo, in his first appearance, is introduced as a flower child; Juliet as a naive teenager who has not yet been radicalized against the insensitivity of her elders. Never before had actual teenagers been permitted to play the protagonists, but in an era when *Hair* had become the most successful show on Broadway, it made sense that Romeo and Juliet were at last depicted as teenagers who want to drop out of the Establishment run by their parents. Their fight is with an unfeeling system and, by the end, they are destroyed by their idealistic actions. Zeffirelli's *Romeo* clicked clearly not only because of its admirable artistic qualities, but also because it re-interpreted a time-honored tale in light of what was happening to society in 1968.

THE KILLING OF SISTER GEORGE

CINERAMA RELEASING CORPORATION

Produced by Robert Aldrich; screenplay by Lukas Heller, from the play by Frank Marcus; directed by Robert Aldrich.

CAST

June Buckridge (Beryl Reid); *Alice "Childie" McNaught* (Susannah York); *Mercy Croft* (Coral Browne); *Leo Lockhart* (Ronald Fraser); *Betty Thaxter* (Patricia Medina); *Freddie* (Hugh Paddick)

With the advent of the new freedom of the screen came a rash of X-rated lovemaking scenes between men and women. Before very long, however, such confrontations lost their ability to shock and titillate. Filmmakers were quick to realize the direction which sex would now take in films, as lesbian love scenes suddenly surfaced as a cinematic turnon for both men and women in the audience. *Therese and Isabelle*, a handsomely photographed European export about two marvelously endowed roommates at an all-girl school and the gradual development of a physical relationship between them, proved amazingly popular; shortly thereafter, an adaptation of D. H. Lawrence's *The Fox* featured Academy Award winner Sandy Dennis coupled with Anne Heywood, thereby giving an aura of respectability to such woman-to-woman confrontations. But the film which most graphically explored—or, in the opinion of some critics, exploited—lesbians on the screen was *The Killing of Sister George*.

Based on the popular stage play by Frank Marcus, the story concerns June Buckridge (Beryl Reid), a stocky, matronly B.B.C. actress who jauntily goes to work every day, waving as she does to the legion of fans that recognize her as the self-sacrificing and courageous "Sister George" on a popular daytime soap opera. But one of her producers, Miss Mercy Croft (Coral Browne), suspects that, by night, the star may in fact be living a secret life as a lesbian, keeping a beautiful but psychologically disturbed child-woman, Alice McNaught (Susannah York), as her live-in lover. Realizing that if this relationship were to become known to the public the ensuing scandal would negatively affect the image of the B.B.C. in general, as well as the series in par-

Beryl Reid as Sister George. *(The Killing of Sister George)*

ticular, Miss Croft takes drastic measures. Her decision is to "kill off" the character of Sister George—as she drives her motorbike to the convent, she will be hit by a convenient truck—thereby ridding everyone of the problem. During the course of the action, though, Miss Croft exposes herself as a closet lesbian with plans of seducing "Childie."

The film version stuck reasonably close to the original play, save only for the final encounter between Mercy and Childie. At this point, the lovemaking that could only be suggested onstage was played in a long, graphic nude sequence. Of this scene, Renata Adler wrote in the New York *Times*: "There is a scene between Coral Browne … playing the seducing studio executive, and Miss York's left breast, which sets a special kind of low in the treatment of sex—any kind of sex—in the movies … Miss Browne approaches the breast with a kind of scholarly interest, like an icthyologist finding something ambivalent that has drifted up on the beach …

It is the longest and most unerotic, cash-conscious scene between a person and a breast that has ever been put on a screen, and outside of a surgeon's office."

That it was the longest and most cash-conscious goes without argument, but most moviegoers found the sequence—in which the camera shoots up and over York's breast at Browne's face, which takes on the look of one of those lush but pallid vampire women in a Hammer horror film about to plunge her teeth into the victim's neck but thoroughly enjoying, and not wishing to rush, the moment of anticipation—highly erotic and very kinky. The film is also interesting as an offbeat version of the sort of film Aldrich had first introduced in 1962 with *What Ever Happened to Baby Jane?* Now, the women are once again tearing away at each other, only in an updating of the situation for the late Sixties, Aldrich gave the conflict an appropriately commercial lesbian approach.

262

Dominance: Beryl Reid and Susannah York. (*The Killing of Sister George*)

Submission: Beryl Reid and Susannah York. (*The Killing of Sister George*)

High Camp: Susannah York and Beryl Reid mimick Laurel and Hardy in *The Killing of Sister George*.

1969

MIDNIGHT COWBOY

UNITED ARTISTS

Produced by Jerome Hellman; screenplay by Waldo Salt, based on the novel by James Leo Herlihy; directed by John Schlesinger.

CAST

Ratso (Dustin Hoffman); *Joe Buck* (Jon Voight); *Cass* (Sylvia Miles); *Mr. O'Daniel* (John McGiver); *Shirley* (Brenda Vaccaro); *Towny* (Barnard Hughes); *Sally Buck* (Ruth White); *Gretel McAlbertson* (Viva)

Instead of an authentic western hero, the focus of *Midnight Cowboy* is on a would-be flimflam man, a naive but hopeful con artist. Joe Buck (Jon Voight) leaves his small town in Texas and travels, by bus, to New York, where he believes his boyish charm and cowboy clothes will make him a hit with the frustrated but wealthy city women, who should be more than willing to pay for his services. Buck's initial optimism is short-lived; classy women cut him dead on the street and the only lady he manages to score with not only fails to pay, but takes most of his meagre funds as "cab fare." Finally, out of sheer desperation, Buck throws in his lot with Enrico "Ratso" Rizzo (Dustin Hoffman), a dying tubercular and street hustler who has thus far survived in the urban no-man's-land of modern Manhattan, and dreams of journeying south to the warm climate of Florida. Together, they move into a deserted, condemned apartment building and, before long, the two unlikely companions have formed a relationship of depth and dignity.

Essentially, *Midnight Cowboy* was, like *Rachel, Rachel*, a film about loneliness. On the surface, sexuality appeared to be the central question as, in order to survive, Buck degenerates from a Park Avenue stud for women in fancy apartments to a 42nd Street hustler of men in rundown movie houses. His sexual fall from grace was underlined by director John Schlesinger in flashbacks which concerned his brutal relationship with an oversexed girlfriend and an earlier, even stranger tie to his flamboyant grandmother. This was underscored later when Ratso insists Joe's cowboy garb proves more attractive to homosexuals than women: Buck retaliates by cruelly suggesting the cripple has never known a woman in his life. The action comes to a head when, after picking up the first woman who is quite willing to pay for his services at a Warholesque

The oddest couple of them all: Jon Voight as the Texas cowboy who teams up with Dustin Hoffman as a denizen of New York's lowlife in *Midnight Cowboy*.

Joe Buck (Jon Voight) confronts Ratso Rizzo (Dustin Hoffman) and demands the return of his stolen money in *Midnight Cowboy*.

party to which he has been invited by accident, Joe finds himself unable to perform in bed. Only when the girl suggests he is perhaps gay and unaware of it is Buck able to finish the job, and then more in a spirit of anger than sensuality. At this point, the audience began to wonder about Joe also: was he really the happy-go-lucky fool we believe him to be when he sets out for New York or rather a deeply troubled man, subconsciously trying to prove something to himself by first proving it to the world around him?

Finally, Joe Buck's position approaches something akin to full tragedy when, at the end, he is left on the Florida bound bus, holding the recently deceased Ratso's body in his arms. Death comes over Ratso quickly and, in fact, could only be considered a blessing: he is at last free of the crippled body, the growing pain, and worst of all the truth that waited for him at the end of the trip: Florida would have come no closer to fulfilling his dream than New York came to fulfilling Joe Buck's. Just as the film began with Joe's symbolic journey it ends with Ratso's; the difference is, Ratso is spared the humiliation of discovering the truth.

The role of Ratso won Dustin Hoffman his sec-ond Academy Award nomination and, while he did not win the trophy, he nonetheless proved his acting abilities to anyone who wondered if *The Graduate* was nothing more than a one-shot. After that film's surprising popularity, Hoffman had at once been offered a dozen Benjamin Braddock–type roles, and was smart enough to turn them all down—realizing that to repeat himself would provide momentary success while ensuring eventual oblivion. Instead, he chose a more risky but ultimately more satisfying route, proving himself as an actor; at the time, audiences were shocked to find the clean-cut youth of *The Graduate* playing a dirty, wasted, aging man. But his artfulness at playing the role assured his lasting stardom as a character lead. Even more significant, the film—originally stamped with an X-rating owing to its nude scenes and overall theme—received the Best Picture of the Year Oscar. Though the X-rating was soon removed (the film was relatively mild, in comparison to what would soon follow!), it was nonetheless a highly mature project, and its acceptance symbolized both the Academy's and the public's acknowledgment that, for better or worse, filmmaking in America had changed.

Would-be stud Joe Buck (Jon Voight) tries his luck with a New York woman (Brenda Vaccaro), who turns out to be a far more experienced wheeler-dealer than he. *(Midnight Cowboy)*

TRUE GRIT

PARAMOUNT PICTURES

Produced by Hal Wallis; screenplay by Marguerite Roberts, based on the novel by Charles Portis; directed by Henry Hathaway.

CAST

Rooster Cogburn (John Wayne); *Le Boeuf* (Glen Campbell); *Mattie Ross* (Kim Darby); *Emmett Quincy* (Jeremy Slate); *Ned Pepper* (Robert Duvall); *Moon* (Dennis Hopper); *Goudy* (Alfred Ryder); *Stonehill* (Strother Martin); *Tom Chaney* (Jeff Corey)

At Long Last Oscar: John Wayne as Rooster Cogburn in *True Grit*.

The members of the Motion Picture Academy of Motion Picture Arts and Sciences managed to split their Oscars for films made during 1969 in a surprisingly felicitous manner. On the one hand they acknowledged the changing face of film by honoring an X-rated picture, *Midnight Cowboy*, as Best Picture. But when it came time to name Best Actor of the Year, the Academy waxed sentimental. There was little doubt in anyone's mind that, even as the majority of the 1969 awards were being passed out to significant new pictures, a very special Oscar would be reserved for the man whose work had, for years, been so natural in its appeal that we had made the mistake of taking it for granted.

True Grit was based on a popular and critically acclaimed short novel by Charles Portis, which concerned a young orphan named Mattie Ross (Kim Darby) who seeks revenge for the death of her parents by a band of killers. Mattie takes up with an egotistic young Texas Ranger (Glen Campbell) and a crusty, conniving old deputy marshal, Rooster Cogburn (John Wayne). The great appeal of the novel derived from Portis' carefully controlled narrative voice: the entire tale is told from the point of view of Mattie, as the less than bright woman puts down her reminiscences about the event on paper at a later date; the book's vast appeal came, as in Mark Twain's classic *Huckleberry Finn*, from the charming quality of the naivete, the high tone Mattie assumes for her story and the vast difference between the way she describes past happenings and the way in which we implicitly understand they must have happened. The book's humor, warmth, and style were all inherent not so much in the story itself, but in the way that story was told.

All of that was, of course, lost in the translation

to the screen. Worse still, filmmaker Henry Hathaway chose to retain the book's constant use of "elevated" dialogue, the effect being that characters were allowed to speak as if they were figures out of a nineteenth-century pulp novel. This might have been played to good effect if the film itself were in some way visually stylized, and audiences were made aware the story was taking place in a literary fairytale conception of the dimly remembered West rather than the actual frontier of history. But the on-location shooting in California and Colorado lent the picture a realism of background which clashed terribly with the stylization of the lines. Hathaway and Wayne were able to salvage only one scene: the climactic moment when Cogburn, holding his horse's reins in his teeth and packing a gun in each hand, rides at the killers like the last of the old knights, out to do battle with the forces of evil around him.

One could easily amass a list of the films for which Wayne *should* have won an Oscar: his idealistic outlaw Ringo in *Stagecoach* (1939), his obsessed cattle baron in *Red River* (1948), his fair-minded cavalry officer in *She Wore a Yellow Ribbon* (1949), his inwardly troubled loner in *The Quiet Man* (1952), and his racist Civil War vet in *The Searchers* (1956) are among the standout performances not only in his career, but in the history of the cinema. Wayne knew his own limitations; he once asserted: "When people ask me if I think I'm a good actor, I just reply, 'What I'm doing isn't acting

No generation gap Here! John Wayne and Kim Darby in *True Grit*.

The Duke in action in *True Grit*.

at all. It's reacting. I react for the camera.'" He stands, in the final analysis, as the greatest of the old stars if only because he, among them, survived the longest; and the success of *True Grit* proved that, even in 1969, when youthful moviegoers were interested in taking trips on *The Yellow Submarine* and running wild with *Joanna,* there was still a large audience that believed in the old values once enshrined by dozens of Hollywood stars—of whom Wayne was the final example. No wonder, then, that even if *True Grit* does not hold up as one of Wayne's best pictures or best performances, the Academy chose, at the end of this most turbulent decade in its history, to honor the most venerable, if least versatile, of its great stars.

THE WILD BUNCH
WARNER BROTHERS–SEVEN ARTS

Produced by Phil Feldman; screenplay by Walon Green and Sam Peckinpah, based on a story by Walon Green and Roy N. Sickner; directed by Sam Peckinpah.

CAST

Pike (William Holden); *Dutch* (Ernest Borgnine); *Thornton* (Robert Ryan); *Sykes* (Edmond O'Brien); *Lyle Gorch* (Warren Oates); *Hector Gorch* (Ben Johnson); *Angel* (Jaime Sanchez); *Menacing Man* (Albert Dekker); *Kid Outlaw* (Bo Hopkins); *Thornton's Companions* (Strother Martin, L. Q. Jones)

In 1962, Sam Peckinpah opened the decade, so far as westerns were concerned, with *Ride the High Country*, a wistful, nostalgic, but never unduly sentimental backward glance at the last days of the open frontier. One way of truly appreciating the changes which the country—and, necessarily, Hollywood—underwent during the intervening decade is to compare that film with Peckinpah's *The Wild Bunch*, the last great western of the period and, importantly, one that looks back at the same turn-of-the-century setting. *The Wild Bunch* apotheosized the violence of an era that barraged us from our city streets and TV news broadcasts of Viet Nam into an epic—and cathartic—unleashing of gore.

The complexity of Peckinpah's vision was clear from the title sequence, in which he introduces four symbolic sets of characters. First, there is the Wild Bunch itself, who ride into the Texas-Mexican border town of San Rafael, disguised as Pershing's expeditionary force out searching for Pancho Villa, and looking like men of the law, rather than out-

William Holden as Pike in *The Wild Bunch.*

269

William Holden and Jaime Sanchez (center) are surprised by *federales* in *The Wild Bunch*.

laws, in their uniforms. Then there are the railroad agents and law enforcement officials, who lie in wait to ambush the Wild Bunch when they attempt to rob the town, and prove themselves every bit as corrupt as the outlaw faction by refusing to warn the endangered citizens about the possible crossfire for fear of giving away their plans. There is the Silent Majority of the city, those middle-Americans who are holding a temperance meeting and parade, marching down the center of town and into the upcoming crossfire between outlaws who look like lawmen and lawmen who act like outlaws. And finally, there is a small group of children at play, who gleefully toss a live scorpion onto a hill full of red ants, and watch the results with demonic glee. The children symbolize the audience watching the film since, once the shooting starts and the action onscreen becomes a terrifying yet, in a strange way, visually beautiful blood bath, we find ourselves in the uncomfortable position of associating with them.

A group portrait: the Wild Bunch.

The question of excessive violence in films was raised at the very onset of the decade, with Hitchcock's *Psycho*, but it did not reach extreme controversy until *Bonnie and Clyde*'s much discussed finale, termed a "ballet of blood" by many critics. *The Wild Bunch* featured an even stronger ending: like *Bonnie and Clyde*, it employed extensions and compressions of time, stop action and slow motion photography, rapid intercutting and repetition of scenes in order to create a totally stylized—and frightfully poetic—experience. Yet the word "excessive" seems wrong, because the filmmaking perfectly fits Peckinpah's conception: the last of the old-time outlaws are anachronistic nonheroes, worthy of tragic stature, and to depict their deaths in a realistic manner would be to cinematically deny their importance. They must go out in the ultimate blaze of glory, and they do. The pity was that so many lesser filmmakers picked up on the style. Within a year, almost all action films contained equal amounts of graphic violence that, in most cases, served no clear purpose but to titillate, in the cheapest manner possible. Peckinpah's film was not so much a violent movie as a movie *about* violence.

The Wild Bunch did have its flaws. Most notably, the relationship between the gang's leader, Pike (William Holden), and his one-time sidekick Thornton (Robert Ryan), now manipulated by the government into tracking down his best friend, is never clearly developed. Still, it rates as one of the great, landbreaking westerns. The Mexican settings were beautifully captured in the film's vivid photography, and one particular sequence—the dynamiting of a bridge with horses and men on it—rates as one of the most spectacular set pieces ever created for a western film. At the same time that *True Grit* tipped its hat to the past traditions of the American western movies, *The Wild Bunch* waved a frantic hello to a new set of rituals that would revolutionize the western film.

William Holden in trouble. *(The Wild Bunch)*

The mystique of the outlaw: Paul Newman and Robert Redford as Butch Cassidy and the Sundance Kid.

BUTCH CASSIDY AND THE SUNDANCE KID

20TH CENTURY–FOX

Produced by John Foreman; screenplay by William Goldman; directed by George Roy Hill.

CAST

Butch Cassidy (Paul Newman); *The Sundance Kid* (Robert Redford); *Etta Place* (Katharine Ross); *Percy Garris* (Strother Martin); *Bike Salesman* (Henry Jones); *Sheriff Bledsoe* (Jeff Corey); *Woodcock* (George Furth); *Agnes* (Cloris Leachman); *Harvey Logan* (Ted Cassidy)

The cult of the outlaw proved one of the more significant movie themes of the Sixties, and in

Butch Cassidy and the Sundance Kid, audiences experienced one of the most delightful variations on that theme. It was inevitably compared with both Arthur Penn's *Bonnie and Clyde* and Sam Peckinpah's *The Wild Bunch*, in that it chronicled the last days of a group of anachronistic highwaymen. But the difference between *Butch Cassidy* and either of those other films was one of mood, texture, and tone. Significantly, both the Barrow Gang and the Wild Bunch are destroyed in a barrage of the very violence they perpetrate throughout; it was an intended irony that Cassidy and the Kid kill no one until they make an attempt to go straight.

Instead of violence, the film made extensive use of comedy, supplied by screenwriter William Goldman. Most writers of westerns work hard to make their films sound as rural as possible; the only word that correctly describes the feeling of *Butch Cassidy* is "urbane," and the results were what might have been achieved if Neil Simon penned a cow-

272

boy story. Director George Roy Hill and Goldman clearly understood that the western is the most cliché ridden of all movie genres and, instead of attempting to demolish those clichés as Peckinpah did in *The Wild Bunch*, they treated them instead with a combination of reverence and wit. Time and again, *Butch Cassidy* begins to execute an old cliché and, at the last possible moment, shatters it.

For example: the town's prim and proper schoolmarm (Katharine Ross) returns to her house one night and begins to slip out of her clothes. Suddenly, she jumps back with a scream of fright, for sitting in her bedroom is Sundance. He draws his pistol, cocks it, and commands her to continue stripping. When she has finished, he rises and approaches the woman, evidently about to force himself upon her. "You know what I wish?" she asks sadly. At this point, it seems unnecessary for her to continue; we already know what she wishes. We've heard it countless times before, in dozens of old movies. She wishes he only knew how sorry she feels for him, how she pities him. That's what our ears are ready to hear; we imagine we *do* hear it, even before she speaks again. "I wish for once you'd get here *on time*," she chides, shoving her tongue into his mouth.

Or better yet: again, night. Cassidy and the Kid are in trouble: a posse is closing in on the hotel where they are hiding out. Quickly, the two slip out the window and over the rooftops. Shades of Henry Fonda and Ty Power as the James boys. Jumping down, they prepare to mount their horses for a getaway. Cassidy sees the posse's horses at a hitching post, only we are one step ahead of him. He is going to shoo them away before escaping himself. "Haaaaaa!" Cassidy screams at the animals, waving his hands wildly in the air; they stand perfectly still, staring at him as though he's lost his mind.

Whereas both the Barrow Gang and the Wild Bunch learned something by the end of their pictures and that, coupled with the graphic way in which their deaths were depicted, was why those films upset audiences so, Butch and Sundance are as lovably stupid at the end as they were at the beginning. Our final reaction turned out to be not an emotional one to their deaths, but a last laugh at their inability to comprehend the reality of the situation around them. In the moment just before death, the non-heroes are suddenly frozen by the camera for all time, allowing the audiences to walk out smiling. The role of Butch allowed Paul Newman to close out his reign as superstar of the Sixties with one of his finest performances. Redford had been acting in pictures since the early Sixties, but despite

his strong screen presence, never really clicked until *Butch Cassidy*. Together, they incarnated one of the great male teams, kicking off a spurt of buddy-buddy movies that would often imitate, but never equal, the success of what may be the most charming western ever made.

Katharine Ross, Paul Newman, and Robert Redford in *Butch Cassidy and the Sundance Kid.*

Robert Redford and Paul Newman: the ultimate buddy-buddy team. *(Butch Cassidy and the Sundance Kid)*

Jane Fonda and Michael Sarrazin: marathon as metaphor. *(They Shoot Horses, Don't They?)*

THEY SHOOT HORSES, DON'T THEY?

CINERAMA RELEASING CORPORATION

Produced by Irwin Winkler and Robert Chartoff; screenplay by James Poe and Robert E. Thompson, based on the novel by Horace McCoy; directed by Sydney Pollack.

CAST

Gloria (Jane Fonda); *Robert* (Michael Sarrazin); *Alice* (Susannah York); *Rocky* (Gig Young); *Sailor* (Red Buttons); *Ruby* (Bonnie Bedelia); *Rollo* (Michael Conrad); *James* (Bruce Dern); *Turkey* (Al Lewis); *Cecil* (Severn Darden)

Horses concerned the dance marathon, that amazingly degrading cross between a contest and a show which flourished during the height of the Great Depression—a period which, in the intensity of its desperation, seemed peculiarly relevant in the equally intense and desperate late Sixties. The setting is the Pacific Ballroom in Los Angeles, but instead of introducing any documentary style footage of the nation racked by poverty, director Sydney Pollack wisely chose to keep us confined in the huge ballroom until the tone and atmosphere of the film became, quite purposefully, claustrophobic. "Yowsa, yowsa, yowsa," the master of ceremonies (Gig Young) roars into a microphone, as the contestants dance on like the mechanical dolls which, by the end of the marathon (and the movie), they have been reduced to. "Round and round we go— one couple only will walk out carrying the grand prize. But isn't that the American way?"

The American way—the *traditional* American way. Never had it been so severely criticized in films as in the late Sixties. Pollack here succeeded in making the marathon a mammoth symbol for life itself, mainly by *not* insisting on it as an abstract metaphor but rather by inebriating us with the concrete experience of the event. The partners dance endlessly in each other's arms until the master of ceremonies grants them a few minutes of unsatisfying sleep, or runs them around in a circle for ten minutes, the last three couples being eliminated from the contest. It thus became our job to extract the message that there are no winners in life, only losers and survivors.

As "Gloria," Jane Fonda finally managed to escape the Vassar girl vocal patterns that had made her so perfect in films like *Sunday in New York* and

Michael Sarrazin and Jane Fonda in *They Shoot Horses, Don't They?*

Barefoot in the Park, but had kept her from being taken seriously as an actress of any depth or variety. Her Academy Award nomination firmly established her as a major star, as well as a forceful young movie presence who reminded many viewers of Bette Davis forty years earlier. Interestingly, audiences at the time considered Fonda's short haircut as a necessity for the role. They missed her long, beautiful hair from *Barbarella* but assumed that, in her next role, Jane would be back to her normal self—extraordinarily beautiful. How surprised they were when it turned out this was "the *new* Jane Fonda"—as an anti-war and pro-Women's Movement activist, she would shun her own classy beauty for the next half decade; then, in the late Seventies, she would strike a fascinating compromise halfway between the two, once again beautiful but maintaining her strong political convictions.

The concept of "the movies" forms an important motif within the film and at the marathon itself. The most obvious example is the way in which Susannah York's character makes herself look as much like Jean Harlow as she can, in hopes the American Dream of being discovered by a Hollywood talent scout might come true. At one point, the master of ceremonies claims to recognize producer Mervyn Le Roy in his audience. Also, Fonda has been

Al Lewis, Gig Young, in his Oscar-winning role in *They Shoot Horses, Don't They?*

Red Buttons and Gig Young in *They Shoot Horses, Don't They?*

276

Michael Sarrazin, Jane Fonda, and Bruce Dern in *They Shoot Horses, Don't They?*

forced into the marathon because of a hassle at central casting which keeps her from making a living as a movie extra. As she dances emotionlessly with Michael Sarrazin, he keeps his mind off their miserable condition by describing in detail a lurid love scene between Anita Louise and Richard Cromwell he once saw. Even the scenery of the marathon correctly reflects America's preoccupation with the movies: one huge poster advertises *Grand Hotel*, while another selling soap proudly pictures Barbara Stanwyck stating, "I prefer it."

The dance marathon may have been an immediate form of American opium which failed to survive, but the movies were just then evolving into a more basic rainbow pattern in the American Dream. Ironically, in the very year that *Horses* represented the roots of movies in American life, the major studios were going bankrupt and auctioning off everything from Judy Garland's slippers from *The Wizard of Oz* to Vivien Leigh's dress from *Gone With the Wind*. Perhaps that is the greatest distinction between the desperate days of the Depression and the even more desperate days of the late Sixties; in the Thirties, we at least had the fantasy image of Hollywood movies to make us feel a sense of community; in 1969, we had lost even that.

ALICE'S RESTAURANT
UNITED ARTISTS

Produced by Hillard Elkins and Joe Manduke; screenplay by Venable Herndon and Arthur Penn, inspired by "The Alice's Restaurant Massacre" record by Arlo Guthrie; directed by Arthur Penn.

CAST

Arlo (Arlo Guthrie); *Alice* (Pat Quinn); *Ray* (James Broderick); *Shelly* (Michael McClanathan); *Roger* (Geoff Outlaw); *Mari-chan* (Tina Chen); *Karin* (Kathleen Dabney); *Officer Obie* (William Obanhein); *Pete Seeger* (Himself); *"Groupie" Reenie* (Shelley Plimpton)

As the Viet Nam War escalated, popular culture reflected the wave of protest growing ever more prevalent among America's young people. By far, the most popular protest song was "Alice's Restaurant," Arlo (son of Woody) Guthrie's walking-talking blues ballad. The song told a good-natured tale from Arlo's own personal experience, in which he enjoyed a Thanksgiving dinner with some friends, dumped the garbage afterwards, and was arrested for littering. Some time later, the presence of that conviction would save him from dreaded induction into the army: because of his criminal record as a litterbug, he was proclaimed morally unfit to serve. Arthur Penn, fresh from his success with *Bonnie and Clyde*, announced plans to make a feature-length film inspired by the song: Penn conceived of the initial idea as a springboard for bigger things, and employed Arlo's ballad as a framework for a tale of the creation of the first authentic "hippie commune."

Penn added extensive episodes drawn from Arlo's life: his early encounter with the draft board, an unhappy stay at college as a music student, singing engagements in New York cellar clubs, various hitchhiking trips, and beatings at the hands of locals who resented the length of his hair. In New York, Arlo turns down a sexual offer from a sniffling, apathetic fourteen-year-old (Shelley Plimpton); she had the dubious distinction of being the first "groupie" to appear onscreen. Equally effective is another scene in which Arlo visits his father, stretched out on a hospital bed and dying of Hodgkins disease. The actual event had taken place only about two years before Penn staged it for his film: here Arlo and Pete Seeger played themselves, while an actor portrayed the deceased Woody.

Arlo Guthrie as himself in *Alice's Restaurant*.

James Broderick as Ray Brock in *Alice's Restaurant*.

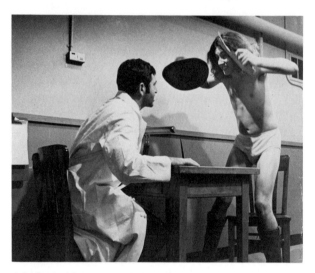

Arlo flunks his army medical examination. *(Alice's Restaurant)*

Officer Obie questions Arlo and fellow hippie. *(Alice's Restaurant)*

Ray and Alice Brock, peripheral characters in the song, quickly emerged as the true focus of the film. We witness their buying a deconsecrated church, gradually turning it into a youth commune for the kids they have come into contact with and cannot let go of, then building the diner called "Alice's Restaurant" to finance the commune. Fortunately, Penn and Guthrie chose not to romanticize the two characters, who could easily have been portrayed as pseudo-saints. The Brocks, we eventually see, were not so much generous as greedy; what appears at first as free love for everybody turns out to be something far more akin to a means of possession. Alice (Pat Quinn) is a compulsive teaser and seducer of young men. When a rehabilitated drug addict named Shelly comes to the church to work on his mobiles and ride his cycle, she pounces on him with the speed of a praying mantis in heat. Ray is no different: Alice quickly matches Arlo up with a girl who, it turns out, has become the object of Ray's interests. Far more serious (and dangerous) than this, however, is Alice's bitchiness and Ray's tendency to fall back on his muscles as a solution to the problems that arise. A pair of emotional cripples, they believe they are doing their best to rehabilitate Shelly while, between the two of them, they manage to destroy him completely by the picture's end—almost destroying themselves in the process.

Arthur Penn's films of the Sixties were, on the surface, about a wide variety of subjects: the 1930s Depression era robbers of *Bonnie and Clyde* may seem pretty far removed from the 1970s hippie subculture living in the Stockbridge, Massachusetts, commune. What Penn brings to his pictures, though, is a basic understanding of life's outlaws, and in each of his films, he deals with some variation of that theme. In *Alice*, Penn didn't so much study the hippie subculture for its own sake (as Arlo had done in his song) but as the latest version of outlaw mentality. Penn cut through all the chic and glamor surrounding the hippies, refusing to either attack or defend them, but instead probing behind the facade of free love and flower power, proving there existed people every bit as ambiguous as those found in the square life.

BOB & CAROL & TED & ALICE
COLUMBIA PICTURES

Produced by Larry Tucker; screenplay by Paul Mazursky and Larry Tucker; directed by Paul Mazursky.

CAST

Carol (Natalie Wood); *Bob* (Robert Culp); *Ted* (Elliott Gould); *Alice* (Dyan Cannon); *Horst* (Horst Ebersberg); *Psychiatrist* (Donald F. Muhich); *Leader of Consciousness Raising Seminar* (Greg Mullavey)

Films like *Alice's Restaurant* were now dealing openly with the effect that the changes in society had on the youth of the nation. But it yet remained for a film to study the shifting lifestyles of early middle-aged people who tried to embrace both the new morality and the youth revolution, attempting to reorder their lifestyles to fit in with the breezy image of how liberated people ought to behave. The film that filled this vacuum was *Bob & Carol & Ted & Alice*, an updating of the Doris Day comedies that had flourished during the first half of the decade, then disappeared when, in 1967, the radical changes going on around us made such pictures seem suddenly obsolete.

Bob (Robert Culp) and Carol (Natalie Wood) return from a consciousness-raising retreat in the mountains with a new outlook on life. They have experimented with the fashionable group encounter sessions, and are now ready to liberate themselves from their old, uptight attitudes by smoking pot and openly enjoying extramarital affairs. When they relate this to their dearest, oldest friends, Ted (Elliott Gould) and Alice (Dyan Cannon), they are surprised to find the two are shocked and outraged by the disclosure. Ted still wears ties and button-down

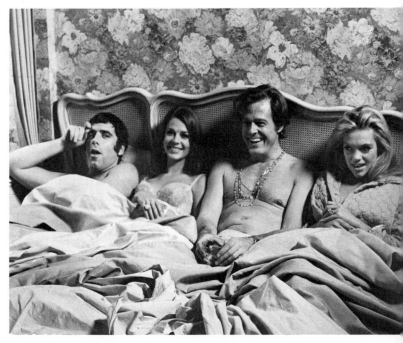

The Sexual Revolution: Elliott Gould, Natalie Wood, Robert Culp, and Dyan Cannon in *Bob and Carol and Ted and Alice*.

Robert Culp and Elliott Gould in *Bob and Carol and Ted and Alice*.

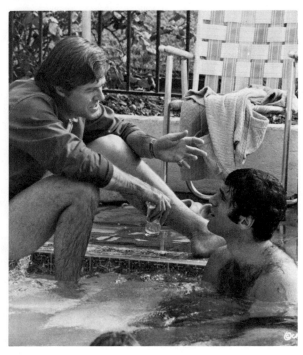

shirts, though he desperately longs to go with a casual open collar like Bob's; Alice retreats to her favorite shrink, where she performs a verbal catharsis by revealing her lack of satisfaction in her sex life with her husband. Finally, after many close encounters with the new morality, the four friends take the ultimate step, and adjourn to a hotel for a wife-swapping session.

At that point, the film turns surprisingly pious, as their passion begins to drain away when they look closely and critically at what they are doing. Silently, they dress and walk out, laughing at their own overly ardent attempt to join the "hip" lifestyle and force themselves to live up to a media-created image of the way in which they should live and relate to one another. Filmmaker Mazursky's great gift—first suggested in his excellent screenplay for *I Love You, Alice B. Toklas*, and in evidence throughout his direction of *B & C & T & A*—was a talent for blending strong social satire with lighthearted situation comedy, and giving the end result an underlying sense of seriousness that elevated his work of entertainment into an "art" film. This would provide the basis for his most satisfying films, including *Blume in Love, Harry and Tonto,* and *An Unmarried Woman*. The great moments in *B & C & T & A* are the ones which demonstrate his

total familiarity with and understanding of the upper-middle-class California scene, which he presents with razor sharp humor but, notably, without the kind of condescension that would diminish the impact of such a film.

Like most American films being made at that time, Mazursky's suffered somewhat from over-reliance on the then-currently trendy styles in moviemaking: endless helicopter shots to give a visual sensation of freedom, offbeat camera angles including bird's-eye-view shots for no particular reason, and soft-focus shots mixed with slow motion effects to add an often unnecessary sense of lyricism. But Mazursky possessed a gift for cataloguing the bits and pieces of the way we live today that set him apart from the majority of the filmmakers whose careers flourished in the youth crazy late Sixties, then proved to be understandably shortlived when the bottom fell out of the youth movement. Importantly, *B & C & T & A* was the film chosen to open the 1969 New York Film Festival, which marked a significant departure from the usual opening night event of the latest import of a film by some respected European auteur. In 1969, critics finally acknowledged that the long-held distinction between honest European art films and synthetic American entertainment films had at last broken down.

Old Friends: Natalie Wood, Dyan Cannon, Elliott Gould, and Robert Culp toast their relationship, which they believe will weather the storm of the current changes in lifestyle. (*Bob and Carol and Ted and Alice*)

The newsman as nonhero: Peter Bonerz and Robert Forster in *Medium Cool*.

MEDIUM COOL

PARAMOUNT PICTURES

Produced by Tully Friedman and Haskell Wexler; screenplay by Haskell Wexler; directed by Haskell Wexler.

CAST

John (Robert Forster); *Eileen* (Verna Bloom); *Gus* (Peter Bonerz); *Ruth* (Mariana Hill); *Harold* (Harold Blankenship)

A team of television cameramen stand by the remains of an automobile accident. Clinically, they photograph every detail, careful in their total professionalism not to miss a drop of blood or speck of "truth" that might prove interesting to channel eight's viewing audience. When the crew is finished, one turns to the other and mutters grimly: "Better call an ambulance."

So began *Medium Cool*, the long-awaited first (and, surprisingly, only) film by Haskell Wexler, best known as the cinematographer who shot other people's best movies. The title referred to Marshall McLuhan's classic statement for the Sixties about television being a "cool medium" of communication, and Wexler's story focused on a TV news photographer (Robert Forster) whose soul has become as cool as the medium which employs him. He is, of course, a second cousin to the anti-hero of Antonioni's *Blow-Up*, but whereas David Hemmings found himself caught in a fantasy-nightmare situation which threatened to become real, Forster is caught in a real situation which threatens to turn into a fantasy nightmare, as he covers the American scene of 1968, from the Poor People's March on Washington to the Siege of Chicago during the Democratic National Convention.

The film revitalized a question as old as art itself: where does fiction leave off and reality begin? In its most striking moment, during the film's chronicle of street fighting between hippies and police in Chicago, a voice can be heard calling out to the director—Wexler, not Forster—to be careful: "Watch out, Haskell! It's *real!*" Unfortunately, what might have been *Medium Cool*'s greatest strength proved its basic weakness. When the historical events are as powerful as those in 1968, the story needs to be equally powerful if it is to command our attention. However, the characters in *Medium Cool* rarely, if ever, engaged the film's audience as much as the national events in which those characters became embroiled.

Ultimately, though, the great value of *Medium Cool* is in the way Wexler, working as both writer and director, attempted to create an organic film, changing the direction of his storyline to fit events as they happened. In this sense, *Medium Cool* marked the most significant attempt to combine

281

Famed photographer Haskell Wexler, making his directorial debut, used camera angles coupled with mirror shots to show the complex psychological relationships of his characters: Verna Bloom (left and in mirror) talks to Peter Bonerz (far right) while Robert Foster, eavesdropping, is picked up by the mirror. *(Medium Cool)*

A time for revolution: Angry blacks discuss their problems with newsmen in *Medium Cool.*

drama with documentary on film since 1945, when Roberto Rossellini and his team of writers improvised a fictional story about a number of characters and shot it against the backdrop of the Nazi evacuation of Italy, thereby creating, in *Open City*, the school of filmmaking known as Neorealism. Rossellini's film was followed by dozens of other similar projects, created by both himself and other gifted Italian filmmakers.

Surprisingly, *Medium Cool* did not spark a major movement, and proved to be the only significant stab at such experimental filmmaking in the late Sixties, despite the amazing—and, at times, downright surrealistic—events then taking place. *Medium Cool* offered an array of images—the civil liberties marches, the assassination of Robert Kennedy, Mayor Richard Daley angrily ordering police into the streets of Chicago—that proved the old adage about fact being stranger than fiction. No wonder Wexler proved unable to create drama that could equal what he documented around him! Few writers possess an imagination that can equal the ever escalating situations that were a part of the everyday reality in 1968.

THE STERILE CUCKOO
PARAMOUNT PICTURES

Produced by Alan J. Pakula; screenplay by Alvin Sargent, based on a novel by John Nichols; directed by Alan J. Pakula.

CAST

Pookie (Liza Minnelli); *Jerry* (Wendell Burton); *Schumacher* (Tim McIntire); *Landlady* (Elizabeth Harrower); *Father* (Austin Green); *Nancy* (Sandra Faison); *Roe* (Chris Bugbee); *Helen Upshaw* (Jawn McKinley)

In Alan J. Pakula's understated—and refreshingly untrendy—*The Sterile Cuckoo*, he told a sensitive love story about two young people that was as far removed from the youth movement as *Rachel, Rachel* was from the sexual revolution. In so doing, he created a picture which proved universal in its appeal, one of the few films made about youth in the late Sixties that lost none of its impact when the revolutionary fervor proved to be a temporary craze rather than a lasting and significant change in society. This simple story about two college kids was shot at the small Hamilton College campus in

The model and the newsman: Marianna Hill and Robert Forster in *Medium Cool.*

upstate New York, but appeared to be out of time altogether; it was not so much the story of a particular era, but the story of first love itself—and the sad, but inevitable, end of an early romance.

Indeed, Pookie (Liza Minnelli) and Jerry (Wendell Burton) live completely in a world of their own making. Pakula managed to create enough interest in them as distinct individuals so that viewers cared what would happen to them, even as they might care about the kids who live down the block. "Let's never be weirdos, huh?" Pookie asks Jerry early in the film. What she means, of course, is the opposite of what she says, for Pookie is the arch kook, the ultimate weirdo. That her schoolmates consider her so is obvious from the looks they throw at her whenever she walks into the bar where the kids hang out. From the weirdo's point of view, of course, it is everyone else who is crazy. Pookie's problem is that Jerry can go either way: he is perfectly capable of being accepted by the society around him. At first he rejects it for his private life with Pookie. When he tries to bring her into the social world with him, the results are disastrous. Obviously, if he's going to join them, it has to be without her: "You're going to become a weirdo soon!" Pookie laments.

What proved ironic about all this—and what made the movie so touching—is that Pookie, weirdo that she is, actually prepares Jerry for the social world at the very moment when she seems to be bringing him deeper into her own private world. At first he is naive, clumsy, unsure of himself. It is

Pookie (Liza Minnelli) daringly checks into a motel for the first time with her equally innocent boyfriend (Wendell Burton) in *The Sterile Cuckoo*.

In one of *The Sterile Cuckoo*'s more mellow moments, Wendell Burton and Liza Minnelli enjoy romance in the country, far from the school setting that constantly threatens their relationship.

283

Woody Allen (far left) pulls off a bank robbery in *Take the Money and Run.*

I Am a Prisoner on a Chain Gang: Woody Allen (second from right) displays the influence an old Paul Muni movie had on his own cinematic sensibility in *Take the Money and Run.*

A family portrait. *(Take the Money and Run)*

284

the presence of the photograph of her that causes his initial acceptance in his dorm; as soon as he is seen as having a girlfriend, he is one of the boys. After they have made love, he displays a new sureness in himself, which leads to his social success. It is part of Pookie's tragedy that the harder she tries to make Jerry her own, the more she ensures the demise of their relationship.

Liza Minnelli's performance was so central to the effect that it had the capacity of making or breaking the film. Fortunately, it was a case of the former. Played too broadly, Pookie would have degenerated into a clown who might have entertained us, but could hardly move us emotionally. Played too heavily, the film would have degenerated into melodrama, without the saving grace of humor. Minnelli steered a steady course between the two: under all her masks of the compulsive wisecracker, we always saw the face of tragedy peeking through. After countless jokes about a dying mother, she finally confides kiddingly to Jerry that her mother died giving birth to her. "My first victim!" she squeals. But Jerry doesn't laugh—and neither did we.

In one particularly memorable scene, Liza ran through a gamut of emotions while talking to Jerry over a phone in a poorly lit booth. It proved to be an actor's dream, and Liza made the most of it, wisecracking desperately, throwing out endless oneliners to cover her tears. Movie fans remembered it as they did Montgomery Clift's classic phone booth sequence in *The Misfits.* Though her co-star Wendell Burton would fade from sight following his only other major film, *Fortune and Men's Eyes,* Liza would establish herself as a significant if offbeat dramatic and musical star, eventually winning the Oscar for her performance in *Cabaret.* Likewise, her director, Alan Pakula, would make his mark. Pakula followed *The Sterile Cuckoo* with *Klute.* His career, like Minnelli's, would flourish mainly because evident in his work was a dedication to the craft of filmmaking and a notable disregard for the flashy, the flamboyant, and the facile.

TAKE THE MONEY AND RUN
CINERAMA RELEASING CORPORATION

Produced by Charles H. Joffe; screenplay by Woody Allen and Mickey Rose; directed by Woody Allen.

CAST

Virgil Starkwell (Woody Allen); *Louise* (Janet Margolin); *Fritz* (Marcel Hillaire); *Miss Blaire* (Jacquelyn Hyde); *Jake* (Lonny Chapman); *Al* (Jan Merlin); *Chain Gang Warden* (James Anderson)

In the late Fifties and early Sixties, Woody Allen was almost indistinguishable from Mort Sahl and a dozen other socially commentative comics who, taken together, might be described as the spawn of Lenny Bruce: with lacerating wit and hip, anti-Establishment delivery, they poked fun at sacred cows and decimated audiences with their mildly shocking jibes at middle America. Their humor is still classic, even though most of their then-controversial targets have since passed out of the public's eye. But only Allen, among them, was meant for superstardom; he alone left the mediums of stand-up comedy and the long playing record behind, in order to conquer motion pictures.

Gore Vidal once commented that the novelists of our time are not influenced nearly so much by reading other writers, as was the case in the past, as they are by going to movies. Whether his statement holds true for our best novelists is arguable; but it was certainly true in the case of Woody Allen. Perhaps no other artist has had his mind so completely conditioned by watching films. Although he did satirize some ''real life'' situations in *Take the Money*—psychiatrists who force complex thoughts into oversimplified patterns, parole officers who cannot admit that the worst criminals are really bad—he appeared much more at home when kidding movies. This was obvious in the form he employed to tell the story of one Virgil Starkwell, a compulsive criminal: the entire film is framed in the form of a pseudo-documentary film about some famous outlaw, complete with the sober, heavy-handed narration and interspersings of news film with such prominent people as Eisenhower and Nixon to set the story in its historical milieu. But as soon as Virgil (Woody) falls in love with a pretty young woman (Janet Margolin), the technique shifts abruptly into something straight out of Claude LeLouch's *A Man and a Woman*: simply, anyone who has been to as many movies as Woody knows a love scene calls for imagery dripping with subdued impressionist coloring.

When the picture shifts to the jail sequence, it is obvious that what we see is not based on any experiences with real jails but with movie jails: the prisoners speak in movie prison jargon right out of *Riot in Cell Block 11, The Last Mile,* and *Inside the Walls of Folsom Prison*, and look like the guys who used to back up George Raft and John Garfield in the days when Woody's mind was being formed in

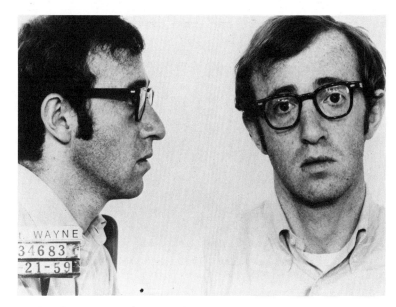

Woody Allen: Wanted, Dead or Alive! *(Take the Money and Run)*

Janet Margolin and Woody Allen in *Take the Money and Run.*

285

The counterculture: Peter Fonda and Dennis Hopper smoke joints. *(Easy Rider)*

EASY RIDER
COLUMBIA PICTURES

Produced by Peter Fonda; screenplay by Peter Fonda, Dennis Hopper, and Terry Southern; directed by Dennis Hopper.

CAST

Wyatt/Captain America (Peter Fonda); *Billy* (Dennis Hopper); *George Hanson* (Jack Nicholson); *Rancher* (Warren Finnerty); *Stranger on Highway* (Luke Askew); *Lisa* (Luana Anders); *Karen* (Karen Black); *Hippie Leader* (Robert Walker); *Hippie Girl* (Sabrina Scharf)

the fifth row of the Bijou Theater. When Virgil is sent out to a road gang in the South, audiences witness a harassing of prisoners by a "Captain" who looked suspiciously like Strother Martin in *Cool Hand Luke*, and later viewed a prison break that harkened all the way back to Paul Muni's in *I Am a Fugitive from a Chain Gang*. This absorption with films came to a head in one of the best scenes in *Take the Money*, when Virgil tries to confuse the police by hiring a rejected European director (who bore more than a fleeting resemblance to Fritz Lang) to pretend he is filming a robbery, and that Virgil's gang members are merely actors. When Virgil's director begins to take his job seriously, and when another gang shows up to rob the bank at the same time, the thin red line between what we think of as reality and the illusions of the film medium rapidly disintegrates. On the surface, this was merely another funny scene—but there was a lot going on beneath that surface.

Take the Money and Run established Woody as the Chaplin of the Seventies: the central comic consciousness of our time, and the single film artist who could take experiences from his own life, combine them with satire on the current scene, and offer them through the medium of homages to memorable movie scenes of past years. His films would brighten the next decade: *Bananas, Sleeper, Love and Death* all proved Allen's intellectual wit, personal warmth, and self-deprecating sense of humor were the hallmarks of the most beloved and respected comic artist since the days of the silent screen. Chaplin's Little Tramp finally met his equal in Allen's insecure survivor of the Sixties and Seventies.

As in the conventional picaresque, viewers were projected into a series of sketches tied together more by mood and theme than by any tight story line, as "Captain America" (Fonda) and "Billy the Kid" (Hopper) quest their way eastward from California to New Orleans. The very sense of direction proved to be at the source of their problems: they share something with Scott Fitzgerald's westerners who journey east in search of sophistication but only find disillusionment and death. Frontiersmen without a frontier, Fonda and Hopper would be better off if, like Cooper's Leatherstocking, they could push away from society into virgin woods. They are unfortunate enough to be born on the West Coast, with no place to go but East—a problem unique to our century, and one shared by the heroes of movies as diverse as *Midnight Cowboy* and *The Wild Bunch*.

The grotesqueness of their journey is underlined when we see the "good" moments (the family dinner with friendly ranchers, the peaceful stay at a hippie commune) take place shortly after leaving California; without knowing it, they are leaving the very thing they most want to find. The closer they come to their destination, the more unpleasant the incidents become (being refused service in a diner, the beating at night during which a friend is killed) until the long-awaited destination—the Mardi Gras—turns out to be obscene, vulgar, and commercialized—the ultimate "bad trip." But this perverse sense of direction is not the only root of their tragedy. Far too much time is spent chronicling the sale of hard drugs through which they finance their trip to let the scene pass lightly. *Easy Rider* was a surprisingly moral tale, for this first scene—the buying and selling of hard drugs—dooms the quest before it starts. A search for truth cannot be financed by an immoral act without disastrous results. The two cyclists depart, laughingly throwing away their watches in a symbolic gesture of freedom from the world and time they have unknowingly bound themselves to in the worst possible way. This is made more explicit near the end, when they try popping pills to take their mind off the ugliness of the Mardi Gras and only worsen the situation by increasing their sense of awareness of how vile it is. "We blew it," Fonda finally admits.

The most important comment *Easy Rider* made was to be found in the vast discrepancy between the visual beauty of the movie, as captured in Laszlo Kovacs' cinematography, and the ugliness of the climate of life in the late Sixties. "This used to be a fine country," Jack Nicholson sighs shortly before his death at the hands of rednecks. "What went

Peter Fonda rolls a joint for a friend in *Easy Rider*.

Peter Fonda as Captain America in *Easy Rider*.

287

wrong?'' He may die not knowing, but (by the end) *Easy Rider* pointed to the answer. At the time of its release, *Time* Magazine referred to this as "the little film that killed the big film." In point of fact, the big film did not die at all, but only went into a state of hibernation during the troubled, overlong winter of 1969. Dozens of imitation *Easy Rider*s were turned out and, almost invariably, they failed at the box office. One year later, *Airport*—a return to the Ross Hunter all-star extravaganzas—broke box-office records.

But if *Easy Rider* did not permanently change the face of American films, it at least stands as a testament to the fact that, for one brief moment, the American cinema was radicalized by the extremity of the times. Hollywood somehow survived that frantic, frenetic period, as it had previously survived the flapper era scandals, the rock bottom economy of the Depression, the difficult days of World War II, and the paranoid mentality of the McCarthy era. However imperfectly, Hollywood reflects the shifting American moods and, to a degree, helps create those ever changing societal shifts by exploiting every latest syndrome and exposing it to the mass audience. In 1969, that mood was best exemplified by *Easy Rider*; a year later, temporary converts to hippiedom would throw away their love beads. And Hollywood, after a few false starts, would once again provide the pictures people wanted to see.

The cult of the rebel, about 1969: Motorcyclists replace cowboys as American popular heroes. *(Easy Rider)*